Legal Aspects of

Building Code Enforcement

in North Carolina

2nd Edition

Philip P. Green, Jr.

1987

INSTITUTE OF GOVERNMENT
The University of North Carolina at Chapel Hill

Cover Design by Ted Clark

FOREWORD

This book is designed as a text to be used in training courses for state and local "code enforcement officials" in North Carolina. As defined in Section 143-151.8 of the General Statutes of North Carolina,

> "Code" means the North Carolina State Building Code and related local building rules and regulations approved by the Building Code Council heretofore or hereinafter enacted, adopted or approved pursuant to G.S. 143-138.
>
> "Code enforcement" means the examination and approval of plans and specifications, or the inspection of the manner of construction, workmanship, and materials for construction of buildings and structures and components thereof as an employee of the State or local government... to assure compliance with the State Building Code and related local building rules and regulations.
>
> "Qualified code enforcement official" means a person qualified under this Article [G.S. Ch. 143, Art. 9B] to engage in the practice of code enforcement.

The officials thus defined include code administrators, building inspectors, plumbing inspectors, mechanical inspectors, and electrical inspectors. They do not include officials whose sole responsibility is to enforce local enactments such as zoning ordinances, sign ordinances, weed ordinances, or minimum housing ordinances.

Since July 1, 1979, all code enforcement officials in North Carolina have been required to hold certificates issued by the North Carolina Code Officials Qualification Board. That Board is charged not only with setting standards for such certification but also with developing programs of instruction through which officials could meet those standards. Hence, this textbook.

It is intended to provide a basic understanding of the governmental and legal system within which every code enforcement official works, with specific reference to source materials wherever possible.

Because of the nature of the subject matter, it is necessary to refer frequently to provisions of the state and federal constitutions, of state statutes, and of the State Building Code and other regulations. Many such provisions are set forth in the text or the Appendix of this book. However, it is desirable that the user have access to other materials.

First, he should have access to a complete set (currently five volumes) of the State Building Code. These volumes cover not only general construction but also residential construction and plumbing, mechanical, and electrical systems.

Second, it would be desirable (but less necessary) that he have access to other regulations of various state and local agencies, as listed in Chapter 3.

Third, he should have access to the regulations of the North Carolina Code Officials Qualification Board. These are available from the Division of Engineering and Building Codes of the North Carolina Department of Insurance, and they are codified in the North Carolina Administrative Code, Title 11, Chapter 8, Sections .0500, .0600, .0700, and .0800.

Fourth, he should have access to North Carolina statutes. These may be found in the North Carolina General Statutes (referred to herein as "G.S.") in codified form and in the Session Laws of North Carolina (referred to as "Sess. Laws") in more complete but uncodified form.

Finally, some users may wish to examine the complete text of the court opinions that are cited. These for the most part may be found in the North Carolina Reports (cited as "N.C.") and the North Carolina Court of Appeals Reports (cited as "N.C. App.").

Readers are urged to notify the author of any mistakes they find or any suggestions they may have for making this book more useful. All such communications should be addressed to the Institute of Government, Knapp Building 059A, The University of North Carolina at Chapel Hill, Chapel Hill, N.C. 27514.

Philip P. Green, Jr.

Chapel Hill
1987

CONTENTS

13 LEGAL RESTRAINTS ON THE CODE ENFORCEMENT OFFICIAL   107

1 OVERVIEW: THE STATE'S COMPREHENSIVE BUILDING REGULATION SYSTEM

Long recognized as a pioneer in the field of building regulation, North Carolina is now coming to have the most comprehensive program in this field of any state. Its many innovations encompass its building codes, its machinery for their enforcement, and its qualification programs for enforcement officials. While these have been widely publicized outside the state, many of our officials are unaware of the significant progress that they represent.

A THUMBNAIL HISTORY

To provide a setting against which to examine the state's current programs, let us take a quick look at some high points in their development.

The earliest building regulations in North Carolina antedated the Revolutionary War and were found in the charters and ordinances of individual cities. Edenton's charter of 1740,[1] for example, prohibited wooden chimneys, and virtually all colonial and early postrevolutionary charters regulated one or more aspects of building construction. This pattern continued through the nineteenth century, as the General Assembly authorized particular cities to deal with fire hazards and later with unsanitary and unhealthful conditions in and around buildings.

A significant change occurred in 1905. Whereas most other states have continued up to the present to rely on local governments to regulate building, 82 years ago North Carolina enacted a state building law that governed construction in all towns over 1,000 population.[2] Further, this law mandated that every such town have a building inspector to enforce the law (in the absence of any other inspector, the statute designated the fire chief as building inspector and made it a misdemeanor for a town board not to appoint a fire chief). And finally, the 1905 law directed the State Commissioner of Insurance to oversee local building inspectors. Although elaborated by the State Building Code and some local regulations

---

1. Laws, 1740, Ch. 1.
2. N.C. Pub. Laws 1905, Ch. 506.

in later years, this law remained in the General Statutes until 1969, and its approach is reflected in today's system. Its major importance lies in the fact that the state recognized for the first time the desirability of having uniform building regulations in all municipalities throughout the state, so that architects, engineers, contractors, and others in the construction industry could move freely from one town to another without having to learn a series of entirely different building codes designed to assure monopolies for local residents. Many states have not yet reached this point.

The next major step forward occurred in 1933, when the General Assembly created the State Building Code Council.[3] This legislation implied recognition that construction technology and materials were changing so rapidly that a legislature—composed of laymen and meeting only once a biennium—could not possibly write, amend, and administer building regulations with understanding and timeliness. The Council was to be composed largely of professional personnel from the construction industry. It was to be responsible for writing a code, amending it to reflect the changes that were occurring, and hearing appeals from local inspectors as to its proper interpretation. The Council published the first State Building Code in 1936, and the General Assembly ratified and adopted the Code in 1941.

In 1957, as a result of recommendations by the Commission on Reorganization of State Government, the statute creating the Building Code Council was largely rewritten to eliminate some legal weaknesses; increase the representation on the Council; make clear the relationship between local governments, state departments with enforcement responsibilities (primarily the departments of Insurance and Labor), and the Council; and broaden the coverage of the State Building Code to include virtually all buildings throughout the state other than certain agricultural structures.[4] Only a minority of states elsewhere, even when they have created arrangements akin to our Building Code Council and State Building Code, have afforded them both the geographical and subject-matter coverage of the North Carolina system.

Two important steps were taken in 1969. The first was passage of acts that provided in detail for the creation, responsibilities, and procedures of city and county inspection departments.[5] This was particularly significant with respect to the counties. In contrast to our cities, North Carolina counties had no authority to appoint inspectors of any type until 1937, when they were empowered to have electrical inspectors. Some (but not all) counties were later given power to have one or more additional kinds

---

3. N.C. Pub. Laws 1933, Ch. 392.
4. N.C. Gen. Stat. Ch. 143, Art. 9; N.C. Sess. Laws 1957, Ch. 1138.
5. N.C. Sess. Laws 1969, Ch. 1065, 1066; now codified as N.C. Gen. Stat. Ch. 153A, Art. 18, Part 4, and *id.* Ch. 160A, Art. 19, Part 5.

of inspectors, but the 1969 act took a giant leap and placed all counties essentially on a par with cities with respect to all types of building inspection. Since enforcement of the State Building Code is dependent in the first instance on local inspectors, this act filled a major gap in protecting the state's citizens against hazards from inferior construction.

The second 1969 action was truly innovative. For years mobile homes (or "trailers") were the one type of residential construction that was totally unregulated. This was true because they were manufactured in factories rather than on-site, so that local inspectors had no opportunity to check construction details, and they frequently were manufactured out of state, where they were believed to be beyond the reach of local legislators. In this situation, it was not surprising that people were shocked and fires were started by faulty electrical installations, floors sagged and sometimes separated from walls, doors were out of plumb, and numerous other problems appeared. Some local inspectors sought to get at such problems by requiring removal of panel sections and other mobile home sections before the structure was placed on a lot, so that details of construction could be checked. Mobile home manufacturers and sellers regarded such requirements to be harassment, and they secured legislation in several states under which a manufacturer would simply affix a sticker to his product certifying that it was properly built, and the mobile home was thereby exempt from the local inspection. Such a bill was introduced in the 1969 General Assembly.

North Carolina officials adamantly opposed this legislation, for obvious reasons. Instead they proposed, and the General Assembly adopted, a system under which the Commissioner of Insurance would adopt regulations for mobile homes (based on standards set by a national organization) and would license recognized testing agencies (a) to approve plans for a manufacturer's products as being in compliance with the regulations, (b) to check the homes as they were manufactured in the factory, and (c) to affix the testing agency's stickers of approval on the homes that were in compliance.[6] This system won almost immediate acceptance and was widely adopted by other states until the federal government pre-empted the field with a generally similar system in 1974.

The final date worthy of mention is 1977. In that year the General Assembly noted that while there was a uniform State Building Code in effect throughout the state, many local governments were not enforcing the Code. Further, the officials who enforced the Code differed widely in their understanding and interpretations. To remedy these situations, the legislature directed *all* local governments to provide for enforcement of the Code within their jurisdiction by dates (1981 through 1985) based on their populations. And it created the North Carolina Code Officials Qualification

---

6. N.C. GEN. STAT. Ch. 143, Art. 9A; N.C. Sess. Laws 1969, Ch. 961.

Board to set up a certification system for local inspectors and to develop uniform educational programs through which those inspectors could qualify for various types of certificates.[7]

Against this historical background, let us turn now to a closer look at the existing North Carolina building regulation system.

ADOPTION AND AMENDMENT OF THE CODE

The leading actor in the adoption of the State Building Code is the Building Code Council. The Council consists of 12 members appointed by the Governor, mostly from the construction industry but also including a local building inspector, a state-employed engineer, an active member of the fire service, and a representative of the general public. Its responsibilities are to (a) prepare and adopt a State Building Code, (b) amend that Code from time to time, (c) approve any local variations from the Code's provisions, (d) hear appeals from decisions of state enforcement agencies under the Code, (e) recommend to the General Assembly desirable changes in statutes relating to construction, and (f) recommend to state agencies improvements in their administrative practices involved in enforcement of building laws.

The Division of Engineering and Building Codes of the North Carolina Department of Insurance is the principal source of staff assistance for the Council. It also draws on the talents of many other professionals through advisory committees.

The first State Building Code was completed and published in 1936, but almost immediately the Council undertook responsibility for amending that Code. This activity took three forms: (1) Over the years the Council made comprehensive revisions of the Code—in 1953, in 1958, in 1967, and in 1978. (2) In almost every quarter the Council has considered and adopted one or more amendments to specific sections of the Code. (3) A unique provision of the statutes allows the Council, in hearing appeals, to permit variations from the Code when it finds that "materials or methods of construction proposed to be used are as good as those required by the Code," provided that it immediately initiates procedures for amending the Code to accord with this decision.

With this steady flow of amendments, the Code has grown in length and complexity. The 1936 Code consisted of a single volume of less than 100 pages. The 1978 Code consists of five volumes—General Construction, Plumbing, Heating, Electrical, and the North Carolina Uniform Residential

---

7. N.C. GEN. STAT. Ch. 143, Art. 9B; N.C. Sess. Laws 1977, Ch. 531.

Building Code; the first volume alone contains almost 700 pages. Basically the Code's various volumes are modeled rather closely after nationally recognized codes. But the Council has carefully considered the applicability of each code's provisions to North Carolina's climate, geography, and other circumstances and has made appropriate changes where indicated.

As noted earlier, the State Building Code applies throughout the state without any necessity for adoption by local governments (their only responsibility is to create inspection departments to enforce it). The 1933 law that originally created the Building Code Council authorized any local government to adopt its own code, provided only that that code be more stringent than the State Building Code. The 1957 statute modified this provision to require Council approval of all local modifications. In furtherance of uniformity throughout the state, the Council has adopted and adhered to a strong policy that it will not approve a complete building code for a local government but will approve limited modifications of the State Code.

The Code now applies to construction of all types of *new* buildings and structures and their systems and facilities except (a) "farm buildings located outside the building-regulation jurisdiction of any municipality"; (b) equipment and facilities for handling, storage, etc., of liquefied petroleum gas or liquid fertilizers; and (c) equipment and facilities, other than buildings, of public utilities. As a result of legislative ratification in 1941 and 1957, the Code applies also to safety features of most *existing* buildings. The Court of Appeals held in *Carolinas-Virginias Association v. Ingram*[8] that special fire protection requirements for existing high-rise buildings exceeded the Council's statutory authority, but the 1981 General Assembly then ratified and itself adopted the challenged requirements.

The General Assembly's foresight in creating a quasi-legislative agency that can react readily to changes in construction techniques and needs is illustrated by the fact that North Carolina has in the recent past been in the forefront of states that have mandated new insulation and energy conservation measures in construction, smoke-detection devices in all new buildings, a wide range of facilities for the handicapped, and extensive fire-protection facilities in new high-rise buildings.

ORGANIZATION FOR ENFORCEMENT

The basic pattern for enforcement prescribed by the statutes is as follows.[9]

(1) Local governments are responsible for most enforcement functions: issuing or denying permits, making necessary inspections, issuing or deny-

---

8. 39 N.C. App. 688 (1979), *rev. denied*, 297 N.C. 299 (1979).
9. N.C. GEN. STAT. § 143-139; *id.* §§ 143-140, -141; *id.* § 153A-352; *id.* § 160A-412.

ing certificates of compliance for completed work, issuing orders to correct violations, bringing judicial actions against actual or threatened violations, keeping records, etc.;

(2) The Insurance Commissioner has general responsibility for supervising local enforcement officials, and appeals from their decisions are taken to him with respect to enforcement of most sections of the State Building Code;

(3) The Bureau of Boiler Inspection of the Department of Labor has general responsibility for supervising local inspectors and hearing appeals with respect to the Code's requirements pertaining to boilers;

(4) The Department of Labor has general responsibility for supervising local inspectors and hearing appeals with respect to the Code's requirements for elevators, escalators, merry-go-rounds, etc.; and

(5) Appeals may be taken from the Department of Insurance or Department of Labor either directly to superior court or first to the Building Code Council and then to the courts.

The General Assembly has given local governments extreme latitude concerning how they may organize to handle their enforcement responsibilities. First, a local government may elect to do nothing at all. In this event, once the scheduled date for action has passed, the Commissioner of Insurance may assume responsibility for enforcing the Code within that unit, either with his department's personnel or through contractual arrangements with another local government.[10] Second, every city and county is authorized to create its own inspection department, with a full range of enforcement powers.[11] Third, any two or more local governments may create a joint inspection department.[12] Fourth, any local government may hire, on a part-time basis, one or more inspectors from another local government, with the approval of that unit's governing board.[13] Fifth, any local government may contract with another local government for the second unit to furnish inspection services to the first.[14] Sixth, a municipality may request the county of which it is a part to provide inspection services throughout the municipality's jurisdiction, without any contract between the two.[15] Seventh, a municipality may enforce the Code over a defined area beyond its boundaries.[16]

Almost all of the above arrangements now exist somewhere within the state. As a result of the certification program described in the section that follows, it is anticipated that a great many more intergovernmental arrange-

10. *Id.* § 153A-351(b); *id.* § 160A-411.
11. *Id.* § 153A-351; *id.* § 160A-411.
12. *Id.* § 153A-353; *id.* §§ 160A-413, -462 ff.
13. *Id.* § 153A-353; *id.* § 160A-413.
14. *Id.* § 160A-461.
15. *Id.* § 160A-360(d), (g).
16. *Id.* § 160A-360(a).

ments will be made in order to provide properly qualified inspectors within every local government. For example, a small town might have its own inspector, who is qualified to handle one- and two-family dwellings. But it might have to share an electrical or plumbing or mechanical inspector with another town. And a number of towns might rely on the county inspection department or a nearby big-city department to provide more highly qualified inspectors certified to inspect the occasional very large or complicated buildings that are constructed within their jurisdiction.

QUALIFICATION OF CODE OFFICIALS

The statutes enacted in 1977 provide that no person may engage in enforcement of the State Building Code as a state or local official after July 1, 1979, without a certificate from the North Carolina Code Officials Qualification Board.[17] This Board consists of twenty members drawn from local government, the construction industry, the ranks of local inspectors, and the academic community. It is responsible for (a) establishing standards for code enforcement officials; (b) creating and administering a system for certifying that officials meet those standards; (c) developing, in cooperation with the state's various educational institutions, programs for training such officials (both pre-service and in-service); (d) certifying the qualifications of instructors in such programs; and (e) administering disciplinary proceedings, if necessary, when inspectors are charged with various abuses.

The Division of Engineering and Building Codes of the North Carolina Department of Insurance also provides staff assistance to this Board, and it has created a number of advisory committees as well.

The Board's first priority after its creation was development of regulations governing the issuance of certificates. This function was accomplished by the July, 1979, deadline, and all known code officials in the state at that time were given their initial certificates.

The statutes call for three general types of certificates: (a) a *limited* certificate, allowing an inspector to continue to hold the position he occupies on a given date but not to move to another position; (b) a *probationary* certificate, allowing a newly appointed or newly promoted inspector to hold a position for a specified period while qualifying for an appropriate standard certificate; and (c) a *standard* certificate, allowing him to hold a position as a particular type of inspector with a given level of competency for any state or local governmental unit.

The original limited certificates were reserved for officials who held a position on June 13, 1977, when the basic law was enacted. However,

---

17. *Id.* § 143-151.13(a).

through a 1979 amendment this type of certificate was also offered to any inspector who held a position on the date when his unit was required to have an inspection department. In either case, the official was required to complete, within two years, the training courses specified by the Board in order to keep his certificate.

Under the initial statute, probationary certificates had only a one-year life. Because of delays in establishing training programs, the 1979 General Assembly allowed the Board to extend this period by regulation to as much as three years. Currently the Board's regulations require the holder of a probationary certificate to qualify for a standard certificate within two years.

The standard certificates are expected to become the basic type of certificates in force throughout the state. Under the Board's regulations, standards have been set for positions in five fields: Code Administrator, Building Inspector, Plumbing Inspector, Mechanical Inspector, and Electrical Inspector. Three levels of competency have been set for each of these types of officials other than the Code Administrator. Level I is basically for officials competent to deal with one- and two-family residences and small buildings of other types. Level III is for officials qualified to deal with buildings and installations of any size. And Level II falls between these two extremes.

For each level and type of position, the Board's regulations prescribe a range of alternative education and experience requirements. A written examination will normally be required from all applicants, together with completion of training courses specified by the Board and the equivalent of a high school education. (Some categories are exempted from the examination—persons who have already passed examinations as county electrical inspectors and persons who hold licenses as architects, engineers, etc. But even these people are required to complete certain short courses.)

Financing and preparing the many educational programs that are required has proved to be a major task for the Board. While the various courses have been prepared under the Board's supervision, they are being offered through community colleges and technical institutes throughout the state at locations most convenient for the inspectors.

These programs will have two major consequences for local governments. First, such governments undoubtedly will want to re-examine their personnel classifications and pay plans in light of the certification system. No one should be hired who does not meet the Board's minimum requirements for certification and cannot be expected to meet those requirements within two years after hiring. Funds must be provided for the various training programs that will be required. And ultimately the local governments must expect to pay more for more highly qualified inspectors.

Second, the certification system will affect how local inspection departments are organized. A great many intergovernmental arrangements, as described earlier in this chapter, may be necessary. The administration and operation of a local department will turn on the types of inspectors it has and their levels of proficiency. It may be difficult, for example, to have "cross-trained" inspectors who can make many types of inspections; it is unrealistic to expect that many inspectors will have level III certificates in all four specialized areas.

Nevertheless, the new system should ultimately result in much improved and more uniform enforcement of the State Building Code throughout the state.

2 THE STRUCTURE OF AMERICAN GOVERNMENT

Many Americans do not understand our nation's governmental structure. They comprehend neither the intricate system of checks and balances among the branches of government that the Founding Fathers created to prevent the rise of autocratic rulers nor the roles of the different levels of government and the interrelationships between them. This chapter will describe the latter area in specific terms—the roles of the different levels in the regulation of building construction.

Chart 1 illustrates the constitutional relationship among the various types of governments in our country today.

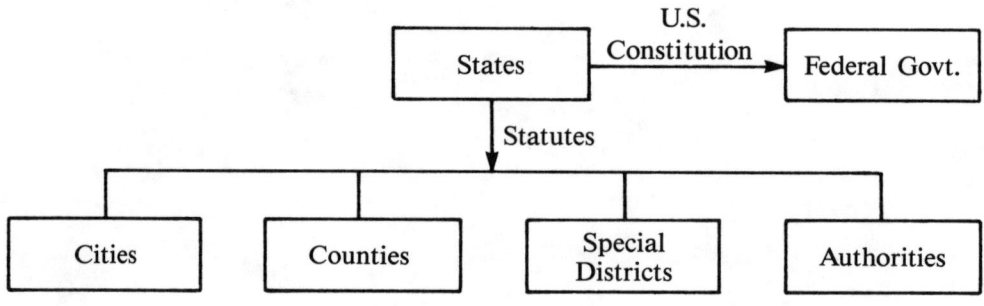

Chart 1

As the diagram shows, the states were the basic building blocks from which our governmental structure was created. They existed as colonies before 1776, and their delegates assembled as the Continental Congress that declared independence in that year. In 1781, through the Articles of Confederation, they created the United States of America to prosecute the Revolution and serve as our first national government. Following the Revolution the states continued to exercise most governmental powers in the new nation. When it became evident that more powers were needed at the national level, in 1787 they drafted and adopted the federal Constitution, which transferred additional powers to the United States. But the states always made clear—expressly so in the Ninth and Tenth Amendments—that the federal government was to have *only* those powers that had specifically been granted to it.

Similarly, the states were the fonts from which all local governments derived their powers. Usually these powers were transmitted through statutes enacted by the state legislature, but in some states twentieth-century amendments to their constitutions transmitted certain powers directly to local governments.

THE FEDERAL GOVERNMENT

The government of the United States is one of delegated powers alone. Its authority is defined and limited by the Constitution. All powers not granted to it by that instrument are reserved to the states or the people.

> Chief Justice Waite in *United States v. Cruikshank*, 92 U.S. 542, 551 (1875).

While undoubtedly the United States as a nation has all the powers which inhere in any nation, Congress is not authorized in all things to act for the nation, and too little effect has been given to the Tenth Article of the amendments to the Constitution, that "the powers not delegated to the United States by the Constitution, nor prohibited by it to the states, are reserved to the states respectively, or to the people." The powers the people have given to the general government are named in the Constitution, and all not there named, either expressly or by implication, are reserved to the people and can be exercised only by them, or upon further grant from them.

> Justice Brewer, concurring in *United States ex rel. Turner v. Williams*, 194 U.S. 279, 295-96 (1904).

Constitution of the United States

Article I, § 8. The Congress shall have power

[1.] *To lay and collect taxes*, duties, imposts and excises, *to* pay the debts and *provide for the* common defence and *general welfare of the United States*; but all duties, imposts and excises shall be uniform throughout the United States;

[2.] To borrow money on the credit of the United States;

[3.] *To regulate commerce* with foreign nations, and *among the several states*, and with the Indian tribes;

[4.] To establish a uniform rule of naturalization, and uniform laws on the subject of bankruptcies throughout the United States;

[5.] To coin money, regulate the value thereof, and of foreign coin, and fix the standard of weights and measures;

[6.] To provide for the punishment of counterfeiting the securities and current coin of the United States;

[7.] To establish post offices and post roads;

[8.] To promote the progress of science and useful arts, by securing for limited times to authors and inventors the exclusive right to their respective writings and discoveries;

[9.] To constitute tribunals inferior to the supreme court;

[10.] To define and punish piracies and felonies committed on the high seas, and offences against the law of nations;

[11.] To declare war, grant letters of marque and reprisal, and make rules concerning captures on land and water;

[12.] To raise and support armies, but no appropriation of money to that use shall be for a longer term than two years;

[13.] To provide and maintain a navy;

[14.] To make rules for the government and regulation of the land and naval forces;

[15.] To provide for calling forth the militia to execute the laws of the union, suppress insurrections and repel invasions;

[16.] To provide for organizing, arming, and disciplining the militia, and for governing such part of them as may be employed in the service of the United States, reserving to the states respectively the appointment of officers and the authority of training the militia according to the discipline prescribed by congress;

[17.] To exercise exclusive jurisdiction in all cases whatsoever, over such district (not exceeding ten miles square) as may, by cession of particular states, and the acceptance of congress, become the seat of the government of the United States, and to exercise like authority over all places purchased by the consent of the legislature of the state in which the same shall be, for the erection of forts, magazines, arsenals, dockyards, and other needful buildings; — and

[18.] *To make all laws which shall be necessary and proper for carrying into execution the foregoing powers, and all other powers vested by this constitution in the government of the United States, or in any department or officer thereof.* [Emphasis added.]

Amendment IX. The enumeration in the constitution of certain rights shall not be construed to deny or disparage others retained by the people.

Amendment X. The powers not delegated to the United States by the constitution, nor prohibited by it to the states, are reserved to the states, respectively, or to the people.

Congress has also been authorized to enforce, by appropriate legislation, the provisions of *Amendment XIII* (prohibiting slavery and involuntary servitude); *Amendment XIV* (prohibiting state action that abridges the privileges or immunities of citizens of the United States, deprives any person of life, liberty, or property without due process of law, or deprives any person of the equal protection of the laws; providing for the apportionment of representatives; and dishonoring officers who have engaged in insurrection or debts incurred in insurrection); *Amendment XV* (forbidding denial of the right to vote on account of race, color, or previous condition of servitude); *Amendment XIX* (forbidding denial of the right to vote on account of sex); *Amendment XXIII* (authorizing selection of presidential electors by the District of Columbia); *Amendment XXIV* (prohibiting denial of voting rights because of failure to pay taxes); and *Amendment XXVI* (prohibiting denial of voting rights to persons 18 or over on account of age). In addition, it was authorized by *Amendment XVI* to levy and collect taxes on income.

The above listing shows that any federal power to directly regulate building construction must be derived from the Interstate Commerce Clause

(Art. I, § 8 [3]), as supported by the Necessary and Proper clause (Art. I, § 8 [18]). Under this authority Congress has regulated the construction of mobile homes, which clearly are sold in interstate transactions. Periodically proposals have been made for adoption of a federal building code. It is not clear whether the courts would find such a move to be regulation of interstate commerce.

Of equal importance has been a device used by Congress for the past 30 or 40 years to extend the reach of federal powers. With its ability to levy the income tax (Amendment XVI), it has gained vast revenues, some of which have been made available as grants to state and local governments pursuant to the General Welfare clause (Art. I, § 8 [1]). It has conditioned many of these grants upon those governments' taking specified actions. An example is the "workable program" requirement that used to be a condition imposed on the grant of federal funds for low-income housing and urban renewal activities; it required that local governments adopt and enforce zoning ordinances, subdivision regulations, housing codes, and building codes, among other things. Since no government is required to accept a grant, it theoretically is free to avoid such requirements by refusing the money. But most governments do comply in order to get their share of these funds.

STATE GOVERNMENTS

Under the Articles of Confederation each state retained its sovereignty, freedom, and independence, and every power, jurisdiction, and right not expressly delegated to the United States. Under the Constitution, though the powers of the states were much restricted, still all powers not delegated to the United States, nor prohibited to the states, are reserved to the states respectively, or to the people. . . . Not only, therefore, can there be no loss of separate and independent autonomy to the states, through their union under the Constitution, but it may be not unreasonably said that the preservation of the states, and the maintenance of their governments, are as much within the design and care of the Constitution as the preservation of the Union and the maintenance of the national government.

Chief Justice Chase in *Texas v. White*, 7 Wall. (U.S.) 700, 725 (1868).

The people of the United States constitute one nation, under one government, and this government, within the scope of the powers with which it is invested, is supreme. On the other hand, the people of each state compose a state, having its own government, and endowed with all the functions essential to separate and independent existence. The states disunited might continue to exist. Without the states in union there could be no such political body as the United States.

Both the states and the United States existed before the Constitution. The people, through that instrument, established a more perfect union by substituting a national government, acting, with ample power, directly upon the citizens, instead of the Confederate government, which acted with powers, greatly restricted, only upon the states. But in many articles of the Constitution the necessary existence of the states, and, within their proper spheres, the independent authority of the states, is distinctly recognized. To them nearly the whole charge of interior regulation is committed or left; to them and to the people all powers not expressly delegated to the national government are reserved.

> Chief Justice Chase in *Lane County v. Oregon*, 7 Wall. (U.S.) 71, 76 (1868).

It is a familiar rule of construction of the Constitution of the Union, that the sovereign powers vested in the state governments by their respective constitutions, remained unaltered and unimpaired, except so far as they were granted to the government of the United States.

> Justice Nelson in *The Collector v. Day*, 11 Wall. (U.S.) 113 (1870).

In contrast to the federal government (which must be able to point to a constitutional provision authorizing a proposed action), a state government inherently has all governmental powers not denied it by provisions of state or federal constitutions. While many state constitutions contain provisions granting the state government particular powers, such provisions are usually enacted in response to a court holding that the state had been denied that power by another provision of its constitution.

As we have seen, the states are the creators of both the federal government and the local governments. The importance of the state in relationship to local governments cannot be overstressed. The state creates these local governments—it specifies their boundaries, their organization, their powers and functions, how they are to be governed and administered, and even details like the salaries to be paid to particular officials. It may abolish existing units, or consolidate them with other units, or turn over some of their functions to different types of units. In short, it has almost complete control over them![1]

The state does all of these things through enactment of statutes by the state legislature. (In some states, but not North Carolina, certain "home rule" powers are granted directly by provisions of the state constitution.)

Grants of power and other legislative enactments may be made to apply generally to all local governments of a given type or class. In North Carolina such statutes are known as "public laws," and ultimately they are codified according to subject matter in the North Carolina General Statutes. (Sometimes statutes granting powers are referred to as "enabling acts," since they "enable" local governments to take specified actions.)

---

1. State v. Jennette, 190 N.C. 96, 129 S.E. 184 (1925).

Some statutes apply only to particular local governments. These may be known in North Carolina as "public-local laws," or "private laws," or "special acts," or "local acts." There is no particular significance to the differences in terminology—they all refer to the same thing: a law passed by the General Assembly that applies only to one or a few local governments. All the special acts that apply to a particular government may be referred to collectively as the "charter" of that government.

In North Carolina both public laws and local laws are published after each legislative session in the Session Laws, where they are called "chapters" —e.g., Sess. Laws 1981, ch. 245. Only public laws are codified in the General Statutes.

The state government's internal organization is based on a wider range of legal instruments. The North Carolina Constitution, the statutes passed by the General Assembly, and the Governor exercising his executive powers create the various state departments and agencies, specify how they are to be organized, and assign powers and duties to them.

Many state agencies have been granted power to adopt regulations governing particular matters. These are "laws" enforceable in the courts, in the same manner as state statutes and local ordinances. North Carolina is now compiling all currently valid regulations in a State Administrative Code, somewhat similar to the General Statutes or to the Code of Federal Regulations.

LOCAL GOVERNMENTS

COUNTIES

The creation of counties as subdivisions of the state originated in England even before the organization of the kingdom itself. *Bignell v. Cummins*, 36 A.L.R. 634; 14 A.J. 185. Their existence and their functions in the administration of the law were so well recognized that those who drafted our original Constitution did not deem it necessary to provide for their creation or to define their powers. Instead they assumed their existence *as a constituent part of the state government*. N.C. Const. of 1776, sec. 38; N.C. Const., Art. VII, sec. 1.

[Counties] are subdivisions of the State, established for the more convenient administration of government and to assure a large measure of local self-government. Their powers which are intrinsically governmental stem from the common law. Legislative acts supplement, modify, or curtail those powers to meet the needs of a changing civilization. Generally speaking they possess such governmental powers as are necessary to be exercised in the enforcement of the law, the maintenance of the peace, and the protection of the people within their boundaries, subject to such limitations as the Legislature may deem it wise to impose, 14 A.J. 185, and are vested by the Constitution with the power to tax for these purposes. N.C. Const., Art. V, sec. 6.[2]

[Counties] are not created for the particular, special, or exclusive benefit of the people having property in them. They are of, and constitute parts of the State government. They are created for political and civil purposes of the State, and may be created without special regard to the will, wish, or convenience of the people who inhabit them. They are instrumentalities of the State government, and subject to its legislative control; they possess such corporate powers and delegated authority as the Legislature may deem fit to confer upon them, and such power and authority must be exercised in the way, and only for the purpose prescribed by legislative enactment; and moreover, they are always subject to legislative control, and their powers may be abolished, enlarged, abridged or modified.[3]

The leading and principal purpose in establishing counties is to effectuate the political organization and civil administration of the state, in respect to its general purposes and policy which require local direction, supervision and control, such as matters of local finance, education, provisions for the poor, the establishment and maintenance of highways and bridges, and in large measure, the administration of public justice. It is through them, mainly, that the powers of government reach and operate directly upon the people, and the people direct and control the government. . . .[4]

Although the original functions of counties were restricted generally to the types of county-wide functions indicated in the above excerpts from court opinions (chiefly relating to welfare, education, roads, the court system, and law enforcement), for the past 30 to 40 years the North Carolina General Assembly has been gradually adding to their powers various municipal functions (largely as a result of increasing urbanization of formerly rural areas and the demands for services made by residents of such areas). Since 1974 North Carolina counties have had almost all powers that our cities have, with the notable exception of responsibility for constructing and maintaining roads (which was taken over by the state during the depression years; counties now function only minimally in this area).

In most states a county government consists of a rather loose confederation of (a) a governing board, such as a board of county commissioners, with primary responsibility for budget-making and tax-levying; (b) numbers of elected officials (frequently prescribed in the state constitution) such as a sheriff, clerk of court, and register of deeds; (c) appointed administrative officials such as a county attorney, treasurer, accountant,

---

2. Railroad v. Mecklenburg County, 231 N.C. 148, 150, 56 S.E.2d 438 (1949).
3. Dare County v. Currituck County, 95 N.C. 189, 191-92 (1886).
4. White v. Commissioners of Chowan, 90 N.C. 437 (1884).

tax supervisor, etc.; and (d) boards responsible for policy-making and administration of particular functions — like the boards of education, elections, health, social services — and their employees. While many North Carolina counties have moved to a county manager system, much of the original pattern is still evident across the state.

CITIES AND TOWNS

Towns and cities organized under charters or particular statutes, and invested with more of the functions of corporate existence, [are] intended to serve, not so much the purposes of the State, as, subject to its general laws, the advantage of particular communities in particular localities in the promotion and regulation more or less of trade, commerce, industries, and the business transactions and relations of the people residing or going there collectively or severally — their purposes are more general, and partake more largely of the purpose and powers of government proper. . . . Cities and towns are incorporated largely and mainly for the particular benefit of the corporators; they have special privileges and advantages and exercise special powers. . . . [5]

Ours would be a strange sort of government if the Legislature could not make a new county without the consent of the people there residing being first had and obtained, or if when, in the opinion of the Legislature, the population of a particular locality has become so dense that it cannot be well governed by the ordinary county regulations, and requires the special "rules and by-laws" of an incorporated town to secure its good order and management, such locality cannot be incorporated into a town or annexed to one already incorporated. . . . [6]

[C]ities and towns are not incorporated for the primary purposes of government, the protection of person and property, since that could be done by the justices of the peace and constables, as in the county districts, without the expensive machinery of municipal government, but municipalities are in fact not so much for governmental purposes as for business needs, such as paving, lights, security against fire, water, sewerage, and the like, which are the necessities of a dense population, and which can be furnished more cheaply and effectively by the representatives of the municipality chosen to administer its common interests, than by subjecting each citizen to the unrestricted demands of private capital. [7]

As the selections above indicate, city functions tend to center around two poles: the enactment and enforcement of *regulations* made necessary by urban conditions and the provision of *services* to people who live closely together, including higher levels of police and fire protection, garbage

---

5. Manuel v. Commissioners of Cumberland, 98 N.C. 9, 10-12, 3 S.E. 829 (1887).
6. Manly v. Raleigh, 57 N.C. 370 (1857).
7. Mayo v. Commissioners, 122 N.C. 5, 25-26, 29 S.E. 343 (1898).

collection, street construction and maintenance, water and sewerage service, recreational facilities, transportation systems, electric power, etc. In general, cities have been delegated a broader range of powers than any other local governmental unit.

Most cities are much more tightly organized than counties, with overall control normally vested in an elected city council or board of aldermen. American cities are usually organized under one of four major plans: (1) strong mayor-council, in which the council fixes policy but the mayor has major executive powers; (2) weak mayor-council, in which the mayor lacks budget power, veto power, or major appointive powers; (3) commission, in which the individual commissioners each administer specified departments in addition to serving together as a policy-making body; and (4) council-manager, in which an elected council fixes policy to be executed under the direction of an appointed manager.

North Carolina has a very strong council-manager tradition, and nearly all but the smallest towns have that form of government.

SPECIAL DISTRICTS AND AUTHORITIES

Most states provide for the creation of special-purpose districts and so-called "authorities." The special district normally includes an area of less than a county (and usually lies outside any incorporated city), and it offers one or a few specialized services to its residents. In return, they pay property taxes or service charges for such services. The most common type of district is the school district; others include sanitary districts, drainage districts, fire protection districts, soil conservation districts, small watershed districts, public health districts, etc. These special units have defined boundaries within which they (or counties or cities on their behalf) may levy and collect property taxes. This form of organization is particularly important in permitting semirural communities to secure and pay for particular services that the rest of the county might neither need nor wish to support.

The "authority" is a special form of agency that normally operates a revenue-producing function more or less in the manner of a private business. It usually has neither defined boundaries nor general taxing powers. It is supported by proceeds from the operations of such enterprises as toll highways and bridges, airports, seaports, housing projects, water systems, etc., and usually it may issue bonds for new construction based on anticipated revenues of these projects.

While certain special districts and authorities in North Carolina have limited regulatory powers, none appears to have authority to regulate construction of buildings.

3 THE GOVERNMENTAL FRAMEWORK FOR BUILDING REGULATION

Building regulation involves two major groups of functions: the adoption and amendment of laws (which we shall refer to as "legislative functions"), and the administration and enforcement of those laws (which we shall call "enforcement functions"). This chapter will examine the allocation of these functions among various governmental units in North Carolina.

LEGISLATIVE FUNCTIONS: THE ADOPTION AND AMENDMENT OF LAWS

Constitution of North Carolina

Article II, Section 1. The legislative power of the state shall be vested in the General Assembly, which shall consist of a Senate and a House of Representatives.

THE GENERAL ASSEMBLY

In the area of building regulation the General Assembly has exercised its constitutional responsibilities in two ways. (1) It has adopted some laws directly regulating particular aspects of construction. (2) It has empowered certain state agencies or departments and local governments to adopt laws regulating other aspects of construction.

As we saw in Chapter 1, the General Assembly in 1905 enacted a complete (by the standards of the time) State Building Law that applied to all North Carolina towns over 1,000 population; this act was repealed in 1969. Among the current examples of direct regulation by statute are Articles 4 (electrical materials, devices, appliances, and equipment), 4A (safety features of hot water heaters), and 4B (safety features of trailers) of General Statutes Chapter 66, and Articles 2 (fire escapes) and 4 (hotels, safety provisions) of Chapter 69.

Usually, however, the General Assembly has recognized the technical complexity of building regulations and has delegated responsibility for developing such regulations to a body with more expertise concerning the issues involved. In some cases it has created new state agencies with responsibility for regulating particular matters. In other cases it has authorized or directed existing state departments to adopt such regulations. And in still other cases it has given this authority to local governments. Examples of these types of delegation are set forth below.

BUILDING CODE COUNCIL

The most significant state agency in the area of building regulation is the Building Code Council. It was created by and derives its powers from Article 9 of General Statutes Chapter 143, set forth in full in the Appendix of this book. It consists of 12 members appointed by the Governor from various segments of the construction industry or the government, and it is staffed by the Division of Engineering [and Building Codes] of the Department of Insurance.[1]

The Council's principal responsibility is to adopt and from time to time amend a State Building Code, in accordance with the detailed provisions of G.S. 143-138. In carrying out this function the Council must also comply with the State Administrative Procedure Act[2] and certain other statutes. Section 107 of Volume I of the State Building Code sets forth procedural rules for hearings on proposed amendments.

A second (and related) responsibility of the Council is approval of local deviations from the Code, pursuant to G.S. 143-138(e). Section 108 of the State Building Code Volume I sets forth procedural rules for handling applications for such approval.

The Council's third major responsibility, although nonlegislative, is to hear appeals from decisions of enforcement agencies under the Code. This duty is discussed in the section on enforcement functions later in this chapter.

Finally, the Council has two less-important legislative responsibilities, assigned by other provisions of the General Statutes. G.S. 153A-235 requires that counties submit their proposed fire prevention codes to the Council for approval before adopting them. And G.S. 143-146 and -147 authorize the Council to regulate licensing of persons or inspection departments that wish to certify compliance of mobile homes with state and federal regulations.

NORTH CAROLINA CODE OFFICIALS QUALIFICATION BOARD

The North Carolina Code Officials Qualification Board is another

---

1. N.C. GEN. STAT. §§ 143-136, -137.
2. *Id.* Ch. 150B, especially Arts. 2 and 5.

agency created to handle a portion of the building regulation field: the certification of code enforcement officials. It was created by and derives its powers from Article 9B of General Statutes Chapter 143, set forth in full in the Appendix of this book. It consists of 20 appointed members from the construction industry, from the ranks of enforcement officials, and from educational institutions, and it too is staffed by the Division of Engineering and Building Codes of the Department of Insurance.[3]

The Board's principal legislative responsibility is to adopt regulations setting education and experience standards for various types and levels of code enforcement officials and specifying how they may be certified as meeting such standards. The provisions guiding the Board as it exercises this responsibility are to be found largely in G.S. 143-151.12 through -151.16. The Board must also comply with the State Administrative Procedure Act.[4]

A second (and related) Board responsibility is to set forth procedures through which a certificate may be denied, suspended, or revoked in cases in which discipline is called for by G.S. 143-151.17.[5]

The Board is also directed to participate in developing courses of instruction through which code officials may qualify for certification, and as a part of this process it may establish qualifications for instructors in such courses.[6]

DEPARTMENT OF INSURANCE

While the Commissioner of Insurance has many *enforcement* functions in the area of building regulation, and the Division of Engineering and Building Codes of his department serves as a staff for the Building Code Council and the North Carolina Code Officials Qualification Board, the Commissioner's only *legislative* function in the area of building regulation has to do with the manufacture of mobile homes. Under Article 9A of General Statutes Chapter 143, he must adopt rules embodying the standards for construction of such units set by the federal Department of Housing and Urban Development, and he may adopt further rules necessary to carry out the provisions of Part 2 of Article 9A.[7]

DEPARTMENT OF LABOR

Article 7A of General Statutes Chapter 95 directs the Commissioner

---

3. *Id.* §§ 143-151.9 and -151.19.
4. *Id.* Ch. 150B, especially Arts. 2 and 5.
5. These rules must also mesh with those set forth in Articles 3A and 4 of the Administrative Procedure Act.
6. N.C. GEN. STAT. § 143-151.12(4), (5), and (6).
7. *Id.* § 143-146.

of Labor, on recommendation of the North Carolina Board of Boiler and Pressure Vessels Rules, to adopt and amend regulations governing the construction, operation, and use of such vessels.

Article 14A of Chapter 95 authorizes the Commissioner to adopt regulations of the construction, etc., of elevators and related devices, and Article 14B grants him similar powers with respect to amusement devices (such as Ferris wheels and roller coasters).

Article 15 of Chapter 95 directs the Commissioner of Labor to adopt regulations as to the construction, operation, and maintenance of passenger tramways—defined as devices to carry passengers uphill (such as ski lifts and cars suspended from cables).

Article 16 of Chapter 95 (the Occupational Safety and Health Act of North Carolina) authorizes the Commissioner of Labor to adopt OSHA regulations differing from those promulgated by the federal Secretary of Labor. Such regulations may cover, among other things, practices during construction of buildings and other facilities.

DEPARTMENT OF AGRICULTURE

Article 4C of General Statutes Chapter 106 directs the Structural Pest Control Committee within the Department of Agriculture to regulate persons in the structural pest control business (control of wood-destroying organisms or household pests).

G.S. 106-673(23) and (24) authorize the Board of Agriculture to regulate installation and operation of facilities for handling and storing liquid fertilizer.

Article 5 of General Statutes Chapter 119 authorizes the Board of Agriculture to adopt regulations for the design, construction, and operation of facilities for storing and utilizing liquefied petroleum gases.

DEPARTMENT OF HUMAN RESOURCES

The Department of Human Resources is a consolidation of the old State Board of Health and the Department of Social Services. Its organization includes a large number of commissions with regulatory powers. Among them are the following, whose powers touch upon particular areas of building construction:

The *Commission for Health Services* is required under G.S. 143B-142 to adopt rules for sanitary privies for schools where water-carried sewage facilities are unavailable[8] and requirements for sanitation of local confinement facilities.[9] In addition it is authorized to adopt rules implementing

---

8. See also *id.* § 115C-522.
9. See also *id.* § 153A-226.

public health programs administered by the Department under G.S. Chapter 130A.[10] It has authority also to regulate day-care facilities,[11] the location and construction of public water and sewer facilities,[12] and meat markets.[13]

The Commission for *Mental Health and Mental Retardation Services* has authority under G.S. 143B-147 to adopt regulations and standards for licensing private hospitals for the mentally disordered.[14]

The *North Carolina Medical Care Commission* has authority under G.S. 143B-165 to adopt regulations to be followed in constructing and maintaining public and private hospitals, medical centers, and related facilities.[15]

The *Social Services Commission* has power under G.S. 143B-153 to establish standards for (1) licensing of maternity homes;[16] (2) licensing of domiciliary homes for aged or disabled persons;[17] (3) licensing of child-care institutions;[18] and (4) jails or local confinement facilities.[19]

DEPARTMENT OF NATURAL RESOURCES AND COMMUNITY DEVELOPMENT

The Department of Natural Resources and Community Development also includes many rule-making commissions of various types. The most significant of these, from the standpoint of building construction, is probably the *Environmental Management Commission.* Under G.S. 143B-282 and Articles 21, 21A, and 21B of G.S. Chapter 143, the Commission has power to establish regulations concerning water and air pollution, the use of water in critical ("capacity use") areas, oil extraction and refinement, the construction of dams, and the delineation of floodways within which construction is largely forbidden.

Other commissions with powers affecting the construction industry are the *North Carolina Mining Commission,* which is empowered by G.S. 143B-290 to adopt regulations implementing the Mining Act of 1971;[20] the *Sedimentation Control Commission,* which is empowered by G.S. 143B-298 to adopt regulations for the control of erosion and sedimentation;[21] and the *Coastal Resources Commission,* which is empowered by Article 7 of

---

10. See *id.* Ch. 130A, Art. 8, Parts 4 (hospitals, nursing homes, and similar facilities), 5 (migrant housing), and 6 (food and lodging facilities).

11. See *id.* Ch. 110, Art. 7.

12. *Id.* Ch. 130A, Arts. 10 and 11.

13. *Id.* Ch. 130A, Art. 8, Part 2.

14. *Id.* Ch. 122C, Art. 2.

15. *Id.* Ch. 131E, Art. 4.

16. *Id.* § 131D-1.

17. *Id.* § 131D-2(b).

18. *Id.* § 131D-10.5.

19. *Id.* § 153A-220, and *id.* Ch. 131D, Art. 2.

20. *Id.* Ch. 74, Art. 7.

21. See also *id.* § 113A-54.

G.S. Chapter 113A to adopt (among other things) regulations for construction in Areas of Environmental Concern in the coastal counties.

DEPARTMENT OF ADMINISTRATION

Among the functions of the Department of Administration under G.S. 143-341 are (1) approval of all plans and specifications for construction or renovation of state buildings and (2) supervision and inspection of work done under such contracts. While there is no explicit regulatory power established in connection with these functions, the Department has issued manuals on "property control and construction" and "instructions to bidders and general conditions of state contracts," which have virtually the same impact as regulations.

LICENSING BOARDS

All licensing boards in the area of the construction industry have power to adopt rules and regulations affecting persons within their jurisdiction. These include the North Carolina Board of Architecture,[22] the State Licensing Board for General Contractors,[23] the State Board of Examiners of Plumbing and Heating Contractors,[24] the State Board of Examiners of Electrical Contractors,[25] the State Board of Refrigeration Contractors,[26] the North Carolina Board of Landscape Architects,[27] the State Board of Registration for Professional Engineers and Land Surveyors,[28] and the North Carolina Landscape Contractors Registration Board.[29]

LOCAL GOVERNMENTS

Historically, North Carolina cities (and later counties) have been granted a much broader range of regulatory powers than individual state departments or agencies. This is still true. Some of these delegations are quite specific and limited, but both cities and counties also possess general regulatory powers.

We have already seen that G.S. 143-138(e) provides for local deviations from the State Building Code, when approved by the Building Code Council. This authority applies to both cities and counties.

---

22. *Id.* Ch. 83A.
23. *Id.* Ch. 87, Art. 1.
24. *Id.* Ch. 87, Art. 2.
25. *Id.* Ch. 87, Art. 4.
26. *Id.* Ch. 87, Art. 5.
27. *Id.* Ch. 89A.
28. *Id.* Ch. 89C.
29. *Id.* Ch. 89D.

Closely related to the building code is a housing code that sets standards for existing as well as new residential structures. G.S. Chapter 160A, Art. 19, Part 6 authorizes both cities and counties to adopt an ordinance of this type, as well as one dealing with certain abandoned buildings. This act is set forth in the Appendix.

Both cities[30] and counties[31] have been authorized to adopt ordinances establishing inspection departments, assigning them duties, specifying fees for various services, and amplifying statutory procedures to be followed in conducting their duties. These statutes are set forth in the Appendix.

The inspection department enabling acts authorize both types of local governments to designate "fire limits" within which wooden buildings may be erected, repaired, altered, or moved only with special permission.[32]

Both cities[33] and counties[34] have been authorized to adopt zoning ordinances that divide the unit into districts and specify what uses may be made of property in each district as well as minimum lot sizes, yard requirements, maximum building heights, and similar matters. These acts are set forth in the Appendix.

The two local units are also allowed to provide within their zoning ordinances for approval of the external appearance of new or altered buildings within a historic district by the historic district commission.[35] This act is set forth in the Appendix.

A specialized type of zoning—airport zoning for areas surrounding airports—is another type of regulation that both cities and counties may adopt.[36]

Both types of units may also adopt floodway regulations to govern construction in stream floodways and ordinances to control sedimentation and erosion.[37]

Counties may adopt fire prevention codes, with the Building Code Council's approval.[38] (Cities may adopt such codes under their general ordinance-making power, G.S. 160A-174.)

And both cities[39] and counties[40] have general power to adopt any ordinance that is consistent with the federal and state constitutions and statutes. While court decisions have in some cases limited the apparent breadth of these provisions, they still authorize a broad range of regulations.

30. *Id.* Ch. 160A, Art. 19, Part 5.
31. *Id.* Ch. 153A, Art. 18, Part 4.
32. Cities: *Id.* §§ 160A-435, -436, -437, -438; counties: *id.* § 153A-375.
33. *Id.* Ch. 160A, Art. 19, Part 3.
34. *Id.* Ch. 153A, Art. 18, Part 3.
35. *Id.* Ch. 160A, Art. 19, Part 3A.
36. *Id.* Ch. 63, Art. 4.
37. *Id.* Ch. 143, Art. 21, Part 6, and *id.* § 160A-458.1; *id.* Ch. 113A, Art. 4; and *id.* § 160A-458.
38. *Id.* § 153A-235.
39. *Id.* § 160A-174.
40. *Id.* § 153A-121.

ENFORCEMENT FUNCTIONS: THE ADMINISTRATION AND ENFORCEMENT OF LAWS

When the General Assembly directly regulates a subject, it sometimes designates the agency or agencies that are to enforce those regulations. For example, the Department of Insurance is charged with enforcing the state laws governing building exits and fire escapes, theater safety, and hotel safety.[41] The Department of Labor is to enforce regulations of elevators, moving stairways, and amusement devices.[42] In the absence of such designation, responsibility for enforcing state laws falls upon the state's criminal justice system: sheriffs, police, and other law enforcement officers; prosecutors in the various courts; the courts themselves; and the correctional system.

In general, state agencies and departments given authority to adopt regulations are also responsible for enforcing those regulations (usually with back-up from the criminal justice system). For example, the Building Code Council, the North Carolina Code Officials Qualification Board, the Department of Insurance, the Department of Labor, the Department of Agriculture, the Department of Human Resources, the Department of Natural Resources and Community Development, and the various licensing boards all have enforcement responsibilities with respect to the regulations described in the preceding section of this chapter.

Similarly, local governments given ordinance-making power have power to enforce those ordinances. See especially G.S. 160A-175 (cities) and G.S. 153A-123 (counties), in addition to enforcement provisions for many of the ordinances specifically authorized by statute.

ENFORCEMENT OF THE STATE BUILDING CODE

GENERAL ALLOCATION OF RESPONSIBILILTY

The statutory pattern for administration and enforcement of the State Building Code is more complex than that prescribed for most other regulations. It is as follows:

Local governments (cities and counties) have initial responsibility for

---

41. *Id.* Ch. 69, Arts. 2 and 4.
42. *Id.* § 143-139(d).

enforcement.[43] This responsibility is to be exercised under general supervision of (and in cooperation with) the Insurance Commissioner (through the Division of Engineering and Building Codes) with respect to most provisions of the Code; the Bureau of Boiler Inspection of the Department of Labor with respect to Code provisions concerning boilers; and the Department of Labor with respect to Code provisions concerning elevators, moving stairways, merry-go-rounds, roller coasters, Ferris wheels, and similar amusement devices.[44]

Appeals may be taken from local inspectors to the Insurance Commissioner with respect to most provisions of the Code, to the Bureau of Boiler Inspection of the Department of Labor with respect to Code provisions concerning boilers, and to the Department of Labor with respect to Code provisions concerning elevators, escalators, and amusement devices.[45]

Further appeals may be taken from the Insurance Commissioner, the Bureau of Boiler Inspection, or the Department of Labor to either a superior court (the Wake County Superior Court or the superior court of the county where the proposed building is to be situated) or the Building Code Council.[46] Further appeals from the Building Code Council also may be taken to a superior court.[47]

Within the court system, further appeals may be taken to the North Carolina Court of Appeals, the North Carolina Supreme Court, and the United States Supreme Court, as with other types of judicial proceedings.

JURISDICTION OF CITIES AND COUNTIES

The territorial areas (jurisdiction) within which cities and counties are empowered to enforce the State Building Code are set by statute.

In general, city jurisdiction includes all areas within the corporate limits, and county jurisdiction includes the areas outside all city limits within the county.[48] However, the statutes also contain provisions under which a city may extend its jurisdiction beyond its limits, and a county may enforce the Code within a city.[49]

Under the provisions of G.S. 160A-360, any city may adopt an ordinance spelling out the boundaries of its extraterritorial jurisdiction, which may extend up to one mile beyond the city limits. Cities with populations of 10,000–25,000 may extend such boundaries as much as two miles beyond their limits, and cities over 25,000 may extend these boundaries as far as

43. Cities: *Id.* §§ 160A-412, -417, -423; counties: *id.* §§ 153A-352, -357, -363; both: State Building Code, Vol. I, § 105.

44. N.C. GEN. STAT. § 143-139.

45. *Id.* § 143-140; *id.* § 153A-374; *id.* § 160A-434; State Building Code, Vol. I, Sec. 106.

46. N.C. GEN. STAT. §§ 143-140, -141; State Building Code, Vol. I, Sec. 106.

47. N.C. GEN. STAT. § 143-141(d).

48. *Id.* § 143-138(e).

49. *Id.* § 160A-360.

three miles; but these larger extensions become effective only if the county commissioners first adopt a resolution approving them.

If the county has already begun to zone, regulate subdivisions, and enforce the State Building Code (all three) within an area outside the city, the city may extend its extraterritorial jurisdiction into *that* area only with the county's permission.

If a city has not adopted an extraterritorial jurisdiction ordinance, the county may exercise its powers right up to the city limits.

Whether or not the city has adopted such an ordinance, it may by resolution authorize the county to exercise particular regulatory powers in any specified areas within its extraterritorial jurisdiction or within the city itself.

In addition to these basic rules setting the territorial jurisdiction of cities and counties, the statutes provide for a variety of contractual arrangements through which two or more local governments may have joint inspection departments or hire services from one another. These possibilities are outlined in the section below.

MANDATORY ARRANGEMENTS FOR ENFORCING THE STATE BUILDING CODE

As a result of legislation passed in 1977, every city and county was required to arrange for enforcing the State Building Code within its jurisdiction by the applicable date (based on 1970 populations) set forth below.[50]

Cities and counties over 75,000 population—July 1, 1979;
Cities and counties between 50,001 and 75,000—July 1, 1981;
Cities and counties between 25,001 and 50,000—July 1, 1983;
Cities and counties 25,000 and under—July 1, 1985.

If a city or county fails to meet this requirement, the Commissioner of Insurance must arrange for such enforcement, either with Department of Insurance personnel or through arrangements with other units.

The statutes allow local governments to meet this requirement in a great many ways:

(1) The unit may do nothing and allow the Insurance Commissioner to make the arrangements.[51]
(2) It may create its own inspection department, charged with enforcing the Code.[52]
(3) Any two or more local governments can create a joint Inspection Department.[53]

---

50. *Id.* § 160A-411; *id.* § 153A-351.
51. *Id.* § 153A-351; *id.* § 160A-411.
52. *Id.* § 153A-351; *id.* § 160A-411.
53. *Id.* § 153A-353; *id.* §§ 160A-413, -462.

(4) The unit may hire, on a part-time basis, one or more inspectors from another local government, with the approval of that unit's governing board. This may be done either to supplement the staff of the first unit or to constitute its total staff.[54]

(5) The local government may contract with another local government for the second to furnish inspection services to the first.[55]

(6) A city may request the county of which it is a part to provide inspection services within its jurisdiction, without the need for a contract between the two.[56]

(7) All the cities in a county might enforce the State Building Code within their defined extraterritorial jurisdiction in such a way that they cover most of the county's developing areas.[57]

INTERNAL ORGANIZATION FOR CODE ENFORCEMENT BY LOCAL GOVERNMENTS

Even though the statutes specifically authorize city and county inspection departments, local governing boards are free to organize the city or county government as they deem most efficient and economical.[58] Using this latitude, some cities and counties have placed enforcement of the State Building Code within an inspection department, while some have made it the responsibility of an inspections division of another department, such as a department of community development, a department of public works, an engineering department, or a planning department.

Furthermore, the statutes do not require any particular internal organization of an inspection department or division. This too is left up to the governing body's discretion (and ultimately to the manager and to the department head).

---

54. *Id.* § 153A-353; *id.* § 160A-413
55. *Id.* § 160A-461.
56. *Id.* § 160A-360(d),(g).
57. *Id.* § 160A-360.
58. City: *Id.* § 160A-146; county: *id.* § 153A-76.

4 THE LEGAL FRAMEWORK OF BUILDING REGULATION

Any regulatory system exists within a framework of constitutional, statutory, and court-created rules that define what can and cannot be regulated and how regulations must be adopted and carried out. North Carolina's system of building regulation is no exception.

CONSTITUTIONAL POWERS AND RESTRAINTS

Most constitutional authorities agree that governmental powers fall into three major divisions: the taxing and spending power, the power of eminent domain, and the police power. There are constitutional restraints upon each of these.

TAXING AND SPENDING POWER

Broadly speaking, the "taxing and spending power" is the government's power to collect funds from its citizens and to spend those funds for various public purposes. In this statement, the word "spending" comprehends all manner of expenditures, and the word "taxing" comprehends all of the means through which governments raise money, including not only taxes but also special assessments, fees and charges, gifts, profits from sales of alcoholic beverages, lotteries, issuance of notes and bonds, and the printing of paper money.

When used in a stricter sense, however, "taxing" takes on a coercive aspect, in which citizens are more or less forcibly separated from their wealth, whether or not they agree with (or directly benefit from) the purposes for which it is to be spent.

The constitutional restraints on the taxing and spending power include both sets of meanings. They restrict the purposes for which governments may spend money, and they restrict the mechanisms through which governments extract that money from their citizens. Such restraints are set forth much more explicitly in the North Carolina Constitution than in the United States Constitution.

Constitution of North Carolina

Article V, Sec. 2. State and local taxation.

(1) *Power of taxation.* The power of taxation shall be exercised in a just and equitable manner, for public purposes only, and shall never be surrendered, suspended, or contracted away.

(2) *Classification.* Only the General Assembly shall have the power to classify property for taxation, which power shall be exercised only on a State-wide basis and shall not be delegated. No class of property shall be taxed except by uniform rule, and every classification shall be made by general law uniformly applicable in every county, city and town, and other unit of local government.

(3) *Exemptions.* Property belonging to the State, counties, and municipal corporations shall be exempt from taxation. The General Assembly may exempt cemeteries and property held for educational, scientific, literary, cultural, charitable, or religious purposes, and, to a value not exceeding $300, any personal property. The General Assembly may exempt from taxation not exceeding $1,000 in value of property held and used as the place of residence of the owner. Every exemption shall be on a State-wide basis and shall be made by general law uniformly applicable in every county, city and town, and other unit of local government. No taxing authority other than the General Assembly may grant exemptions, and the General Assembly shall not delegate the powers accorded to it by this subsection.

(4) *Special tax areas.* Subject to the limitations imposed by Section 4, the General Assembly may enact general laws authorizing the governing body of any county, city, or town to define territorial areas and to levy taxes within those areas, in addition to those levied throughout the county, city, or town, in order to finance, provide, or maintain services, facilities, and functions in addition to or to a greater extent than those financed, provided, or maintained for the entire county, city, or town.

(5) *Purposes of property tax.* The General Assembly shall not authorize any county, city or town, special district, or other unit of local government to levy taxes on property, except for purposes authorized by general law uniformly applicable throughout the State, unless the tax is approved by a majority of the qualified voters of the unit who vote thereon. . . .

Article I, Sec. 32. Exclusive emoluments. No person or set of persons is entitled to exclusive or separate emoluments or privileges from the community but in consideration of public services.

As the above provisions show, the major constitutional restraints are that money may be collected and spent only for "public purposes," public funds may not be paid to individuals as "exclusive or separate emoluments" that they have not earned through public service, and taxes generally must be levied in a uniform manner.

Although the taxing and spending power has little direct application to building regulation, it supplies the wherewithal for the regulatory system to function. And the government's ability to make loans and grants may supplement regulations in programs to upgrade the quality of housing.

POWER OF EMINENT DOMAIN

Eminent domain is the power to take (or "condemn") private property for public use. Because it was originally used by the king of England to acquire strategically located lands whose possession was essential to defense of the country, eminent domain has been referred to as an inherent power of government, necessary for the government's own preservation. Most present-day uses of eminent domain are much more prosaic, such as the acquisition of street rights-of-way or a site for a new city hall. The utility of eminent domain is primarily to keep property owners from "holding up" the government by demanding an excessive price for property the government needs for the public good.

The constitutional restraints on the exercise of eminent domain, some stemming directly from constitutional language and some imposed by the courts, require that property be taken only for a "public use" (akin to the "public purpose" for which public funds may be spent) and that fair compensation be paid for it.[1]

In general this power may be exercised only through the court system, and the statutes authorizing it normally include a range of mandatory procedures designed to assure fair treatment for the property owner.

Eminent domain need not be exercised in ordinary building regulation programs. But it may be a critical element in programs of public housing, urban renewal, or community development designed to upgrade the quality of slum areas.

POLICE POWER

Building regulation involves an exercise of the third of the major powers: the "police power." The police power has been described as "the broadest of all governmental powers" and as "all governmental powers which do not fall into the categories of taxing and spending or eminent domain." Usually it is thought of as government's regulatory power. Its exercise does not normally necessitate payment of compensation to the regulated parties (although its abuse may), and it is not used for the purpose of collecting money for government operations (although some of its penalty provisions have that effect).

The range of subjects regulated in the 24 volumes of the North Carolina General Statutes (not to mention the United States Code and the thousands and thousands of pages of federal, state, and local regulations and

---

1. U.S. CONST. amend. V; N.C. CONST. art. I, § 19.

ordinances) indicates the importance attached to this type of power by governmental officials and the citizens who elect them or their superiors. In the eyes of many, no problem is too complex to be dealt with by simply "adopting a law."

The restraints upon abuse of such power are to be found in a number of federal and state constitutional provisions and the interpretations placed upon them by the courts. The major provisions with which we shall be concerned are those below.

Constitution of the United States

Amendment XIV, § 1. All persons born or naturalized in the United States, and subject to the jurisdiction thereof, are citizens of the United States and of the state wherein they reside. No state shall make or enforce any law which shall abridge the privileges or immunities of citizens of the United States; nor shall any state deprive any person of life, liberty, or property, without due process of law; nor deny to any person within its jurisdiction the equal protection of the laws. . . .

Constitution of North Carolina

Article I, Sec. 19. *Law of the land; equal protection of the laws.* No person shall be taken, imprisoned, or disseized of his freehold, liberties, or privileges, or outlawed, or exiled, or in any manner deprived of his life, liberty, or property, but by the law of the land. No person shall be denied the equal protection of the laws; nor shall any person be subjected to discrimination by the State because of race, color, religion, or national origin.

Article I, Sec. 32. *Exclusive emoluments.* No person or set of persons is entitled to exclusive or separate emoluments or privileges from the community but in consideration of public services.

Article I, Sec. 34. *Perpetuities and monopolies.* Perpetuities and monopolies are contrary to the genius of a free state and shall not be allowed.

Article II, Sec. 1. *Legislative power.* The legislative power of the State shall be vested in the General Assembly, which shall consist of a Senate and a House of Representatives.

The constraints derived from the above provisions fall under three main headings: "due process," "equal protection," and "delegation of legislative power."

Due Process. Our courts have held that the provisions of the "due process" clause in the federal Constitution's Fourteenth Amendment and the "law of the land" clause in Article I, Section 19, of the North Carolina Constitution are essentially identical.

Originally the due process provisions were understood to require *fair procedures:* notably the citizen's right to notice, a hearing, and a right to appeal to the courts when he is subjected to regulation. Collectively, these requirements have come to be known as "procedural due process." Their impact is to be found in many statutory provisions affording such rights with respect to particular types of regulation.[2]

More recently our courts have begun to use the "due process" provisions as a test of the constitutionality of the *substance* of legislation, and the term "substantive due process" has been applied to the rules governing such review.

The major substantive due process rules require that regulations:

(a) bear a reasonable and substantial relationship to the public health, safety, morals, or general welfare (which are sometimes known as the "police power objectives" that describe the proper areas for governmental regulation);

(b) be "reasonable" in their extent (i.e., must not go so far as to become a "taking" of property rights or other rights as viewed by the courts);

(c) be specific enough that they can be understood both by those who are regulated and those who are enforcing the regulations (i.e., they must not be "unconstitutionally vague"); and

(d) not be "arbitrary and capricious" in their application.

For example, front-yard requirements in a zoning ordinance might be justified on a health basis because they keep residences far enough from the street that their occupants will not be subjected to high concentrations of carbon monoxide or other noxious fumes; or they might be justified on a safety basis, either as fire lanes between residences or in affording motorists better views of driveways and intersections and of children dashing from the front door into the street; or they might be justified on a general-welfare basis, insofar as they hold down the density of development to a level that can be served by existing water, sewerage, and street facilities and require a degree of openness and greenery that helps preserve tax values.

If those regulations go so far as to prohibit any reasonable use of a piece of property, however, the courts will hold that they amount to a "taking," which is impermissible under the police power. And they must not be "arbitrary" or "capricious" in their application.

And if the regulations are so imprecise in their wording that the property owner cannot understand what is required of him, it would be unjust to punish him for their violation or to require him to forego legitimate conduct for fear that it might be proscribed.

Equal Protection. Both the Fourteenth Amendment of the federal Constitution and Article I, Section 19, of the North Carolina Constitution

---

2. See, for example, N.C. Gen. Stat. §§ 143-138(a), (d),(g), -140, and -141 of the enabling act authorizing the State Building Code, set forth in the Appendix.

contain "equal protection" clauses. These provisions are essentially aimed at enforcing the basic principle that everyone should be treated the same under the law. The provisions of Article I, Sections 32 and 34, of the North Carolina Constitution supplement the "equal protection" clauses in support of this principle.

Our courts have recognized, however, that laws cannot operate exactly the same upon everyone because of basic differences in circumstance. Even the fundamental laws prohibiting persons from killing one another have to make distinctions among deliberate and intentional killings, killings while under the influence of alcohol, killings in defense of one's home or family against intruders, accidental killings, or killings of enemy soldiers in time of war. But our courts have required that when distinctions are made, they must be based on reasonable criteria or reasonable classifications (not be "arbitrary" or "capricious"); if there is such a basis, they will not be held to violate equal protection requirements. It should be noted that in certain areas involving "fundamental rights"—such as the right to vote—the courts require a higher level of justification for a classification ("suspect classification").

The major type of "equal protection" cases in the courts has involved discrimination against groups of people, such as discrimination on the basis of race, religion, sex, age, or handicap. Not only the courts but many agencies of our government at all levels have been actively engaged in identifying and eliminating such discrimination from our laws.

Other types of "equal protection" violations also have been struck down by our courts. One of these has to do with discrimination among similar types of activities. For example, is it a violation of equal protection to exclude "farm buildings located outside the building-regulation jurisdiction of any municipality" from coverage of the State Building Code,[3] or is that a valid classification? Is it a violation of equal protection for the State Building Code to divide structures into the occupancy or use classifications set forth in Section 401 of Volume I of that Code and to prescribe different regulations for each classification, or are these valid classifications? Is it a violation of equal protection to set different construction standards for mobile homes from those applied to conventional dwellings, or is that a valid classification?

Another type of possible discrimination is regulation of similar properties in different manners. This is the basis of the so-called "spot zoning" rule in zoning law, which invalidates zoning a particular piece of property differently from generally similar properties in the same area. Similarly, is it valid for our stream pollution laws to require a manufacturing plant that discharges its wastes into a particular segment of a river to meet higher standards of treatment than a manufacturing plant downstream that discharges its wastes into another segment of that same river?

---

3. See N.C. Gen. Stat. § 143-138(b).

In all of these cases, the issue boils down to whether there is a reasonable, nonarbitrary basis for treating one person, one activity, or one piece of property in a manner different from the treatment of other persons, activities, or properties.

Delegation of Legislative Power. One feature of the constitutional structure of both the federal and state governments is the separation of powers among the legislative, executive, and judicial branches. Article II, Section 1, of the North Carolina Constitution, above, reflects this doctrine.

An outgrowth of this doctrine has been the development of a judicial rule that a legislative body may not "delegate" its power to an administrative agency in the executive branch. Strictly speaking, this rule would mean that the General Assembly could not authorize the Building Code Council to adopt a State Building Code or any other state department or agency to adopt rules and regulations. However, the courts have recognized the practical necessity for such delegation, especially in matters requiring technical expertise, and have held that when the statute that makes the delegation contains adequate "standards" to limit the discretion of the regulatory agency, it is no longer a delegation of legislative power but rather an assignment of administrative responsibility for carrying out the law passed by the legislature. And some courts, especially at the federal level, have enunciated a further loosening-up doctrine that there is no "delegation" if adequate procedural safeguards are included in the enabling legislation—regardless of the adequacy of the standards.

Obviously it is difficult to draft restrictive standards to govern regulations in complicated fields, and the courts have recognized this fact by not requiring more than is reasonably feasible in light of the complexity of the subject matter.

An illustration of a legislative attempt to provide such standards appears in G.S. 143-138(c) of the State Building Code enabling act. The basic approach here was to use the provisions of many model, nationally recognized codes to set the general parameters within which the Building Code Council could operate. The procedural provisions alluded to earlier (under "due process") also provide support for this delegation.

STATUTORY POWERS AND RESTRAINTS

When a state agency or local government derives its power from a state enabling act, that act in itself becomes a sort of "constitution" for the affected agency or unit.

Chapter 3 cited many of the enabling acts under which various state agencies and departments have been granted regulatory powers. To illustrate how such acts operate as constraints upon an agency, let us re-examine Article 9 of G.S. Chapter 143—the enabling act (set forth in the Appendix) under which the Building Code Council adopts and amends the State Building Code.

First, there are procedural requirements. As we have seen, G.S. 143-138(a) and (d) require that before adopting the Code or any amendment thereto, the Building Code Council must hold at least one public hearing in the City of Raleigh. At a minimum, notice of this public hearing must be given once a week for two successive calendar weeks in a newspaper published in Raleigh, beginning at least 15 days before the hearing. Further, G.S. 143-138(g) requires that the Code and its amendments be published and made available to the public after adoption. Our courts have repeatedly held that where there are such statutory requirements concerning procedures, failure to comply with these requirements will invalidate the purported action. Even a relatively minor violation, such as advertising only 14 instead of 15 days before the hearing, will have this effect.[4]

Second, the enabling act by its terms may limit what can be regulated. Sometimes this requires an interpretation. G.S. 143-138(b) originally spoke only of regulation of "buildings." Following an Attorney General's ruling that this meant the Code could not regulate structures *other than* buildings, the act was amended in 1971 to allow regulation of other structures. More recently, the North Carolina Court of Appeals held in *Carolinas-Virginias Association v. Ingram,*[5] that the act does not authorize the Code to include certain fire-protection requirements for *existing* buildings, although it may make such requirements for new buildings. This led to 1981 amendments ratifying and adopting those Code requirements.

In other cases no interpretation is required, because the act very specifically exempts certain structures from coverage by the Code: (a) farm buildings located outside the building-regulation jurisdiction of any municipality; (b) equipment for storing, handling, transporting, and using liquefied petroleum gases for fuel purposes or anhydrous ammonia or other liquid fertilizers; (c) equipment or facilities, other than buildings, of a public utility or an electric or telephone membership corporation.[6]

Third, the enabling act may by its terms specify the nature as well as the scope of the regulations. G.S. 143-138(c), while providing "standards" to counter any charge of an unlawful delegation of legislative power, requires that provisions contained in the Code have a demonstrable connection to one of the police power objectives and "conform to good engineering practice" (as evidenced generally by the model codes cited).

[It will be noted that G.S. 143-138(b) states that "the Code may contain provisions regulating every type of building or structure, wherever it might be situated in the State," and that G.S. 143-138(e) says that "The North Carolina State Building Code shall apply throughout the State, from the time of its adoption"—unless the Building Code Council has approved a

---

4. George v. Town of Edenton, 31 N.C. App. 648, 230 S.E.2d 695 (1977), *partially reversed on other grounds*, 294 N.C. 679, 242 S.E.2d 877 (1978).
5. 39 N.C. App. 688, 251 S.E.2d 910 (1979), *rev. denied*, 297 N.C. 299, 254 S.E.2d 925 (1979).
6. N.C. GEN. STAT. § 143-138(b).

local provision that supersedes a portion of the State Code. There is no need under the enabling act for local adoption of the Code.]

Of perhaps equal importance to local code officials are the provisions of G.S. Chapter 153A, Article 18, Part 4 and G.S. Chapter 160A, Article 19, Part 5, which authorize counties and cities to create inspection departments and assign certain responsibilities and powers to those departments. Analysis of these acts (found in the Appendix) shows that they too specify the procedures for adopting the ordinances that create such departments, the permissible subjects to be included in those ordinances, and many of the procedures that must be followed by code officials who are members of such departments.

The rest of this book is devoted in large measure to the detailed requirements of these and other statutes that pertain to the area of code enforcement.

JUDICIAL DECISIONS

Beginning many years before the American Revolution, our forebears in England established the concept of the courts' creating a body of law independent of the legislature. They did this by according precedential value to earlier decisions that dealt with similar factual situations; if one court had held a man liable, either civilly or criminally, for injuring his neighbor in a given manner, another court would use this decision as a basis for holding another man liable in a similar case. The body of precedents came to be known as the "common law."

While American legislatures have increasingly converted the principles thus developed by the courts into written statutes, the courts have continued to play a vital role. Under our constitutional system, the courts may be called on occasionally to determine whether a particular legislative enactment is constitutional. But there are many less dramatic cases in which the courts have held a particular statute or ordinance invalid because it was not properly enacted or exceeded the authority of the body that enacted it, and cases in which a court ruling is necessary to interpret the meaning of a statutory or ordinance provision.

Unlike some areas of the law, building regulation has not produced many North Carolina appellate cases, and those that we have fall into only a few categories.

First, there is the important holding in *State v. J. A. Tenant,*[7] which has had a marked impact on the law in other areas. In that case the defendant was charged with violating a local ordinance that required anyone who constructed, altered, or added to any building in town first to

---

7. 110 N.C. 609, 12 S.E. 387 (1892).

secure a building permit from the board of aldermen. While noting that the regulation of buildings was constitutionally permissible, the court held that the bare requirement of a permit with no indication as to the circumstances in which the permit would be granted or denied was unconstitutional. It said that this lack of standards allowed the aldermen complete freedom to grant or deny permits according to their arbitrary will, and it therefore amounted to a denial of due process.

Next come a number of cases dealing with municipal fire-limits ordinances. These ordinances commonly define an area by "fire limits" and prohibit the erection, alteration, or repair of any wooden building within those limits. Such regulations were developed to prevent conflagrations like those that had swept through the centers (and beyond) of many major cities of the world. While most buildings already standing in North Carolina cities were built of wood, it was contemplated that these would eventually be removed by natural causes and replaced with more fireproof structures. (While fire limits were an early type of building regulation, they are still authorized in cities by G.S. 160A-435 through -438, and in counties by G.S. 153A-375.)

State v. Johnson[8] first upheld the validity of such ordinances. In *State v. Eubanks,*[9] the ordinance required that anyone who undertook to construct a wooden building in the fire limits first secure a building permit from the board of aldermen. The court held that this requirement conflicted with a general state law that provided for a local building inspector to issue all building permits; furthermore, the court said, the requirement would probably be invalid under the reasoning of *State v. Tenant*, described earlier.

Two cases dealt with the application of fire-limits provisions to particular situations. In *State v. Lawing,*[10] the roof of a wooden two-story ell on a brick hotel was composed of rotting wood shingles. The owner sought to replace it with a sheet-iron roof. The court held that even though the sheet-iron roof itself was more fireproof than the wooden shingles, it violated the intent of the ordinance by making the wooden ell more permanent. In *State v. Shannonhouse,*[11] the court held that a hotel owner's attempt to replace a part of a wooden piazza without a permit violated the fire limits ordinance. (In *State v. Johnson, State v. Lawing,* and *State v. Shannonhouse* the court stated a rule that fire-limits restrictions could not impede minor repairs like replacing broken windows, hanging a shutter, or fixing steps, but they would prevent repairs that would insure the continuance of the building.)

---

8. 114 N.C. 846, 19 S.E. 599 (1894).
9. 154 N.C. 628, 70 S.E. 466 (1911).
10. 164 N.C. 492, 80 S.E. 69 (1913).
11. 166 N.C. 241, 80 S.E. 881 (1914).

The next group of cases generally established the validity of the State Building Code without directly raising issues concerning it. This group includes *Lutz Industries, Incorporated v. Dixie Home Stores,*[12] *Pinnix v. Toomey,*[13] *In re O'Neal,*[14] *Drum v. Bisaner,*[15] *Jenkins v. Leftwich Electric Company,*[16] *Jenkins v. Starrett Corporation,*[17] and *Lindstrom v. Chesnutt.*[18] All but *In re O'Neal* (essentially a zoning case) were suits between private parties (usually an owner and a contractor) in which one alleged that negligent construction or installation by the other had caused damage to him. In several of these cases the court traced the complete history of the State Building Code. Each decision affirmed the Code's validity and held that violating it would amount to negligence.

A large group of cases stemmed from one situation. The Charlotte inspection department, finding that a residential building was unsafe, ordered that it be demolished or removed. The owner challenged the con-stitutionality of the state statute that authorized condemnation of unsafe buildings (now part of the city and county enabling acts for inspection departments) and the city's ordinance provisions (a) authorizing inspections to ascertain building safety, (b) directing the department to condemn or remove unsafe buildings, and (c) requiring building permits. Altogether the owner carried four cases to the North Carolina Supreme Court and another through the chain of federal courts to the United States Supreme Court. Ultimately he lost on all points![19]

Greene v. Winston-Salem[20] challenged the validity of a Winston-Salem fire prevention ordinance requiring that certain high-rise buildings have sprinklers and other devices for fire protection. The North Carolina Supreme Court held that the state had "pre-empted" the field of such regulation and that the only way in which a local government could enact a valid ordinance of this type was with the approval of the Building Code Council as provided by G.S. 143-138(e). Since Winston-Salem had not secured such approval, its ordinance was invalid.

As we have already seen, *Carolinas-Virginias Association v. Ingram*[21] held that the State Building Code's enabling act allowed it to regulate only new construction and not existing buildings (except as its regulations

---

12. 242 N.C. 332, 88 S.E.2d 333 (1955).

13. 242 N.C. 359, 87 S.E.2d 893 (1955).

14. 243 N.C. 714, 92 S.E.2d 189 (1956).

15. 252 N.C. 305, 113 S.E.2d 560 (1960).

16. 254 N.C. 553, 119 S.E.2d 767 (1961).

17. 13 N.C. App. 437, 186 S.E.2d 198 (1972).

18. 15 N.C. App. 15, 189 S.E.2d 749 (1972).

19. Walker v. Charlotte, 262 N.C. 697, 138 S.E.2d 501 (1964); State v. Walker, 265 N.C. 482, 144 S.E.2d 419 (1965); James R. Walker v. North Carolina, 262 F. Supp. 102 (W.D.N.C. 1966), *aff'd per curiam*, 372 F.2d 129 (4th Cir. 1967), *cert. denied*, 388 U.S. 917 (1967); Walker v. Charlotte, 268 N.C. 345, 150 S.E.2d 493 (1966); Walker v. City of Charlotte, 276 N.C. 166, 171 S.E.2d 431 (1970).

20. 287 N.C. 66, 213 S.E.2d 231 (1975).

21. 39 N.C. App. 688, 251 S.E.2d 910 (1979), *rev. denied*, 297 N.C. 299, 254 S.E.2d 925 (1979).

of such buildings were ratified by the General Assembly in 1941 or 1957). The specific provisions invalidated were new fire protection requirements for high-rise buildings, somewhat similar to those involved in the *Greene* case. (The General Assembly responded to this ruling by itself adopting those regulations, now codified as G.S. 143-138(i).)

Finally, among a group of cases that pertain to minimum housing ordinances and their enforcement, several bear on Building Code enforcement. *Dale v. Morganton,*[22] held that a municipality can cut off electricity from a building only for reasons of safety in the electrical system, for nonpayment of the electrical bill, or for some other factor related to the electrical system; it cannot use such a cutoff to enforce a regulation that has no such relationship. *Horton v. Gulledge,*[23] held that an owner of a structure that has been declared unfit for human habitation cannot be ordered to demolish it without first being given an opportunity to bring it up to code standards. *In re Dwelling of Properties, Incorporated,*[24] held that only the occupant's consent (and not the nonresident owner's) is required in order to enter property for the purpose of making a housing inspection.

Very few U.S. Supreme Court cases bear on the validity of building regulations. Of these, the most notable is *Queenside Hills Realty Company v. Saxl,*[25] which upheld the constitutionality of fire protection measures required of existing multi-family dwellings by New York State (against claims that they amounted to a denial of due process and equal protection).

---

22. 270 N.C. 567, 155 S.E.2d 136 (1967).
23. 277 N.C. 353, 177 S.E.2d 885 (1971).
24. 24 N.C. App. 17, 210 S.E.2d 73 (1974).
25. 328 U.S. 80 (1946).

ENFORCEMENT
5 RESPONSIBILITIES OF LOCAL
INSPECTION DEPARTMENTS

The basic enforcement responsibilities of local inspection departments are set forth in the general enabling acts that authorize cities and counties to create such departments, occasionally in special acts relating to particular cities or counties, and in the ordinances adopted by a particular city or county.

The enabling acts for city and county inspection departments set forth the general duties of such a department as follows:

§ 160A-412. Duties and responsibilities.

The duties and responsibilities of an inspection department and of the inspectors therein shall be to enforce within their territorial jurisdiction State and local laws relating to
   (1) The construction of buildings and other structures;
   (2) The installation of such facilities as plumbing systems, electrical systems, heating systems, refrigeration systems, and air-conditioning systems;
   (3) The maintenance of buildings and other structures in a safe, sanitary, and healthful condition;
   (4) Other matters that may be specified by the city council.
These duties shall include the receipt of applications for permits and the issuance or denial of permits, the making of any necessary inspections, the issuance or denial of certificates of compliance, the issuance of orders to correct violations, the bringing of judicial actions against actual or threatened violations, the keeping of adequate records, and any other actions that may be required in order adequately to enforce those laws. The city council shall have the authority to enact reasonable and appropriate provisions governing the enforcement of those laws.

(The above pertains to cities; the essentially identical county provisions appear in G.S. 153A-352.)

The major state law that a local inspection department is charged with enforcing is the State Building Code, with its various volumes. A local department may also have some responsibilities in enforcing other state laws, such as G.S. Chapter 66, Articles 4 (electrical equipment), 4A (hot water heaters), and 4B (mobile homes); Chapter 69, Articles 2 (fire escapes, theater safety, etc.) and 4 (hotel safety); Chapter 95, Article 7A (boilers and pressure vessels); and Chapter 143, Article 9A (mobile homes). In coastal counties it may have responsibilities under the Coastal Area Management Act (Chapter 113A, Article 7). And it may be called on to participate in enforcing many of the state departmental and agency regulations described in Chapter 3.

Locally it may be responsible for enforcing a great range of ordinances, such as the zoning ordinance, minimum housing ordinance, floodway ordinance, sedimentation and erosion control ordinance, sign ordinance, curb-cut ordinance, service station ordinance, weed-control ordinance, abandoned-car ordinance, explosives-storage ordinance, hazardous substances ordinance, animal-control ordinance, etc.

The major functions that may be involved in administering and enforcing such laws are set forth in G.S. 160A-412, above, for cities and G.S. 153A-352 for counties.

The inspection department must:

(1) Receive applications for building permits;
(2) Issue or deny permits;
(3) Make necessary inspections;
(4) Issue or deny certificates of compliance;
(5) Issue orders to correct violations and take other nonjudicial measures;
(6) Revoke permits;
(7) Bring judicial actions against actual or threatened violations;
(8) Keep adequate records;
(9) Take other appropriate enforcement actions.

The chapters that follow deal with the legal and practical considerations affecting each of these functional responsibilities.

6 PERMITS

The building permit is the basic administrative device used in enforcing the laws that relate to building construction, repair, or alteration. It is used to enforce the State Building Code, the National Electrical Code, the various plumbing codes, fire-limits ordinances, zoning ordinances, sign ordinances, and many other local ordinances relating to such activities.

The merit of the building permit as an enforcement device is that it puts the burden on the citizen to come forward with information concerning his plans, from which the code enforcement official can determine whether they would violate the relevant laws. The official thus is spared the need to seek such information on his own initiative. If the information that is presented is inadequate, he may refuse to issue a permit until further information is produced. If the citizen does not come forward and secure a permit before taking action, he can be prosecuted for that fact alone; this eliminates any difficulties in proving that the construction actually violated any law.

LEGAL VALIDITY

The legal validity of requiring a building permit in a given situation turns on (a) the validity of the regulations that it is being used to enforce, and (b) whether there are adequate standards to guide the enforcement official in deciding whether to issue the permit. If these tests are met, the building permit as an enforcement device is clearly valid.

This is illustrated by the following passages quoted in a decision of the North Carolina Supreme Court:[1]

> Municipal corporations may, in the proper exercise of their police power, require that permits or certificates be obtained as a prerequisite to the erection, alteration, improvement, or use of buildings or other property in a particular manner or in a particular area; and such provisions will generally be upheld if they are reasonable and within the limitations of the exercise of municipal powers generally.
> 62 C.J.S., Municipal Corporations, § 227(3), p. 507.

> An ordinance requiring a permit to alter or repair...buildings...is regarded as a reasonable exercise of the police power.
> McQuillin, Municipal Corporations, 3d Ed., Vol. 9, p. 529.

> The purpose of requiring a permit is to enable the municipality to make sure that the proposed building conforms to the pertinent ordi-

---

1. State v. Walker, 265 N.C. 482, 484 (1965).

nances. Provisions for permits are for the benefit and protection of the municipality, not the property owner.

> *Tremarco Corp. v. Garzio*, 55 N.J. Super. 320, rev'd o.g. 32 N.J. 448.

In the case from which these quotes were taken, the State Supreme Court upheld the conviction of a property owner for "remodeling and repairing his residence...without first applying for and obtaining a written permit from the Building Inspection Department of the City...."

ROLE OF THE CODE ENFORCEMENT OFFICIAL

The basic rule that the code enforcement official must follow in deciding whether to issue a building permit is that he must comply with the provisions of the law he is enforcing. As our State Supreme Court said in a zoning case, "In the issuing of building permits the building inspector, a purely administrative agent, must follow the literal provisions of the zoning regulations."[2]

In another case, the Court said:

In fact, the defendants concede in their answer that prior to the commencement of this action the Building Inspector of the City of Durham, who is the administrative official charged with the enforcement of the zoning ordinance, examined the application of the plaintiffs for the building permit, and ascertained that it complied "with the building and zoning regulations of the City of Durham." These things being true, the plaintiffs had a clear legal right to the building permit sought by them, and the defendants had no discretionary power to withhold it....

The defendants asserted at the trial that the governing body of the City of Durham caused the permit to be withheld from plaintiffs because it concluded that they intended to use the proposed building as a nursing home, infirmary, or hospital, and not as a hotel as recited in their application....[It] is to be noted that the municipal authorities had no legal power to refuse a building permit for the cause assigned even if they had grounds for believing such cause to exist. The law declares that "if the right of the applicant to erect the building for which the permit is sought is otherwise absolute, it is no ground for the denial of the permit or of a mandate to compel its issuance that the applicant intends to put the building when erected to an improper use; the question as to the legality of the alleged intended use must await determination in proper proceedings after such use is attempted to be made of the building." 34 Am. Jur., Mandamus, section 188.[3]

---

2. Lee v. Board of Adjustment, 226 N.C. 107, 110 (1946).
3. Mitchell v. Barfield, 232 N.C. 325, 326-27 (1950).

In this case, as well as in an earlier one in Winston-Salem, the relief given to the property owner was simply a court order that the permit be issued; no damages were granted. In the Winston-Salem case the Court said:

> The exercise of the power to grant or refuse the license to erect a building was a governmental function, and if, as a jury finds in this case, the reason given for the refusal of the license was erroneous, the plaintiffs' remedy was by a mandamus [an order to issue the permit] which has been awarded them; but in no aspect would the city be liable in an action for damages. . . .

> If the officials charged with the exercise of the duty should have corruptly or oppressively refused the license asked, an action might have been laid against them individually; but there is no such allegation in the pleadings. . . .The city, even in that event, would not be liable in damages for such conduct on the part of its officials.[4]

STATUTES BEARING ON ISSUANCE OR DENIAL OF PERMITS

The following statutory provisions (from the municipal and county enabling acts for an inspection department) can be regarded as the basic, most comprehensive provisions governing the issuance or denial of permits. Further statutory and State Building Code provisions bearing on particular provisions of these statutes are set forth and described in subsequent subsections.

§ 160A-417. Permits.

No person shall commence or proceed with
    (1) The construction, reconstruction, alteration, repair, movement to another site, removal, or demolition of any building or structure,
    (2) The installation, extension, or general repair of any plumbing system,
    (3) The installation, extension, alteration, or general repair of any heating or cooling equipment system, or
    (4) The installation, extension, alteration, or general repair of any electrical wiring, devices, appliances, or equipment,
without first securing from the inspection department with jurisdiction over the site of the work any and all permits required by the State Building Code and any other State or local laws applicable to the work. A permit shall be in writing and shall contain a provision that the work done shall comply with the State Building Code and all other applicable State and local laws. No permits shall be issued unless the plans and specifications are identified by the name and address of the author thereof, and if the General Statutes of North Carolina require that plans for certain types of work be prepared only by a registered architect or registered engineer, no permit shall be issued unless the plans and specifications bear the North Carolina seal of a registered architect or of a registered engineer. When any provision of the General Statutes of North Carolina or of any ordinance requires that work be done by

---

4. Clinard v. Winston-Salem, 173 N.C. 356, 358 (1917).

a licensed specialty contractor of any kind, no permit for the work shall be issued unless the work is to be performed by such a duly licensed contractor. No permit issued under Articles 9 or 9C of Chapter 143 shall be required for any construction, installation, repair, replacement, or alteration costing five thousand dollars ($5,000) or less in any single family residence or farm building unless the work involves: the addition, repair or replacement of load bearing structures; the addition (excluding replacement of same size and capacity) or change in the design of plumbing; the addition, replacement or change in the design of heating, air conditioning, or electrical wiring, devices, appliances, or equipment; the use of materials not permitted by the North Carolina Uniform Residential Building Code; or the addition (excluding replacement of like grade of fire resistance) of roofing. Violation of this section shall constitute a misdemeanor.

(County: G.S. 153A-357)

§ 160A-418. Time limitations on validity of permits.

A permit issued pursuant to G.S. 160A-417 shall expire by limitation six months, or any lesser time fixed by ordinance of the city council, after the date of issuance if the work authorized by the permit has not been commenced. If after commencement the work is discontinued for a period of 12 months, the permit therefor shall immediately expire. No work authorized by any permit that has expired shall thereafter be performed until a new permit has been secured.

(County: G.S. 153A-358)

§ 160A-419. Changes in work.

After a permit has been issued, no changes or deviations from the terms of the application, plans and specifications, or the permit, except where changes or deviations are clearly permissible under the State Building Code, shall be made until specific written approval of proposed changes or deviations has been obtained from the inspection department.

(County: G.S. 153A-359)

"[P]ERMITS REQUIRED BY THE STATE BUILDING CODE...."

Section 105 of Volume I (General Construction) of the State Building Code sets forth the responsibilities of local inspectors in enforcing the Code. Section 105.3 specifies that the following permits are required:

105.3 — PERMITS REQUIRED

(a) *New Building:* No person shall commence or proceed with construction of any new building or structure covered by this Code without first applying for and receiving one or more permits covering all work to be done.

(b) *Existing Buildings:* No person shall commence or proceed with reconstruction, alteration, repair, moving or demolition of any existing building or structure without first applying for and receiving one or more permits covering all such work. (Reference: Chapter X, Section 2604.)

(c) *Buildings within Fire Limits:* A special permit is required for any alteration, repair, or movement of a wood frame building inside fire limits. (References: Section 302; G.S. 153A-375, 160A-436, 160A-437, 160A-438.)

(d) *Signs:* A permit is required to install signs. (Reference: Section 2301.)

(e) *Marquees, etc.:* A permit is required to install marquees, awnings, etc. (Reference: Section 2601.)

(f) *A permit is required whenever the use of an existing building is changed.* This permit shall not be issued until the inspector has made an inspection of the building to determine whether it must be altered or repaired in order to meet the requirements of the Code with respect to the new use. (G.S. 143-138(b), 143-139, 153A-357, 160A-417.)

A corresponding Section 105 appears in Volume II (Plumbing). Its Section 105.3 deals with required permits:

105.3 — PERMITS REQUIRED

(a) *New Building:* No person shall commence or proceed with the installation of any plumbing system covered by this Code without first applying for and receiving one or more permits covering all work to be done.

(b) *Existing Buildings:* No person shall commence or proceed with reconstruction, alteration, repair, moving or demolition of any existing plumbing system without first applying for and receiving one or more permits covering all such work. (Reference: Chapter X, Section 2604. (Volume 1)

(c) *A permit is required whenever the use of an existing building is changed.* This permit shall not be issued until the inspector has made an inspection of the building to determine whether it must be altered or repaired in order to meet the requirements of the Code with respect to the new use. (G.S. 143-138 (b), 143-139, 153A-357, 160A-417.)

(d) *Minor Repairs:* The provisions of this code shall not apply to those who make minor repairs or replacements to an already installed system of plumbing, on the house side of a trap, provided such repairs or replacements in no way disrupts the original water supply, waste or ventilating system. In the event a fixture is replaced, a permit shall be secured and same shall be inspected by the plumbing inspector.

Note especially the exemptions from the permit requirement under subsection (d).

Section 105 of Volume III (Heating, Air Conditioning, Refrigeration, & Ventilation) likewise contains a Section 105.3 concerning required permits:

105.3 — PERMITS REQUIRED

No person may commence or proceed with the installation, extension, alteration, or general repair of any heating or cooling equipment system without first securing from the inspection department with jurisdiction over the site of the work each permit required by the State Building Code and any other State or local law or local ordinance or regulation applicable to the work.

If the provisions of a General Statute of North Carolina or of any ordinance requires that work be done by a licensed contractor, no permit for the work may be issued unless such work is to be performed by such a duly licensed contractor.

Apparently there is no exemption of electrical installations from permit requirements under Volume IV of the Code.

All of the above provisions are subject to the 1981 and 1983 amendments to the enabling act for the State Building Code, which state:

Provided further, that no building permit shall be required under the Code or any local variance thereof approved under subsection (e) for any construction, installation, repair, replacement, or alteration costing five thousand dollars ($5,000) or less in any single family residence or farm building unless the work involves: the addition, repair, or replacement of load bearing structures; the addition (excluding replacement of same size and capacity) or change in the design of plumbing; the addition, replacement or change in the design of heating, air conditioning, or electrical wiring, devices, appliances, or equipment; the use of materials not permitted by the North Carolina Uniform Residential Building

Code; or the addition (excluding replacement of like grade of fire resistance) of roofing.[5]

"[IF] THE GENERAL STATUTES OF NORTH CAROLINA REQUIRE THAT PLANS FOR CERTAIN TYPES OF WORK BE PREPARED ONLY BY A REGISTERED ARCHITECT OR REGISTERED ENGINEER..."

The following section of the General Statutes requires that registered architects or engineers prepare plans for certain buildings:

§ 133-1.1. Certain buildings involving public funds to be designed, etc., by architect or engineer.

(a) In the interest of public health, safety and economy, every officer, board, department, or commission charged with the duty of approving plans and specifications or awarding or entering into contracts involving the expenditure of public funds in excess of one hundred thousand dollars ($100,000) for the repair of public buildings where such repair does not include major structural change, or in excess of forty-five thousand dollars ($45,000) for the construction of, or additions to, public buildings or State-owned and operated utilities shall require that such plans and specifications be prepared by a registered architect, in accordance with the provisions of Chapter 83 of the General Statutes, or by a registered engineer, in accordance with the provisions of Chapter 89C of the General Statutes, or by both architect and engineer, particularly qualified by training and experience for the type of work involved, and that the North Carolina seal of such architect or engineer together with the name and address of such architect or engineer, or both, be placed on all such plans and specifications.

(b) On all projects requiring the services of an architect or engineer, or both, the architect or engineer, or both, whose names and seals appear on the plans and specifications shall conduct frequent and regular inspections or such inspections as required by the contract and shall issue a signed and sealed certificate of compliance to the awarding authority that:

    (1) The inspections of the construction, repairs, or installations have been conducted with the degree of care and professional skill and judgment ordinarily exercised by a member of that profession; and

    (2) To the best of his knowledge and in the professional opinion of the architect or engineer the contractor has fulfilled the obligations of such plans, specifications, and contract.

No certificate of compliance shall be issued until the architect and/or engineer is satisfied that the contractor has fulfilled the obligations of such plans, specifications, and contract.

(c) The following shall be excepted from the requirements of subsection (a) of this section:

    (1) Dwellings and outbuildings in connection therewith, such as barns and private garages.

---

5. N.C. Sess. Laws 1981, Ch. 677, and N.C. Sess. Laws 1983, Ch. 614, amending N.C. GEN. STAT. § 143-138(b); *id.* § 153A-357; *id.* § 160A-417.

(2) Apartment buildings used exclusively as the residence of not more than two families.

(3) Buildings used for agricultural purposes other than schools or assembly halls which are not within the limits of a city or an incorporated village.

(4) Temporary buildings or sheds used exclusively for construction purposes, not exceeding 20 feet in any direction, and not used for living quarters.

(d) On repair projects involving the expenditures of public funds in an amount of one hundred thousand dollars ($100,000), or less, or on construction or addition projects involving the expenditures of public funds in an amount of forty-five thousand dollars ($45,000), or less, and on which no registered architect or engineer is employed, the governing board or awarding authority shall require a certificate of compliance with the State Building Code from the city or county inspector for the specific trade or trades involved or from a registered architect or engineer, except that the provisions of this subsection shall not apply on projects wherein plans and specifications are approved by the Department of Administration, Division of State Construction, and the completed project is inspected by the Division of State Construction.

(e) All plans and specifications for public buildings of any kind shall be identified by the name and address of the author thereof.

(f) Neither the designer nor the contractor involved shall receive his final payment until the required certificate of compliance shall have been received by the awarding authority.

(g) On all facilities which are covered by this Article, other than those listed in subsection (c) of this section and which require any job-installed finishes, the plans and specifications shall include the color schedule.

Other plans are required to have such seals when their preparation falls under the statutory definitions of the practice of architecture or engineering:

§ 83A-1. Definitions.

When used in this Chapter, unless the context otherwise requires:

(1) "Architect" means a person who is duly licensed to practice architecture.

• • •

(7) "Practice of architecture" means performing or offering to perform or holding oneself out as legally qualified to perform professional services in connection with the design, construction, enlargement or alteration of buildings, including consultations, investigations, evaluations, preliminary studies, the preparation of plans, specifications and contract documents, administration of construction contracts and related services or combination of services in connection with the design and construction of buildings, regardless of whether these services are performed in person or as the directing head of an office or organization.

§ 83A-12. Prohibited practice.

The purpose of the Chapter is to safeguard life, health and property. It shall be unlawful for any individual, firm or corporation to practice or offer to practice architecture in this State as defined in this Chapter, or to use the title "Architect" or any form thereof, except as provided in Chapter 89A for Landscape Architects, or to display or use any words, letters, figures, titles, sign, card, advertisement, or other device to indicate that such individual or firm practices or offers to practice architecture as herein defined or is an architect or architectural firm qualified to perform architectural work, unless such person holds a current individual or corporate certificate of admission to practice architecture under the provisions of this Chapter.

§ 83A-13. Exemptions.

(a) Nothing in this Chapter shall be construed to prevent the practice of general contracting under the provisions of Article 1 of Chapter 87, or the practice by any person who is qualified under law as a "registered professional engineer" of such architectural work as is incidental to engineering projects or utilities, or the practice of any other profession under the applicable licensure provisions of the General Statutes.

(b) Nothing in this Chapter shall be construed to prevent a duly licensed general contractor, professional engineer or architect, acting individually or in combination thereof, from participating in a "Design/Build" undertaking including the preparation of plans and/or specifications and entering individual or collective agreements with the owner in order to meet the owner's requirements for pre-determined costs and unified control in the design and construction of a project, and for the method of compensation for the design and construction services rendered; provided, however, that nothing herein shall be construed so as to allow the performance of any such services or any division thereof by one who is not duly licensed to perform such service or services in accordance with applicable licensure provisions of the General Statutes; provided further, that full disclosure is made in writing to the owner as to the duties and responsibilities of each of the participating parties in such agreements; and, provided further, nothing in this Chapter shall prevent the administration by any of the said licensees of construction contracts and related services or combination of services in connection with the construction of buildings.

(c) Nothing in this Chapter shall be construed to require an architectural license for the preparation, sale, or furnishing of plans, specifications and related data, or for the supervision of construction pursuant thereto, where the building, buildings, or project involved is in one of the following categories:

   (1) A family residence, up to eight units attached with grade level exit, which is not a part of or physically connected with any other buildings or residential units;
   (2) A building upon any farm for the use of any farmer, unless the building is of such nature and intended for such use as to substantially involve the health or safety of the public;
   (3) An institutional or commercial building if it does not have a total value exceeding ninety thousand dollars ($90,000);
   (4) An institutional or commercial building if the total building area does not exceed 2,500 square feet in gross floor area;
   (5) Alteration, remodeling or renovation of an existing building which is exempt under this section, or alteration,

remodeling, or renovation of an existing building or building site which does not alter or affect the structural system of the building;

(6) The preparation and use of details and shop drawings, assembly or erection drawings, or graphic descriptions utilized to detail or illustrate a portion of the work required to construct the project in accordance with the plans and specifications prepared or to be prepared under the requirements or exemptions of this Chapter.

(d) Nothing in this Chapter shall be construed to prevent any individual from making plans or data for buildings for himself.

(e) Plans and specifications prepared by persons or corporations under these exemptions shall bear the signature and address of such person or corporate officer.

§ 89C-2. Declarations; prohibitions.

In order to safeguard life, health, and property, and to promote the public welfare, the practice of engineering and the practice of land surveying in this State are hereby declared to be subject to regulation in the public interest. It shall be unlawful for any person to practice or to offer to practice engineering or land surveying in this State, as defined in the provisions of this Chapter, or to use in connection with his name or otherwise assume or advertise any title or description tending to convey the impression that he is either a professional engineer or a registered land surveyor, unless such person has been duly registered as such. The right to engage in the practice of engineering or land surveying shall be deemed a personal right, based on the qualifications of the individual as evidenced by his certificate of registration, which shall not be transferable.

§ 89C-3. Definitions.

When used in this Chapter, unless the context otherwise requires:

• • •

(2) "Engineer". — The term "engineer," within the intent of this Chapter, shall mean a person who, by reason of his special knowledge and use of the mathematical, physical and engineering sciences and the principles and methods of engineering analysis and design, acquired by engineering education and engineering experience, is qualified to practice engineering.

• • •

(6) "Practice of Engineering". —
   a. The term, "practice of engineering," within the intent of this Chapter, shall mean any service or creative work, the adequate performance of which requires engineering education, training, and experience, in the application of special knowledge of the mathematical, physical, and engineering sciences to such services or creative work as consultation, investigation, evaluation, planning, and design of engineering works and systems, planning the use of land and water, engineering surveys, and the observation of construction for the purposes of assuring compliance with drawings and

specifications, including the consultation, investigation, evaluation, planning, and design for either private or public use, in connection with any utilities, structures, buildings, machines, equipment, processes, work systems, projects, and industrial or consumer products or equipment of a mechanical, electrical, hydraulic, pneumatic or thermal nature, insofar as they involve safeguarding life, health or property, and including such other professional services as may be necessary to the planning, progress and completion of any engineering services.

A person shall be construed to practice or offer to practice engineering, within the meaning and intent of this Chapter, who practices any branch of the profession of engineering; or who, by verbal claim, sign, advertisement, letterhead, card, or in any other way represents himself to be a professional engineer, or through the use of some other title implies that he is a professional engineer or that he is registered under this Chapter; or who holds himself out as able to perform, or who does perform any engineering service or work not exempted by this Chapter, or any other service designated by the practitioner which is recognized as engineering.

b. The term "practice of engineering" shall not be construed to permit the location, description, establishment or reestablishment of property lines or descriptions of land boundaries for conveyance.

§ 89C-19. Public works; requirements where public safety involved.

This State and its political subdivisions such as counties, cities, towns, or other political entities or legally constituted boards, commissions, public utility companies, or authorities, or officials, or employees thereof shall not engage in the practice of engineering or land surveying involving either public or private property where the safety of the public is directly involved without the project being under the supervision of a professional engineer for the preparations of plans and specifications for engineering projects, or a registered land surveyor for land surveying projects, as provided for the practice of the respective professions by this Chapter.

An official or employee of the State or any political subdivision specified in this section, holding the positions set out in this section as of June 19, 1975, shall be exempt from the provisions of this section so long as such official or employee is engaged in substantially the same type of work as is involved in his present position.

Nothing in this section shall be construed to prohibit inspection, maintenance and service work done by employees of the State of North Carolina, any political subdivision thereof, or any municipality therein including construction, installation, servicing, and maintenance by regular full-time employees of, secondary roads and drawings incidental thereto, streets, street lighting, traffic-control signals, police and fire alarm systems, waterworks, steam, electric and sewage treatment and disposal plants, the services of superintendents, inspectors or foremen regularly employed by the State of North Carolina or any political subdivision thereof, or municipal corporation therein.

The provisions in this section shall not be construed to alter or modify the requirements of Article 1 of Chapter 133 of the General Statutes.

"WHEN ANY PROVISION OF THE GENERAL STATUTES OF NORTH CAROLINA OR OF ANY ORDINANCE REQUIRES THAT WORK BE DONE BY A LICENSED SPECIALTY CONTRACTOR OF ANY KIND..."

The licensing acts for general contractors, plumbing and heating contractors, electrical contractors, and refrigeration contractors contain provisions as to what type of work requires a license:

§ 87-1. "General contractor" defined; exceptions.

For the purpose of this Article any person or firm or corporation who for a fixed price, commission, fee or wage, undertakes to bid upon or to construct or who undertakes to superintend or manage, on his own behalf or for any person, firm or corporation that is not licensed as a general contractor pursuant to this Article, the construction of any building, highway, public utilities, grading or any improvement or structure where the cost of the undertaking is thirty thousand dollars ($30,000) or more, shall be deemed to be a "general contractor" engaged in the business of general contracting in the State of North Carolina.

This section shall not apply to persons or firms or corporations furnishing or erecting industrial equipment, power plant equipment, radial brick chimneys, and monuments.

This section shall not apply to any person or firm or corporation who constructs a building on land owned by that person, firm or corporation when such building is intended for use by that person, firm or corporation after completion.

§ 87-13. Unauthorized practice of contracting; impersonating contractor; false certificate; giving false evidence to Board; penalties.

Any person, firm, or corporation not being duly authorized who shall contract for or bid upon the construction of any of the projects or works enumerated in G.S. 87-1, without having first complied with the provisions hereof, or who shall attempt to practice general contracting in the State, except as provided for in this Article, and any person, firm, or corporation presenting or attempting to file as his own the licensed certificate of another or who shall give false or forged evidence of any kind to the Board or to any member thereof in maintaining a certificate of license or who falsely shall impersonate another or who shall use an expired or revoked certificate of license, and any architect or engineer who recommends to any project owner the award of a contract to anyone not properly licensed under this Article, shall be deemed guilty of a misdemeanor and shall for each such offense of which he is convicted be punished by a fine of not less than five hundred dollars ($500.00) or imprisonment of three months, or both fine and imprisonment in the discretion of the court. And the Board may, in its discretion, use its funds to defray the expense, legal or otherwise, in the prosecution of any violations of this Article. No architect or engineer shall be guilty of a violation of this section if his recommendation to award a contract is made in reliance upon current written information received by him from the appropriate Contractor Licensing Board of this State which information erroneously indicates that the contractor being recommended for contract award is properly licensed.

§ 87-14. Regulations as to issue of building permits.

Any person, firm or corporation, upon making application to the building inspector or such other authority of any incorporated city, town or county in North Carolina charged with the duty of issuing building or other permits for the construction of any building, highway, sewer, grading or any improvement or structure where the cost thereof is to be thirty thousand dollars ($30,000) or more, shall, before he be entitled to the issuance of such permit, furnish satisfactory proof to such inspector or authority that he or another person contracting to superintend or manage the construction is duly licensed under the terms of this Article to carry out or superintend the same, and that he has paid the license tax required by the Revenue Act of the State of North Carolina then in force so as to be qualified to bid upon or contract for the work for which the permit has been applied; and it shall be unlawful for such building inspector or other authority to issue or allow the issuance of such building permit unless and until the applicant has furnished evidence that he is either exempt from the provisions of this Article or is duly licensed under this Article to carry out or superintend the work for which permit has been applied; and further, that the applicant has paid the license tax required by the State Revenue Act then in force so as to be qualified to bid upon or contract for the work covered by the permit; and such building inspector, or other such authority, violating the terms of this section shall be guilty of a misdemeanor and subject to a fine of not more than fifty dollars ($50.00).

---

§ 87-21. Definitions; contractors licensed by Board; examination; posting license, etc.

(a) Definitions. — For the purpose of this Article:
  (1) The word "plumbing" is hereby defined to be the system of pipes, fixtures, apparatus and appurtenances, installed upon the premises, or in a building, to supply water thereto and to convey sewage or other waste therefrom.
  (2) The phrase "heating, group number one" shall be deemed and held to be the heating system of a building, which requires the use of high or low pressure steam, vapor or hot water, including all piping, ducts, and mechanical equipment appurtenant thereto, within, adjacent to or connected with a building, for comfort heating.
  (3) The phrase "heating, group number two" means an air conditioning system which consists of an assemblage of interacting components producing conditioned air for comfort cooling by the lowering of temperature, and having a mechanical refrigeration capacity in excess of fifteen tons, and which circulates air.

(4) The phrase "heating, group number three" shall be deemed and held to be a direct heating system of a building which produces heat to raise the temperature of the space within the building for the purpose of comfort in which electric heating elements or products of combustion exchange heat either directly with the building supply air or indirectly through a heat exchanger and using an air distribution system of ducts. A heating system requiring air distribution ducts and supplied by ground water or utilizing a coil supplied by water from a domestic hot water heater not exceeding 150° Fahrenheit requires either plumbing or heating group number one license to extend piping from valved connections in the domestic hot water system to the heating coil and requires either heating group number one or heating group number three license for installation of coil, duct work, controls, drains and related appurtenances.

(5) Any person, firm or corporation, who for a valuable consideration, installs, alters or restores, or offers to install, alter or restore, either plumbing, heating group number one, or heating group number two, or heating group number three, or any combination thereof, as defined in this Article, shall be deemed and held to be engaged in the business of plumbing or heating contracting. Any person who installs a plumbing or heating system on property which at the time of installation was intended for sale or to be used primarily for rental is deemed to be engaged in the business of plumbing or heating contracting without regard to receipt of consideration, unless exempted elsewhere in this Article.

(6) The word "contractor" is hereby defined to be a person, firm or corporation engaged in the business of plumbing or heating contracting.

(7) The word "heating" shall be deemed and held to mean heating group number one, heating group number two, heating group number three, or any combination thereof.

(8) The obtaining of a license, as required by this Article, shall not of itself authorize the practice of another profession or trade for which a State qualification license is required.

(9) The word "Board" means the State Board of Examiners of Plumbing and Heating Contractors.

(b) Classes of Licenses; Eligibility and Examination of Applicant; Necessity for License. — In order to protect the public health, comfort and safety, the Board shall establish two classes of licenses: Class I covering all structures and systems to which this Article applies, and Class II covering plumbing and heating systems in single-family detached residential dwellings.

• • •

(c) To Whom Article Applies. — The provisions of this Article shall apply to all persons, firms, or corporations who engage in, or attempt to engage in, the business of plumbing or heating contracting, or any combination thereof as defined in this Article. The provisions of this Article shall not apply to those who make minor repairs or minor replacements to an already installed system of plumbing or heating.

• • •

§ 87-25. Violations made misdemeanor; employees of licensees excepted.

Any person, firm or corporation who shall engage in or offer to engage in, or carry on the business of either plumbing or heating contracting, or both, as defined in G.S. 87-21, without first having been licensed to engage in such business, or businesses, as required by the provisions of this Article; or any person, firm or corporation holding a limited heating license under the provisions of this Article who shall practice or offer to practice or carry on any type of heating contracting not authorized by said limited license; or any person, firm or corporation who shall give false or forged evidence of any kind to the Board, or any member thereof, in obtaining a license, or who shall falsely impersonate any other practitioner of like or different name, or who shall use an expired or revoked license, or who shall violate any of the provisions of this Article, shall be guilty of a misdemeanor and upon conviction fined not less than one hundred dollars ($100.00) or imprisoned for not more than three months, or both, in the discretion of the court. Employees, while working under the supervision and jurisdiction of a person, firm or corporation licensed in accordance with the provisions of the Article, shall not be construed to have engaged in the business of either plumbing or heating contracting, or both.

§ 87-43. Electrical contracting defined; licenses.

Electrical contracting shall be defined as engaging or offering to engage in the business of installing, maintaining, altering or repairing any electric work, wiring, devices, appliances or equipment. No person, firm or corporation shall engage, or offer to engage, in the business of electrical contracting within the State of North Carolina without having received a license from the State Board of Examiners of Electrical Contractors in compliance with the provisions of this Article. In each separate place of business operated by an electrical contractor at least one person must be regularly on active duty who has passed the examination required by this Article and who has the specific duty and authority to supervise and direct all electrical wiring or electrical installation work done or made by such separate place of business. Every person, firm or corporation engaging in the business of electrical contracting shall display a current certificate of license in his principal place of business and in each branch place of business which he operates. Licenses issued hereunder shall be signed by the chairman and the secretary-treasurer of the Board, under the seal of the Board. A registry of all licenses issued to electrical contractors shall be kept by the secretary-treasurer of the Board, and said registry shall be open for public inspection during ordinary business hours.

§ 87-43.1. Exceptions.

The provisions of this Article shall not apply:
  (1) To the installation, construction or maintenance of facilities for providing electric service to the public ahead of the point of delivery of electric service to the customer;
  (2) To the installation, construction, maintenance, or repair of telephone, telegraph, or signal systems, by public utilities, or their corporate affiliates, when said work pertains to the services furnished by said public utilities;

(3) To any person in the course of his work as a bona fide employee of a licensee of this Board;

(4) To the installation, construction or maintenance of electrical equipment and wiring for temporary use by contractors in connection with the work of construction;

(5) To the installation, construction, maintenance or repair of electrical wiring, devices, appliances or equipment by persons, firms or corporations, upon their own property when such property is not intended at the time for rent, lease, sale or gift, who regularly employ one or more electricians or mechanics for the purpose of installing, maintaining, altering or repairing of electrical wiring, devices or equipment used for the conducting of the business of said persons, firms or corporations;

(5a) To any person who is himself and for himself installing, maintaining, altering or repairing electric work, wiring, devices, appliances or equipment upon his own property when such property is not intended at the time for rent, lease, or sale;

(6) To the installation, construction, maintenance or repair of electrical wiring, devices, appliances or equipment by State institutions and private educational institutions which maintain a private electrical department;

(7) To the replacement of lamps and fuses and to the installation and servicing of cord-connected appliances and equipment connected by means of attachment plug-in devices to suitable receptacles which have been permanently installed or to the servicing of appliances connected to a permanently installed junction box. This exception does not apply to permanently installed receptacles or to the installation of the junction box.

§ 87-43.3. Classification of licenses.

An electrical contractor's license shall be issued in one of the following classifications: *Limited,* under which a licensee shall be permitted to engage in a single electrical contracting project of a value not in excess of ten thousand dollars ($10,000) and on which the equipment or installation in the contract is rated at not more than 600 volts; *Intermediate,* under which a licensee shall be permitted to engage in a single electrical contracting project of a value not in excess of fifty thousand dollars ($50,000); *Unlimited,* under which a licensee shall be permitted to engage in any electrical contracting project regardless of value; and such other special Restricted classification as the Board may establish from time to time to provide for the licensing of persons, firms or corporations wishing to engage in special restricted electrical contracting, under which license a licensee shall be permitted to engage only in a specific phase of electrical contracting of a special, limited nature; and for the licensing of persons, firms or corporations wishing to engage in electrical contracting work as an incidental part of their primary business, which is a lawful business other than electrical contracting, under which license a licensee shall be permitted to engage only in a specific phase of electrical contracting of a special, limited nature directly in connection with said primary business. The Board may establish appropriate standards for each classification, such standards not to be inconsistent with the provisions of G.S. 87-42.

§ 87-43.4. Residential dwelling license.

There is hereby created a separate license for electrical contractors which shall permit an electrical contractor to engage in electrical contracting projects pertaining to single-family detached residential dwellings. The Board shall establish appropriate standards for this new license. The standards of knowledge, experience and proficiency shall be those appropriate for that license.

§ 87-57. License required of persons, firms or corporations engaged in the refrigeration trade.

In order to protect the public health, safety, morals, order and general welfare of the people of this State, all persons, firms or corporations, whether resident or nonresident of the State of North Carolina, before engaging in refrigeration business or contracting, as defined in this Article, shall first apply to the Board and shall procure a license.

§ 87-58. Definitions; contractors licensed by Board; towns excepted; examinations.

(a) As applied in this Article, "refrigeration trade or business" is defined to include all persons, firms or corporations engaged in the installation, maintenance, servicing and repairing of refrigerating machinery, equipment, devices and components relating thereto and within limits as set forth in the codes, laws and regulations governing refrigeration installation, maintenance, service and repairs within the State of North Carolina or any of its political subdivisions, provided however, that this Article shall not apply to the replacement of lamps and fuses and to the installation and servicing of appliances and equipment connected by means of attachment plug-in devices to suitable receptacles which have been permanently installed, "or devices using gas as a fuel, or ice using or storing equipment"; and provided, further, that the provisions of this Article shall not repeal any wording, phrase, or paragraph as set forth in North Carolina General Statutes, Chapter 87, Article 2; and provided, further, that this Article shall not apply to employees of persons, firms, or corporations or persons, firms or corporations, not engaged in refrigeration contracting as herein defined, that install, maintain and service their own refrigerating machinery, equipment and devices. The provisions of this Article shall not apply to any person, firm or corporation engaged in the business of selling, repairing and installing any air-conditioning units, devices or systems for the purpose of cooling offices, buildings, houses, works, manufacturing plants, or any machinery, manufactured article or processing of material.

(b) The phrase "refrigeration contractor" is hereby defined to be a person, firm or corporation engaged in the business of refrigeration contracting.

(c) Any person, firm or corporation who for valuable consideration engages in the refrigeration business or trade as herein defined shall be deemed and held to be in the business of refrigeration contracting.

(d) In order to protect the public health, comfort and safety, the Board shall prescribe the standard of efficiency to be required of an applicant for license and shall give an examination designed to ascertain the technical and practical knowledge of the applicant concerning the analysis of plans and specifications, estimating cost, fundamentals of installation and design as same pertain to refrigeration; and as a result of such examination, the Board shall issue a certificate of license in refrigeration to applicants who pass the required examination and a license shall be obtained in accordance with the provisions of this Article, before any person, firm or corpo-ration shall engage in, or offer to engage in the business of refrigeration contracting as herein defined. Each application for examination shall be accompanied by a check, post-office money order or cash in the amount of the annual license fee required by this Article. Regular examinations shall be given in the months of April and October of each year and additional examinations may be given at such other times as the Board may deem wise and necessary. Any person may demand in writing a special examination and upon payment by the applicant of the cost of holding such examination and the deposit of the amount of the annual license fee, the Board in its discretion will fix a time and place for such examination. A person who fails to pass any examination shall not be reexamined until the next regular examination.

(e) Repealed by Session Laws 1979, c. 843, s. 1, effective July 1, 1979.

(f) Licenses Granted without an Examination. — Persons who had an established place of business prior to July 1, 1979, and who produce satisfactory evidence that they are engaged in the refrigeration business as herein defined in any city, town or other area in which Article 5 of Chapter 87 of the General Statutes did not previously apply shall be granted a certificate of license, without examination, upon application to the Board and payment of the license fee, provided such completed applications shall be made prior to June 30, 1981.

(g) The current license issued in accordance with the provisions of this Article shall be posted in the business location of the licensee, and its number shall appear on all proposals or contracts and requests for permits issued by municipalities.

"PRIORITY" STATUTES

Certain statutes grant priority to the issuance of particular permits before other permits. Two of these follow. G.S. 143-215.59 is from the statute that authorizes regulation of construction in floodways:

§ 143-215.59. Other approvals required.

(a) The granting of a permit under the provisions of this Part shall in no way affect any other type of approval required by any other statute or ordinance of the State or any political subdivision of the State, or of the United States, but shall be construed as an added requirement.

(b) No permit for the construction of any structure to be located within a floodway shall be granted by a political subdivision unless the applicant has first obtained the permit required by this Part.

G.S. 130A-338 gives similar treatment to permits or authorizations issued by local health departments with respect to sanitary sewage systems serving proposed structures.

§ 130A-338. Improvement permit or authorization required before other permits to be issued.

Where construction, location or relocation is proposed to be done upon a residence, place of business or place of public assembly, no permit required for electrical, plumbing, heating, air conditioning or other construction, location or relocation activity under any provision of general or special law shall be issued until an improvement permit has been issued under G.S. 130A-336 or authorization has been obtained under G.S. 130A-337(c).

STATE BUILDING CODE PROVISIONS CONCERNING ISSUANCE OF PERMITS

The various volumes of the State Building Code contain provisions concerning applications for permits and their issuance. The most extensive are to be found in Volume I, General Construction:

105.4—APPLICATION FOR PERMIT

(a) Each application for a permit shall be filed with the appropriate local Inspection Department, in writing, on a form furnished for that purpose, and shall contain a general description of the proposed work and its location. The application shall be signed by the owner or his authorized agent.

(b) Each application shall indicate the proposed use or occupancy of all parts of the building and of that portion of the site or lot, if any, not covered by the building, and shall contain such other information as may be required by the Inspection Department.

(c) When required by the Inspection Department, two or more copies of specifications and of drawings drawn to scale with sufficient clarity and detail to indicate the nature and character of the work shall accompany each application. Such drawings and specifications shall contain information, in the form of notes or otherwise, as to the quality of materials, where quality is essential to conformity with this Code. The Inspection Department may require details, computations, stress diagrams, and other data necessary to describe the construction and basis of calculations, and they shall bear the signature of the person responsible for the design. Plans for all buildings shall indicate how required structural and fire-resistive integrity will be maintained where a penetration of a required fire-resistive wall, floor, or partition will be made for electrical, mechanical, plumbing, and communication conduits, pipes, and systems and also indicate in sufficient detail how the fire integrity will be maintained where required fire-resistive floors intersect the exterior walls.

(d) No permit shall be issued unless the plans and specifications are identified by the name and address of the author thereof.

(e) Where the General Statutes require that plans for certain types of construction be prepared only by a registered architect or a registered engineer, no permit shall be issued unless the plans and specifications bear the North Carolina seal of a registered architect or registered engineer.

(f) Where the General Statutes require a licensed contractor for certain types of construction, no permit shall be issued for such construction except in compliance with these statutes.

(g) The Inspection Department may require drawings showing the location of the proposed building and of every existing building on the site or lot. He may also require a boundary line survey, prepared by a qualified surveyor. (Authority: G.S. 143-139, 153A-357, 160A-417, 83-12, Ch. 87, Ch. 89C, 133-1.1.)

(h) Where necessary to determine compliance with Code standards, the Inspection Department may require tests or test reports. Such tests must be made by an approved testing laboratory or other approved agency, at the expense of the applicant. Copies of test reports or the results of tests shall be kept on file in the Inspection Department. (Authority: same as (g) above.).

105.5 — PERMITS

(a) If the Inspection Department is satisfied that the work described in an application for permit and the drawings and specifications filed therewith conforms to the requirements of this Code and all other applicable State and local laws, it shall issue a permit therefor to the applicant.

(b) The permit shall be in writing and shall contain a provision that the work done shall comply with the State Building Code and all other applicable State and local laws.

(c) A permit issued for work under this Code shall expire by limitation six months (or such lesser period fixed by local ordinance) after the date of issuance if the work authorized has not been commenced. If after commencement the work is discontinued for a period of 12 months, the permit therefor shall immediately expire. No work authorized by any permit that has expired shall thereafter be performed until a new permit has been secured.

(d) After a permit has been issued, no changes or deviations from the terms of the application, plans and specifications, or the permit (except changes or deviations clearly permissible under this Code) shall be made until specific written approval of proposed changes or deviations has been obtained from the Inspection Department. (Authority: G.S. 143-139, 153A-357, 153A-358, 153A-359, 160A-417, 160A-418, 160A-419.)

(e) When the Inspection Department issues a permit, it shall endorse in writing or by stamping "APPROVED" all sets of plans which have been submitted. One set of plans so approved shall be retained by the Inspection Department, and the other set or sets shall be returned to the applicant; one set of which shall be kept at the site of the work and shall be open to inspection by any authorized member of the Inspection Department.

The North Carolina Uniform Residential Building Code volume contains the following:

SECTION 2. Application, plans and permits.

Before the erection, construction or alteration of any building or structure, or part of same, there shall be submitted to the Building Inspector, by the owner or authorized agent, an application on appropriate blanks to be furnished by the Building Inspector, containing a detailed statement of the specifications, and accompanied by a full and complete copy of all necessary plans of such proposed work. Each application for a building permit shall be accompanied by a plat, drawn to scale, showing accurate dimensions of the lot to be built upon, accurate dimensions of the building to be erected and its location on the lot. If it shall appear to the Building Inspector that the provisions of this code and the State building laws have been complied with, and all requirements of fees has been paid, he will then issue the building permit. A copy of the plans as approved by the Building Inspector shall be kept at the building during the progress of the work and shall be open to inspection by the Building Inspector. Plans and specifications submitted to the Building Inspector shall be kept in files in his office or returned to the owner. It shall be within the discretion of the Building Inspector to issue permits for minor construction work without plans and specifications.

Volume II (Plumbing) provides:

105.4-APPLICATION FOR PERMIT

(a) Each application for a permit shall be filed with the appropriate local Inspection Department, in writing, on a form furnished for that purpose, and shall contain a general description of the proposed work and its location. The application shall be signed by the owner or his authorized agent.

(b) Each application shall indicate the proposed use or occupancy of all parts of the building and of that portion of the site or lot, if any, not covered by the building, and shall contain such other information as may be required by the Inspection Department.

(c) When required by the Inspection Department, two or more copies of specifications and of drawings drawn to scale with sufficient clarity and detail to indicate the nature and character of the work shall accompany each application. Such drawings and specifications shall contain information, in the form of notes or otherwise, as to the quality of materials, where quality is essential to conformity with this Code. The Inspection Department may require details, computations, and other data necessary to describe compliance with this code, and they shall bear the signature of the person responsible for the design. Plans for all buildings shall indicate how required structural and fire-resistive integrity will be maintained where a penetration of a required fire-resistive wall, floor, or partition will be made for plumbing, pipes, and systems.

(d) No permit shall be issued unless the plans and specifications are identified by the name and address of the author thereof.

(e) Where the General Statutes require that plans for certain types of construction be prepared only by a registered architect or a registered engineer, no permit shall be issued unless the plans and specifications bear the North Carolina seal of a registered architect or registered engineer.

(f) Where the General Statutes require a licensed contractor for certain types of construction, no permit shall be issued for such construction except in compliance with these statutes.

(g) The Inspection Department may require drawings showing the location of the proposed building and of every existing building on the site or lot. He may also require a boundary line survey, prepared by a qualified surveyor. (Authority: G.S. 143-139, 153A-357, 160A-417, 83-12, Ch. 87, Ch. 89C, 133-1.1.)

(h) Where necessary to determine compliance with Code standards, the Inspection Department may require tests or test reports. Such tests must be made by an approved testing laboratory or other approved agency, at the expense of the applicant. Copies of test reports or the results of tests shall be kept on file in the Inspection Department. (Authority: same as (g) above.).

105.5-PERMITS

(a) If the Inspection Department is satisfied that the work described in an application for permit and the drawings and specifications filed therewith conforms to the requirements of this Code and all other applicable State and local laws, it shall issue a permit therefor to the applicant.

(b) The permit shall be in writing and shall contain a provision that the work done shall comply with the State Building Code and all other applicable State and local laws.

(c) A permit issued for work under this Code shall expire by limitations six months (or such lesser period fixed by local ordinance) after the date of issuance if the work authorized has not been commenced. If after commencement the work is discontinued for a period of 12 months, the permit therefor shall immediately expire. No work authorized by any permit that has expired shall thereafter be performed until a new permit has been secured.

(d) After a permit has been issued, no changes or deviations from the terms of the application, plans and specifications, or the permit (except changes or deviations clearly permissible under this Code) shall be made until specific written approval of proposed changes or deviations has been obtained from the Inspection Department. (Authority: G.S. 143-139, 153A-357, 153A-358, 153A-359, 160A-417, 160A-418, 160A-419.)

(e) When the Inspection Department issues a permit, it shall endorse in writing or by stamping "APPROVED" all sets of plans which have been submitted. One set of plans so approved shall be retained by the Inspection Department, and the other set or sets shall be returned to the applicant; one set of which shall be kept at the site of the work and shall be open to inspection by any authorized member of the Inspection Department.

Volume III (Heating, Air Conditioning, Refrigeration & Ventilation) provides:

105.4-APPLICATION FOR PERMIT

(a) Each application for a permit shall be filed with the appropriate local Inspection Department, in writing, on a form furnished for that purpose, and shall contain a general description of the proposed work and its location. The application shall be signed by the owner or his authorized agent.

(b) When required by the Inspection Department, two or more copies of specifications and of drawings drawn to scale with sufficient clarity and detail to indicate the nature and character of the work shall accompany each application. Such drawings and specifications shall contain information, in the form of notes or otherwise, as to the quality of materials, where quality is essential to conformity with this Code. The Inspection Department may require details, computations, and other data necessary to describe the system, and they shall bear the signature of the person responsible for the design. Plans for all buildings shall indicate how required structural and fire-resistive integrity will be maintained where a penetration of a required fire-resistive wall, floor, or partition will be made for electrical, mechanical, plumbing, and communication conduits, pipes, and systems and also indicate in sufficient detail how the fire integrity will be maintained where required fire-resistive floors intersect the exterior walls.

(c) No permit shall be issued unless the plans and specifications are identified by the name and address of the author thereof.

(d) Where the General Statutes require that plans for certain types of construction be prepared only by a registered architect or a registered engineer, no permit shall be issued unless the plans and specifications bear the North Carolina seal of a registered architect or registered engineer.

(e) Where the General Statutes require a licensed contractor for certain types of construction, no permit shall be issued for such construction except in compliance with these statutes.

(f) Where necessary to determine compliance with Code standards, the Inspection Department may require tests or test reports. Such tests must be made by an approved testing laboratory or other approved agency, at the expense of the applicant. Copies of test reports or the results of tests shall be kept on file in the Inspection Department. [Authority: G.S. 143-139, 153A-357, 160A-417, 83-12, CH 87, CH 89c, 133.1.1]

105.5-PERMITS

(a) If the Inspection Department is satisfied that the work described in an application for permit and the drawings and specifications filed therewith conforms to the requirements of this Code and all other applicable State and local laws, it shall issue a permit therefor to the applicant.

(b) The permit shall be in writing and shall contain a provision that the work done shall comply with the State Building Code and all other applicable State and local laws. Inspection fees shall be as designated by the local governing authority.

(c) A permit issued for work under this Code shall expire by limitation six months (or such lesser period fixed by local ordinance) after the date of issuance if the work authorized has not been commenced. If after commencement the work is discontinued for a period of 12 months, the permit therefor shall immediately expire. No work authorized by any permit that has expired shall thereafter be performed until a new permit has been secured.

(d) After a permit has been issued, no changes or deviations from the terms of the application, plans and specifications, or the permit (except changes or deviations clearly permissible under this Code) shall be made until specific written approval of proposed changes or deviations has been obtained from the Inspection Department. [Authority: G.S. 143-139, 153A-357, 153A-358, 153A-359, 160A-417, 160A-418, 160A-419.]

(e) When the Inspection Department issues a permit, it shall endorse in writing or by stamping "APPROVED" all sets of plans which have been submitted. One set of plans so approved shall be retailed by the Inspection Department, and the other set or sets shall be returned to the applicant; one set of which shall be kept at the site of the work and shall be open to inspection by any authorized member of the Inspection Department.

LOCAL ORDINANCE PROVISIONS CONCERNING ISSUANCE OF PERMITS

G.S. 160A-412, which outlines the responsibilities of municipal inspection departments (see G.S. 153A-352 for the counties' counterpart), provides that "[t]he city council shall have the authority to enact reasonable and appropriate provisions governing the enforcement of those laws." G.S. 160A-414 (county: G.S. 153A-354) provides that "[the city council] shall have power to fix reasonable fees for issuance of permits, inspections, and other services of the inspection department." Under these grants of authority, many local ordinances contain at least a few provisions bearing on applications for and issuance of permits. Each code enforcement official should check his local code for such provisions.

7 INSPECTIONS

In carrying out his duties the code enforcement official may be called on to make three main types of inspections: (1) inspections of construction work in progress and when finished to assure that it is being carried out in accordance with the relevant laws; (2) periodic areawide inspections of existing buildings to locate hazardous and unhealthful conditions or violations of law; and (3) inspections of particular buildings where there is reason to believe such conditions may exist. As we shall see, there is ample statutory and Code authority for making such types of inspections.

CONSTITUTIONAL REQUIREMENTS

The major legal issues confronting a code enforcement official as he makes (or attempts to make) inspections arise from provisions of the federal and state constitutions.

The Fourth Amendment to the Constitution of the United States provides as follows:

> The right of the people to be secure in their persons, houses, papers, and effects, against unreasonable searches and seizures, shall not be violated, and no warrants shall issue but upon probable cause, supported by oath or affirmation and particularly describing the place to be searched and the persons or things to be seized.

This amendment is part of the Bill of Rights of the federal Constitution (which North Carolina would not ratify until the document contained a bill of rights). While originally thought to apply only to the federal government, these provisions have been made to apply to the states (through the Fourteenth Amendment) by a series of U.S. Supreme Court decisions.

In addition to these federal provisions, Article I, Section 20 of the Constitution of North Carolina provides as follows:

> General warrants, whereby any officer or other person may be commanded to search suspected places without evidence of the act committed, or to seize any person or persons not named, whose offense is not particularly described and supported by evidence, are dangerous to liberty and shall not be granted.

For many years it was believed that these provisions applied only to searches for the purpose of enforcing criminal laws (such as prohibition laws, laws against illicit possession of drugs, etc.) and not to "administrative" inspections for unsafe or unhealthful conditions. When this view was finally challenged, the U.S. Supreme Court first held in two narrowly divided decisions—*Frank v. Maryland*,[1] a 5-4 decision, and *Ohio ex rel. Eaton v. Price*,[2] a 4-4 decision that let stand a decision of the Ohio Supreme Court—that the Fourth Amendment did not apply to "administrative" inspections. But in June 1967, it reversed itself in two major decisions: *Camara v. San Francisco*[3] and *See v. Seattle*.[4] These two decisions were summarized as follows:

(1) *Frank v. Maryland*, 359 U.S. 360 (1959), is overruled to the extent that *Frank* permitted routine *warrantless* inspections in connection with enforcement of administrative codes such as housing, building, health and fire ordinances or regulations and upheld punishment of property owners or possessors who obstructed such entry.

(2) Administrative inspections of residential (*Camara*) and commercial establishments (*See*) can be performed without a warrant upon the consent of the owner or possessor.

(3) Administrative inspections of residences and commercial establishments can be conducted without the consent of the owner or possessor only when (a) the inspection is of an emergency nature, that is, in connection with special, emergency health or safety problems such as epidemics, seizure of putrid food, quarantines, or fire, or (b) the inspector secures a warrant issued by a judicial officer.

(4) Warrants may be issued in particular cases when the search is deemed "reasonable" by the issuing authority; but "probable cause" (in the standard criminal sense) for believing a violation exists is not required.

(5) A search is "reasonable" when it is required (a) in order to achieve the legitimate goals of the administrative code sought to be enforced, and (b) by application of the legitimate standards of the administrative code which prescribes the inspection. [The Court mentioned that the basis of such standards may be passage of time, general condition of the area, nature of the buildings; but specific knowledge of the condition of a particular building is not required.]

(6) A search warrant should ordinarily be issued only after refusal of consent. But when the element of surprise is a reasonable goal of the inspection, the warrant may be issued in advance of such refusal.

(7) Although a search warrant is necessary to force entry into areas of business premises not open to the public, the Court indicated that business premises may reasonably be inspected in many more situations than private homes.[5]

Thus code enforcement officials became subject for the first time to the laws governing other law enforcement officials who find it necessary to inspect property during their investigations. Under the general range of cases dealing with searches of property, law enforcement officials may

---

1. 359 U.S. 360 (1959).
2. 364 U.S. 263 (1960).
3. 387 U.S. 523 (1967).
4. 387 U.S. 541 (1967).
5. David G. Warren, *Health Law Bulletin* No. 13 (Institute of Government, 1967).

enter those portions of private property that are generally open to the public. If they wish to go beyond such areas, they may do so with the "informed consent" of the property's legal occupant.[6] If he refuses this consent, they may enter the property only with the backing of a search warrant, issued by a judicial officer.

What are the risks of entering property without either valid consent or a search warrant? The occupant may collect civil damages from the official for a trespass. The official also may be held guilty of a criminal trespass. Any evidence gathered during such an unauthorized entry will not be admissible in a court proceeding to enforce the law that the official is seeking to carry out.

Obviously, this issue will not often arise in enforcing the State Building Code. The owner and the contractor know that unless the enforcement official makes his inspections, he will not issue a certificate of compliance when the work is done (see Chapter Nine), and the owner will not be permitted to move into the building. On the other hand, when the inspector attempts to make an inspection for the purpose of enforcing the minimum housing code as it applies to existing buildings, enforcing the zoning ordinance, making fire prevention or sanitary inspections, or enforcing a local nuisance ordinance, he must be aware of this area of the law. That is why it is covered in this publication.

ADMINISTRATIVE SEARCH AND INSPECTION WARRANTS

Before the recent Supreme Court decisions, there was no authority in the North Carolina General Statutes for the issuance of administrative search warrants. But after those decisions the General Assembly acted promptly to fill this gap by enacting Article 4A of G.S. Chapter 15, which provides as follows:

§ 15-27.2. Warrants to conduct inspections authorized by law.

(a) Notwithstanding the provisions of Article 11 of Chapter 15A, any official or employee of the State or of a unit of county or local government of North Carolina may, under the conditions specified in this section, obtain a warrant authorizing him to conduct a search or inspection of property if such a search or inspection is one that is elsewhere authorized by law, either with or without the consent of the person whose privacy would be thereby invaded, and is one for which such a warrant is constitutionally required.

(b) The warrant may be issued by any magistrate of the general court of justice, judge, clerk, or assistant or deputy clerk of any court of record whose territorial jurisdiction encompasses the property to be inspected.

---

6. *In re* Dwelling of Properties, 24 N.C. App. 17, 210 S.E.2d 73 (1974), held that the constitutional protection is afforded to the tenant rather than the landlord if the owner does not occupy the property.

(c) The issuing officer shall issue the warrant when he is satisfied the following conditions are met:

    (1) The one seeking the warrant must establish under oath or affirmation that the property to be searched or inspected is to be searched or inspected as part of a legally authorized program of inspection which naturally includes that property, or that there is probable cause for believing that there is a condition, object, activity or circumstance which legally justifies such a search or inspection of that property;

    (2) An affidavit indicating the basis for the establishment of one of the grounds described in (1) above must be signed under oath or affirmation by the affiant;

    (3) The issuing official must examine the affiant under oath or affirmation to verify the accuracy of the matters indicated by the statement in the affidavit;

(d) The warrant shall be validly issued only if it meets the following requirements:

    (1) Except as provided in subsection (e), it must be signed by the issuing official and must bear the date and hour of its issuance above his signature with a notation that the warrant is valid for only 24 hours following its issuance;

    (2) It must describe, either directly or by reference to the affidavit, the property where the search or inspection is to occur and be accurate enough in description so that the executor of the warrant and the owner or the possessor of the property can reasonably determine from it what person or property the warrant authorizes an inspection of;

    (3) It must indicate the conditions, objects, activities or circumstances which the inspection is intended to check or reveal;

    (4) It must be attached to the affidavit required to be made in order to obtain the warrant.

(e) Any warrant issued under this section for a search or inspection shall be valid for only 24 hours after its issuance, must be personally served upon the owner or possessor of the property between the hours of 8:00 A.M. and 8:00 P.M. and must be returned within 48 hours. If the warrant, however, was procured pursuant to an investigation authorized by G.S. 69-1, the warrant may be executed at any hour, is valid for 48 hours after its issuance, and must be returned without unnecessary delay after its execution or after the expiration of the 48 hour period if it is not executed. If the owner or possessor of the property is not present on the property at the time of the search or inspection and reasonable efforts to locate the owner or possessor have been made and have failed, the warrant or a copy thereof may be affixed to the property and shall have the same effect as if served personally upon the owner or possessor.

(f) No facts discovered or evidence obtained in a search or inspection conducted under authority of a warrant issued under this section shall be competent as evidence in any civil, criminal or administrative action, nor considered in imposing any civil, criminal, or administrative sanction against any person, nor as a basis for further seeking to obtain any warrant, if the warrant is invalid or if what is discovered or obtained is not a condition, object, activity or circumstance which it was the legal purpose of the search or inspection to discover; but this shall not prevent any such facts or evidence to be so used when the warrant issued is not constitutionally required in those circumstances.

(g) The warrants authorized under this section shall not be regarded as search warrants for the purposes of application of Article 11 of Chapter 15A of the General Statutes of North Carolina.

The constitutionality of this act has been upheld and its requirements rigorously enforced in at least two cases.[7]

On this page and the next three pages are forms for two types of administrative search warrants. The first two pages are a warrant for use in carrying out a general program of inspection; the last two are a warrant for inspection for a particular health, safety, or other hazard.

STATE OF NORTH CAROLINA
In the General Court of Justice

_____ County

AFFIDAVIT TO OBTAIN ADMINISTRATIVE INSPECTION WARRANT FOR PERIODIC INSPECTION

I, _____ , being duly
(write your name and position)

sworn and examined under oath, state under oath that there is a program of inspection authorized

by _____ which
(identify statute or regulation authorizing inspection)

naturally includes the property owned or possessed by _____
(name owner or possessor)

_____ and described as follows: _____

_____
(precisely describe the property to be inspected)

The program of inspection referred to covers the area _____

_____
(indicate town, county, or portion thereof, or other specific territory covered

_____
by inspection program)

and is being conducted for the purpose of checking or revealing the following:

_____
(state conditions, objects, activities, or circumstances covered by inspection program)

_____

_____

This inspection program is a legal function of _____
(name agency)

and is under the supervision of _____
(identify person responsible for inspection program)

Signature of Applicant

SWORN AND SUBSCRIBED TO BEFORE ME

Date

Signature

☐ Assistant CSC   ☐ DeputyCSC   ☐ Clerk of Superior Court
☐ Magistrate   ☐ Superior Court Judge   ☐ District Court Judge

AOC-CR-914M
Rev. 7-85   **IMPORTANT:** Attach the Affidavit to the WARRANT if not on reverse side.

---

7. Brooks v. Taylor Tobacco Enterprises, Inc., 39 N.C. App. 529, 251 S.E.2d 656 (1979), *rev'd*, 298 N.C. 759, 260 S.E.2d 419 (1979); Gooden v. Brooks, 39 N.C. App. 519, 251 S.E.2d 698 (1979).

STATE OF NORTH CAROLINA
In the General Court of Justice

_____ County

**ADMINISTRATIVE INSPECTION WARRANT
FOR PERIODIC INSPECTION**

G.S. 15-_._.2

TO ANY LAWFUL OFFICIAL EMPOWERED TO CONDUCT THE INSPECTION AUTHORIZED BY THIS WARRANT:

The applicant named on the accompanying affidavit, being duly sworn, has stated to me that the property described in that affidavit is to be inspected as part of a legally authorized program of inspection which naturally includes that property. I have examined this applicant under oath or affirmation and have thereby verified the accuracy of the matters in the affidavit establishing the legal grounds for this warrant. THEREFORE, YOU ARE HEREBY COMMANDED TO INSPECT THE PROPERTY DESCRIBED IN THE ACCOMPANYING AFFIDAVIT.

This inspection is authorized to check or reveal the conditions, objects, activities, or circumstances indicated in the accompanying affidavit as a purpose of the inspection program.

This warrant must be served upon the owner or possessor of the property described in the accompanying affidavit. If the owner or possessor is not present on the property at the time of inspection and you have made reasonable but unsuccessful efforts to locate the owner or possessor, you may instead serve it by affixing this warrant or a copy to the property.

THIS WARRANT MAY BE EXECUTED ONLY BETWEEN THE HOURS OF 8:00 A.M. AND 8:00 P.M. AND ONLY WITHIN 24 HOURS AFTER IT WAS ISSUED. IT MUST BE RETURNED WITHIN 48 HOURS AFTER IT WAS ISSUED.

Date Issued	Time Issued ☐ A.M. ☐ P.M.
Signature	

☐ Assistant CSC ☐ Deputy CSC ☐ Clerk of Superior Court
☐ Magistrate ☐ Superior Court Judge ☐ District Court Judge

OFFICER'S RETURN

I certify that this WARRANT was executed on the date and time shown below.

Date of Execution	Signature of Inspecting Official
Time of Execution ☐ A.M. ☐ P.M.	

CLERK'S ACCEPTANCE

This WARRANT has been returned to this office on the date and time shown below.

Date of return	Signature
Time of return ☐ A.M. ☐ P.M.	☐ Assistant CSC ☐ Deputy CSC ☐ Clerk of Superior Court

AOC-CR-914M, Side Two
Rev 7-85

IMPORTANT: Attach Affidavit to Warrant if not on reverse side.

STATE OF NORTH CAROLINA
In the General Court of Justice

_____ County

AFFIDAVIT TO OBTAIN ADMINISTRATIVE INSPECTION WARRANT FOR PARTICULAR CONDITION OR ACTIVITY

I, _____ , being duly
(write your name and position)

sworn and examined under oath, state under oath that there is probable cause for believing that

there is _____
(describe condition, object, activity, or circumstance which the

_____
search is intended to check or reveal)

_____

at the property owned or possessed by _____

and described as follows: _____

_____
(precisely describe the property to be inspected)

The facts which establish probable cause to believe this are: _____

_____

_____

_____

_____

_____

_____

_____

Signature of Applicant

SWORN AND SUBSCRIBED TO BEFORE ME

Date

Signature

☐ Assistant CSC   ☐ DeputyCSC   ☐ Clerk of Superior Court
☐ Magistrate   ☐ Superior Court Judge   ☐ District Court Judge

IMPORTANT: Attach the Affidavit to the WARRANT if not on reverse side.

AOC-CR-913M
Rev. 7-85

STATE OF NORTH CAROLINA In the General Court of Justice _____ County	ADMINISTRATIVE INSPECTION WARRANT FOR PARTICULAR CONDITION OR ACTIVITY G.S. 15-27.2

TO ANY LAWFUL OFFICIAL EMPOWERED TO CONDUCT THE INSPECTION AUTHORIZED BY THIS WARRANT:

The applicant named on the accompanying affidavit, being duly sworn, has stated to me that there is a condition, object, activity, or circumstance legally justifying an inspection of the property described in that affidavit. I have examined this applicant under oath or affirmation and have verified the accuracy of the matters in the affidavit establishing the legal grounds for this warrant. YOU ARE HEREBY COMMANDED TO INSPECT THE PROPERTY DESCRIBED IN THE ACCOMPANYING AFFIDAVIT.

This inspection is authorized to check or reveal the conditions, objects, activities, or circumstances indicated in the accompanying affidavit.

This warrant must be served upon the owner or possessor of the property described in the accompanying affidavit. If the owner or possessor is not present on the property at the time of inspection and you have made reasonable but unsuccessful efforts to locate the owner or possessor, you may instead serve it by affixing this warrant or a copy to the property.

THIS WARRANT MAY BE EXECUTED ONLY BETWEEN THE HOURS OF 8:00 A.M. AND 8:00 P.M. AND ONLY WITHIN 24 HOURS AFTER IT WAS ISSUED. IT MUST BE RETURNED WITHIN 48 HOURS AFTER IT WAS ISSUED. HOWEVER, IF THIS WARRANT IS ISSUED PURSUANT TO A FIRE INVESTIGATION AUTHORIZED BY G.S. 69-1, IT MAY BE EXECUTED AT ANY TIME WITHIN 48 HOURS AFTER IT IS ISSUED. IT MUST BE RETURNED WITHOUT UNNECESSARY DELAY AFTER ITS EXECUTION OR AFTER 48 HOURS FROM THE TIME IT WAS ISSUED IF IT WAS NOT EXECUTED.

Date	Time ☐ A.M. ☐ P.M.
Signature	

☐ Assistant CSC   ☐ Deputy CSC   ☐ Clerk of Superior Court
☐ Magistrate   ☐ Superior Court Judge   ☐ District Court Judge

OFFICER'S RETURN

I certify that this WARRANT was executed on the date and time shown below.

Date of Execution	Signature of Inspecting Official
Time of Execution ☐ A.M. ☐ P.M.	

CLERK'S ACCEPTANCE

This WARRANT has been returned to this office on the date and time shown below.

Date of return	Signature
Time of return ☐ A.M. ☐ P.M.	☐ Assistant CSC ☐ Deputy CSC ☐ Clerk of Superior Court

AOC-CR-913M. Side Two
Rev. 7-85

IMPORTANT: Attach Affidavit to Warrant if not on reverse side.

STATUTES CONCERNING INSPECTIONS

Besides the statutory provisions for search warrants and the constitutional provisions requiring such warrants, the code enforcement official must have specific authority under the statutes, the State Building Code, or local ordinances to make inspections. These statutes grant such authority:

§ 160A-420. Inspections of work in progress.

As the work pursuant to a permit progresses, local inspectors shall make as many inspections thereof as may be necessary to satisfy them that the work is being done according to the provisions of any applicable State and local laws and of the terms of the permit. In exercising this power, members of the inspection department shall have a right to enter on any premises within the jurisdiction of the department at all reasonable hours for the purposes of inspection or other enforcement action, upon presentation of proper credentials.

(County: G.S. 153A-360)

§ 160A-424. Periodic inspections.

The inspection department shall make periodic inspections, subject to the council's directions, for unsafe, unsanitary, or otherwise hazardous and unlawful conditions in structures within its territorial jurisdiction. In addition, it shall make inspections when it has reason to believe that such conditions may exist in a particular structure. In exercising this power, members of the department shall have a right to enter on any premises within the jurisdiction of the department at all reasonable hours for the purposes of inspection or other enforcement action, upon presentation of proper credentials.

(County: G.S. 153A-364)

§ 69-4. Inspection of premises; dangerous material removed.

The Commissioner of Insurance, or the chief of fire department or chief of police where there is no chief of fire department, or the city or county building inspector, electrical inspector, heating inspector, or fire prevention inspector has the right at all reasonable hours, for the purpose of examination, to enter into and upon all buildings and premises in their jurisdiction. When any of such officers find in any building or upon any premises overcrowding in violation of occupancy limits established pursuant to the North Carolina State Building Code, combustible material or inflammable conditions dangerous to the safety of such building or premises they shall order the same to be removed or remedied, and this order shall be forthwith complied with by the owner or occupant of such buildings or premises. The owner or occupant may, within twenty-four hours, appeal to the Commissioner of Insurance from the order, and the cause of the complaint shall be at once investigated by his direction, and unless by his authority the order of the officer above named is revoked it remains in force and must be forthwith complied with by the owner or occupant. The Commissioner of Insurance, fire chief, or building inspector, electrical inspector, heating inspector, or fire prevention inspector shall make an immediate investigation as to the presence of combustible material or the existence of inflammable conditions in any building or upon any premises under their jurisdiction upon complaint of any person having an interest in such building or premises or property adjacent thereto. The Commissioner may, in person or by deputy, visit any municipality or county and make such inspections alone or in company with the local officer.

§ 160A-448. Additional powers of public officer.

An ordinance adopted by the governing body of the city may authorize the public officer to exercise any powers necessary or convenient to carry out and effectuate the purpose and provisions of this Part, including the following powers in addition to others herein granted:

• • •

(3) To enter upon premises for the purpose of making examinations in a manner that will do the least possible inconvenience to the persons in possession;

• • •

STATE BUILDING CODE PROVISIONS CONCERNING INSPECTIONS

The State Building Code essentially duplicates the statutory grants of authority and adds some additional powers.

Volume I (General Construction) contains the following provisions:

105.6 — INSPECTIONS REQUIRED

(a) As the work covered by permit progresses, local inspectors shall make as many inspections thereof as necessary to satisfy them that the work is being done in accordance with this Code, any other applicable State and local laws, and the terms of the permit.

(b) When required, the Inspection Department shall make at least the following inspections of all work being performed under the permit and shall either approve that portion of the construction as completed or shall notify the permit holder or his agent wherein the same fails to comply with the law. The permit holder or his agent shall give timely notice to the Inspection Department when the work for these inspections are ready:

Foundation Inspection: To be made after excavation and forms, if any are erected and reinforcing steel, if any, is placed and prior to placement of concrete.

Frame Inspection: To be made after the roof, all framing, fire-blocking and bracing is in place and all pipes, chimneys, and vents are complete.

Insulation Inspection: To be made after framing is complete with insulation being installed and prior to finish being applied.

Final Inspection: To be made after the building or structure is completed and ready for occupancy.

(c) Work shall not proceed on any part of a building or structure beyond the point indicated for each inspection described in subsection (b) above until written approval has been received from the inspection department.

(d) Reinforcing steel or structural framework of any part of any building shall not be covered or concealed in any manner whatsoever without first obtaining the approval of the Inspection Department and, where appropriate, the designing architect or engineer.

(e) In all buildings where plaster is used for fire protection purposes, the permit holder or his agent shall notify the Inspection Department after all lathing and backing is in place. Plaster shall not be applied until the approval of the Inspection Department has been received.

(f) Where necessary to determine compliance of any work with Code standards, the Inspection Department may require tests or test reports. Such tests must be made by an approved testing laboratory or other approved agency, at the expense of the owner. Copies of test reports or the results of tests shall be submitted to and kept on file in the Inspection Department.

(g) *Periodic Inspections:* Local Inspection Department shall make periodic inspections (subject to direction of the local governing board) of existing buildings to determine their compliance with this Code and to determine whether they meet minimum requirements for safety to life. In addition, they shall make inspections when they have reason to believe that unsafe, unsanitary, hazardous, or unlawful conditions may exist in a particular structure. (Reference: Chapter X, Volume 1.)

(h) Change of Use: When an existing building is to be converted to another use of occupancy, it shall be the responsibility of the owner or his agent to notify the Inspection Department to make an inspection of such building to assure that it will be in compliance with the safety requirements of this Code as they would apply to the new use or occupancy. (Authority: G.S. 153A-360, 153A-364, 160A-420, 160A-424, 143-139.)

105.7 — RIGHT OF ENTRY

Authorized personnel of a local Inspection Department shall have a right to the extent provided by the N.C. General Statutes to enter on any premises within the Department's jurisdiction, including entry into or upon all buildings or structures, for the purpose of inspection or other enforcement action, upon presentation of proper credentials. (Authority: G.S. 69-4, 69-13, 143-139, 153A-360, 153A-364, 160A-420, 160A-424.)

Volume II (Plumbing) contains the following:

105.6 — INSPECTIONS REQUIRED

(a) *Inspection Required:* All plumbing installed in accordance with the provisions of this code shall be inspected by the plumbing inspector and no part of the plumbing system shall be covered until same has been so inspected and approved as herein prescribed.

(b) *Request For Inspection:* Requests for inspection of plumbing, as required in this code shall be filed by the master plumber or the installer of same in the office of the plumbing inspector at such time as the local governing authority may determine.

(c) *Final Inspection:* When the installation, alteration or restoration of plumbing has been completed in accordance with the provisions of this code, a request for final inspection shall be filed at the office of the plumbing inspector by the master plumber or installer.

(d) *Final Certificate of Inspection Issued By Plumbing Inspector:* If, after the final inspection and tests of plumbing, as provided for in this code, the plumbing inspector approves of same, he shall issue a certificate of compliance to the master plumber or installer. A property owner or his agent shall be entitled to a copy of said certificate of compliance upon request to the plumbing inspector.

105.7 — TESTING

(a) *Plumbing System To Be Tested:* In order to prevent the use of defective materials and to provide for water tight or air tight joints, the piping of the entire drainage and venting system shall be tested in the presence of the plumbing inspector by application of the water test as follows. If such test is applied to the entire system, all openings in the piping shall be tightly closed, except the highest openings above the roof, and the entire system shall be filled with water to the point of overflow. If the system is tested in sections, each opening shall be tightly plugged, except the highest opening of the section under test, and each section shall be completely filled with water. No section shall be tested with less than a ten (10) foot head of water. In testing successive sections, at least the upper ten (10) feet of the next succeeding section shall be tested so that no joint or pipe in the building shall have been submitted to a test of less than a ten (10) foot head of water. In lieu of the above water test, the plumbing inspector may require an air test, to consist of not less than five (5) pounds per square inch of pressure in the system. In either of the above tests, the plumbing system shall sustain a constant water level or air pressure per square inch for a period of not less than fifteen (15) minutes. If either of the above tests reveals defective materials or workmanship, same shall be replaced or corrected and tests, as provided in this section, shall be repeated. A roughing-in test shall be required before any piping of the plumbing system is concealed or fixtures set.

(b) *Test of Existing Plumbing:* In event the plumbing inspector has reason to believe that insanitary conditions exist, in habitable buildings or on premises, he may require the owner or agent thereof to provide for tests, as described in Section 105.6(a) thereof, and in event defective materials or workmanship are revealed by such tests, the said owner or agent shall immediately repair the plumbing system in accordance with the directions of the plumbing inspector.

(c) *Materials and Labor for Tests:* All equipment, material, power and labor necessary for inspection and tests shall be furnished by the master plumber or installer.

105.8 – RIGHT OF ENTRY

Authorized personnel of a local Inspection Department shall have a right to the extent provided by the N.C. General Statutes to enter on any premises within the Department's jurisdiction, including entry into or upon all buildings or structures, for the purpose of inspection or other enforcement action, upon presentation of proper credentials. (Authority: G.S. 69-4, 69-13, 143-139, 153A-360, 153A-364, 160A-420, 160A-424.)

Volume III (Heating, Air Conditioning, Refrigeration and Ventilation) provides:

105.6 – INSPECTIONS REQUIRED

(a) As the work covered by permit progresses, local inspectors shall make as many inspections thereof as necessary to satisfy them that the work is being done in accordance with this Code, any other applicable State and local laws, and the terms of the permit.

(b) All heating, air conditioning, refrigeration and ventilation installed in accordance with the provisions of this Code shall be inspected and/or tested by the inspector and no part of the heating, air conditioning, refrigeration or ventilation system shall be covered until same has been so inspected and approved as herein prescribed.

(c) Work shall not proceed on any part of the system beyond the point indicated for each inspection described in subsection (b) above until written approval has been received from the Inspection Department.

(d) Where necessary to determine compliance of any work with Code standards, the Inspection Department may require tests or test reports. Such test must be made by an approved testing laboratory or other approved agency, at the expense of the owner. Copies of test reports or the results of tests shall be submitted to and kept on file in the Inspection Department.

(e) *Periodic Inspections:* Local Inspection Department shall make periodic inspections (subject to direction of the local governing board) of existing buildings to determine their compliance with this Code and to determine whether they meet minimum requirements for safety to life. In addition, they shall make inspections when they have reason to believe that unsafe, unsanitary, hazardous, or unlawful conditions may exist in a particular structure. [Reference: Chapter X, Volume 1.)

(f) Change of Use: When an existing building is to be converted to another use of occupancy, it shall be the responsibility of the owner or his agent to notify the Inspection Department to make an inspection of such building to assure that it will be in compliance with the safety requirements of this Code as they would apply to the new use or occupancy. [Authority: G.S. 153A-360, 153A-364, 160A-420, 160A-424, 143-139.]

105.7 – RIGHT OF ENTRY

Authorized personnel of a local Inspection Department shall have a right to the extent provided by the N.C. General Statutes to enter on any premises within the Department's jurisdiction, including entry into or upon all buildings or structures, for the purpose of inspection or other enforcement action, upon presentation of proper credentials. [Authority: G.S. 69-4, 69-13, 143-139, 153A-360, 153A-364, 160A-420, 160A-424.]

LOCAL ORDINANCE PROVISIONS CONCERNING INSPECTIONS

Local ordinances creating inspection departments may contain further provisions concerning inspections—particularly the types of inspections to be made and the timing of those inspections—pursuant to G.S. 160A-412 (municipal) and G.S. 153A-352 (county).

8 NONJUDICIAL ENFORCEMENT ACTIONS

In the course of his various inspections, of either work in progress or existing buildings, the code enforcement official will encounter violations of the laws he is enforcing. When this happens, he ordinarily can begin enforcement actions in the courts — as outlined in Chapter 10. But he also has powers to correct some violations through actions short of going to court. (Following this course does not preclude his *later* going to court, if he encounters a recalcitrant violator.)

His primary nonjudicial powers are the issuance of a "stop order" and the revocation of a permit. Both apply only to violations discovered while work is actually under way. Issuance of a stop order is possible whether or not a permit has been procured for the work (indeed, one type of violation for which a stop order can be issued is simply that no permit was given for the work). But obviously, the enforcement official can "revoke" only a permit that has been issued.

The statutes that authorize these actions set forth certain required procedures.

STOP ORDERS

§ 160A-421. Stop orders.

Whenever any building or structure or part thereof is being demolished, constructed, reconstructed, altered, or repaired in a hazardous manner, or in substantial violation of any State or local building law, or in a manner that endangers life or property, the appropriate inspector may order the specific part of the work that is in violation or presents such a hazard to be immediately stopped. The stop order shall be in writing, directed to the person doing the work, and shall state the specific work to be stopped, the specific reasons therefor, and the conditions under which the work may be resumed. The owner or builder may appeal from a stop order involving alleged violation of the State Building Code or any approved local modification thereof to the North Carolina Commissioner of Insurance within a period of five days after the order is issued. Notice of appeal shall be given in writing to the Commissioner of Insurance, with a copy to the local inspector. The Commissioner of Insurance shall promptly conduct a hearing at which the appellant and the inspector shall be permitted to submit relevant evidence, and shall rule on the appeal as expeditiously as possible. Pending the ruling by the Commissioner of Insurance on an appeal no further work shall take place in violation of a stop order. Appeals from a stop order based on violation of any other local ordinance relating to buildings shall be taken to the local official designated by that ordinance and shall be taken, heard, and decided in the same manner as prescribed herein for appeals to the Commissioner. Violation of a stop order shall constitute a misdemeanor.

(County: G.S. 153A-361)

Note that the stop order must be "in writing." An oral order is not enough. The stop order must be directed to the "person doing the work" (rather than to the owner). It must state "the specific work to be stopped" (in some circumstances this might be *all* work—for example, where no permits had been issued). It must state "the specific reasons" for stopping the work (which in most cases should include citations of the specific laws being violated and how). And it must state the conditions under which the work can be resumed (for example, only after permits have been issued).

The law provides that appeals with respect to State Building Code are to be taken to the North Carolina Commissioner of Insurance.

It should be noted that violation of a stop order constitutes a misdemeanor. G.S. 160A-432 (county: G.S. 153A-372) states that the unit may also go to court for equitable relief in such cases. So if the stop order is ignored, there are some "teeth" behind it.

REVOCATION OF PERMITS

§ 160A-422. Revocation of permits.

The appropriate inspector may revoke and require the return of any permit by notifying the permit holder in writing stating the reason for the revocation. Permits shall be revoked for any substantial departure from the approved application, plans, or specifications; for refusal or failure to comply with the requirements of any applicable State or local laws; or for false statements or misrepresentations made in securing the permit. Any permit mistakenly issued in violation of an applicable State or local law may also be revoked.

(County: G.S. 153A-362)

This statutory provision codifies court decisions around the country that as a matter of "common law" have authorized permit revocation on these bases even though no statute could be cited.

Note that the statute *requires* ("shall") revocation in the following circumstances:

(1) When there has been a substantial departure from the approved application, plans, or specifications;[1]

(2) When the permit-holder has refused or failed to comply with the requirements of any applicable state or local laws;

(3) When the permit holder has made false statements or misrepresentations in securing the permit.[2]

And the statute *permits* ("may") revocation when a permit has been mistakenly issued in violation of applicable state or local law.[3]

---

1. Crudele v. Cook, 165 S.2d 424 (Fla. App. 1963).

2. Rosenbush v. Keller, 247 App. Div. 748, 285 N.Y.S. 636 (1936).

3. Giordano v. Dumont, 141 N.J. Eq. 34, 55 A.2d 671 (Ch. 1947); Godson v. Surfside, 150 Fla. 614, So.2d 497 (1942); Wood v. Boston, 256 Mass. 238, 152 N.E. 63 (1926); Milwaukee v. Leavitt, 142 N.W.2d 169 (Wis. 1966). *Cf.* Raleigh v. Fisher, 232 N.C. 629 (1950).

It will be noted that when a revocation is made pursuant to the statutory authority set forth above, the code enforcement official must give the permit holder *written* notice that *states the reason for the revocation.* Failure to do this will nullify the attempted revocation.

Once the permit has been revoked, the property owner will violate G.S. 160A-417 (county: G.S. 153A-357) if he attempts to proceed further without a new permit.

Again, under G.S. 160A-434 (municipal) and G.S. 153A-374 (county) appeals are to be taken from such an action to the State Commissioner of Insurance rather than to a local board.

ORDER TO CORRECT DEFECTS UNDER BUILDING LAWS

A third statutory provision gives local code enforcement officials authority to order corrections of law violations:

§ 160A-425. Defects in buildings to be corrected.

When a local inspector finds any defects in a building, or finds that the building has not been constructed in accordance with the applicable State and local laws, or that a building because of its condition is dangerous or contains fire hazardous conditions, it shall be his duty to notify the owner or occupant of the building of its defects, hazardous conditions, or failure to comply with law. The owner or occupant shall each immediately remedy the defects, hazardous conditions, or violations of law in the property he owns.

(County: G.S. 153A-365)

Unfortunately, it should be noted, there are no "teeth" behind this provision if the order is ignored.

9 CERTIFICATES OF COMPLIANCE

The certificate of compliance (also sometimes known as a "certificate of occupancy"—a term that is most common in zoning ordinances) represents the final "sign-off" by the code enforcement official in most situations involving construction, repair, or movement of a building. It signifies to the owner and the contractor that all work has been completed in compliance with the law, and they may reasonably take this as the point at which the owner makes his final payment and moves in.

The statutory provisions for issuance of this certificate are as follows:

§ 160A-423. Certificates of compliance.

At the conclusion of all work done under a permit, the appropriate inspector shall make a final inspection, and if he finds that the completed work complies with all applicable State and local laws and with the terms of the permit, he shall issue a certificate of compliance. No new building or part thereof may be occupied, and no addition or enlargement of an existing building may be occupied, and no existing building that has been altered or moved may be occupied, until the inspection department has issued a certificate of compliance. A temporary certificate of compliance may be issued permitting occupancy for a stated period of specified portions of the building that the inspector finds may safely be occupied prior to final completion of the entire building. Violation of this section shall constitute a misdemeanor.

(County: G.S. 153A-363)

The State Building Code contains essentially identical provisions.

It should be noted that this certificate is not to be issued until all work under the permit has been completed and the code enforcement official has made a final inspection. (G.S. 160A-416 and G.S. 153A-356 make it a misdemeanor for the official to issue the certificate without making the inspection.) However, in some situations the owner may wish to use part of a building before the structure has been completed. Examples of this would be use of a segment of a shopping center or several floors of an office building, while the remainder of the building was under construction. In such a case, the statute allows the enforcement official to issue a "temporary" certificate permitting occupancy for a *stated period* of *specified portions* of the building.

Note also that the statute speaks of compliance "with all applicable State and local laws." At a minimum these would include the requirements of all volumes of the State Building Code—general construction, plumbing, heating and air conditioning, and electrical. But this provision may also be used as a basis for coordinating the efforts of a variety of departments and agencies. For example, a city might require that the departments enforcing the zoning ordinance, curb-cut ordinance, sign ordinance, utility-connection regulations, the traffic code, the fire prevention code, the erosion-control ordinance, the flood-plain ordinance, various health regulations, etc., all approve the completed job insofar as they are concerned before the inspection department will issue the certificate.

Some code enforcement officials are concerned at the breadth of this provision, fearing that they might be prosecuted for issuing a certificate when there were violations of some law of which they were unaware. They should note that G.S. 160A-416 and G.S. 153A-356 speak only of "willful" violations (for all situations other than issuance of a certificate without having made an inspection), and they therefore need not fear prosecution if they have made good-faith efforts to enforce all those laws that they might reasonably be expected to know about.

Finally, the statute makes it a misdemeanor for anyone to occupy a new, altered, or moved building until this certificate has been issued, and G.S. 160A-432 (municipal) and G.S. 153A-372 (county) provide for issuance of an injunction to reinforce the criminal penalty.

10 JUDICIAL ENFORCEMENT

As enforcement officer for particular laws, the code enforcement official is responsible for initiating whatever court actions become necessary when someone refuses to comply with one of those laws.

Judicial enforcement may be through a *criminal action*, in which the violator may be fined or imprisoned if convicted, or through a *civil action*, in which the court may order him either to take certain affirmative actions ("mandamus" or "mandatory injunction") or to cease violations ("injunction").

PROCEDURAL ASPECTS

PRELIMINARY PROCEDURES

Some statutes will direct the enforcement officer to give written notice to a violator before bringing a court action. Even when written notice is not a statutory requirement, considerations of "fair play" suggest that the officer should give the violator both informal and formal notice of observed violations and an opportunity to correct them before taking the serious step of bringing a court action.

As a matter of policy, the officer should also consult with his superiors and with the city or county attorney before bringing a legal action. On the basis of this consultation, he should take whatever steps are indicated to assure that he has all necessary evidence to support his case.

CHOICE OF CIVIL VS. CRIMINAL ACTION

Where he has a choice between a civil action and a criminal action, the code enforcement official will usually want to use the former because the nature of the violation is such that an injunction usually would be more appropriate and effective relief than a relatively small criminal penalty. Furthermore, the burden of proof of a violation in a criminal case is greater ("beyond a reasonable doubt") than it is in a civil case ("by a preponderance of the evidence").

To bring a civil suit, the officer should contact the city attorney, set forth the facts of the case, and request that he file a complaint against the violator that seeks an injunction against further violations and an order that existing violations be corrected.

To bring a criminal action, the officer should contact the district attorney for the local district court with jurisdiction over misdemeanors and ask that the violator be charged. Or he may directly appear before a magistrate to present sworn testimony in support of issuance of a criminal summons or warrant for arrest.

STATUTES OF LIMITATIONS

The officer should not delay too long in bringing legal action against a violator. Under G.S. 15-1, no action for a misdemeanor may be brought before a grand jury later than two years after the violation took place. More time is available in a civil action, since G.S. 1-56 provides a ten-year limitation that apparently applies to the types of proceedings that might be brought for enforcement of building laws.

It should be noted that while the statute of limitations commences to "run" when the violation occurs, some sorts of violations are "continuing" (i.e., a building might violate the building code for as long as it remains standing). This means that while a statute of limitations might have "run out" against a contractor who violated the Building Code when he erected the building, it has not expired against the owner, who is responsible for as long as the building remains in a defective condition.

Regardless of limitations placed by the law, it is always wise to initiate court actions promptly, once they have been decided upon, because the problem of proof grows more difficult as time passes and people's memory fades.

EVIDENCE

In addition to initiating a court action, the code enforcement official normally has major responsibility for providing evidence of the violation. He will probably be the chief witness at the trial and therefore must have the facts to prove the alleged violation.

The basic rule of evidence is that the witness may testify only as to facts that he knows about personally. The enforcement officer may not report what he has heard from others concerning the construction techniques of a building, for example; nor may he surmise as to what probably took place. He must actually see with his own eyes the factors that establish the violation, if he is to testify concerning them in the courtroom. He will be permitted, under certain circumstances, to "refresh his memory" by consulting his records made at the time of the investigation, but he may not supply facts that he did not think to look for.

It cannot be stressed too much that evidence must be gathered and preserved very carefully and that adequate records must be kept. Because a layman cannot be expected to know the legal pitfalls in this area, it is very desirable that the enforcement officer consult with the city or county attorney as soon as he suspects a violation and accept his guidance as to the facts that must be ascertained and the methods that should be followed in preserving evidence. As soon as the district attorney is brought into the case, he will (of course) assume a primary role, for he will be responsible for actually trying the case.

STATUTORY PROVISIONS SETTING PENALTIES

The following excerpts from statutes relating to construction show the penalties (civil or criminal) prescribed for various violations:

GENERAL

§ 160A-417. Permits.

No person shall commence or proceed with
   (1) The construction, reconstruction, alteration, repair, movement to another site, removal, or demolition of any building or structure,
   (2) The installation, extension, or general repair of any plumbing system,
   (3) The installation, extension, alteration, or general repair of any heating or cooling equipment system, or
   (4) The installation, extension, alteration, or general repair of any electrical wiring, devices, appliances, or equipment,
without first securing from the inspection department with jurisdiction over the site of the work any and all permits required by the State Building Code and any other State or local laws applicable to the work. A permit shall be in writing and shall contain a provision that the work done shall comply with the State Building Code and all other applicable State and local laws. No permits shall be issued unless the plans and specifications are identified by the name and address of the author thereof, and if the General Statutes of North Carolina require that plans for certain types of work be prepared only by a registered architect or registered engineer, no permit shall be issued unless the plans and specifications bear the North Carolina seal of a registered architect or of a registered engineer. When any provision of the General Statutes of North Carolina or of any ordinance requires that work be done by a licensed specialty contractor of any kind, no permit for the work shall be issued unless the work is to be performed by such a duly licensed contractor. No permit issued under Articles 9 or 9C of Chapter 143 shall be required for any construction, installation, repair, replacement, or alteration costing five thousand dollars ($5,000) or less in any single family residence or farm building unless the work involves: the addition, repair or replacement of load bearing structures; the addition (excluding replacement of same size and capacity) or change in the design of plumbing; the addition, replacement or change in the design of heating, air conditioning, or electrical wiring, devices, appliances, or equipment; the use of materials not permitted by the North Carolina Uniform Residential Building Code; or the addition (excluding replacement of like grade of fire resistance) of roofing Violation of this section shall constitute a misdemeanor.

(County: G.S. 153A-357)

§ 160A-421. Stop orders.

Whenever any building or structure or part thereof is being demolished, constructed, reconstructed, altered, or repaired in a hazardous manner, or in substantial violation of any State or local building law, or in a manner that endangers life or property, the appropriate inspector may order the specific part of the work that is in violation or presents such a hazard to be immediately stopped. The stop order shall be in writing, directed to the person doing the work, and shall state the specific work to be stopped, the specific reasons therefor, and the conditions under which the work may be resumed. The owner or builder may appeal from a stop order involving alleged violation of the State Building Code or any approved local modification thereof to the North Carolina Commissioner of Insurance within a period of five days after the order is issued. Notice of appeal shall be given in writing to the Commissioner of Insurance, with a copy to the local inspector. The Commissioner of Insurance shall promptly conduct a hearing at which the appellant and the inspector shall be permitted to submit relevant evidence, and shall rule on the appeal as expeditiously as possible. Pending the ruling by the Commissioner of Insurance on an appeal no further work shall take place in violation of a stop order. Appeals from a stop order based on violation of any other local ordinance relating to buildings shall be taken to the local official designated by that ordinance and shall be taken, heard, and decided in the same manner as prescribed herein for appeals to the Commissioner. <u>Violation of a stop order shall constitute a misdemeanor.</u>

(County: G.S. 153A-361)

§ 160A-423. Certificates of compliance.

At the conclusion of all work done under a permit, the appropriate inspector shall make a final inspection, and if he finds that the completed work complies with all applicable State and local laws and with the terms of the permit, he shall issue a certificate of compliance. No new building or part thereof may be occupied, and no addition or enlargement of an existing building may be occupied, and no existing building that has been altered or moved may be occupied, until the inspection department has issued a certificate of compliance. A temporary certificate of compliance may be issued permitting occupancy for a stated period of specified portions of the building that the inspector finds may safely be occupied prior to final completion of the entire building. <u>Violation of this section shall constitute a misdemeanor.</u>

(County: G.S. 153A-363)

§ 160A-427. Removing notice from condemned building.

If any person shall remove any notice that has been affixed to any building or structure by a local inspector of any municipality and that states the dangerous character of the building or structure, <u>he shall be guilty of a misdemeanor.</u>

(County: G.S. 153A-367)

§ 160A-431. Failure to comply with order.

If the owner of a building or structure fails to comply with an order issued pursuant to G.S. 160A-429 from which no appeal has been taken, or fails to comply with an order of the city council following an appeal, <u>he shall be guilty of a misdemeanor</u> and shall be punished in the discretion of the court.

(County: G.S. 153A-371)

§ 160A-432. Equitable enforcement.

Whenever any violation is denominated a misdemeanor under the provisions of this Part, the city, either in addition to or in lieu of other remedies, may initiate any appropriate action or proceedings to prevent, restrain, correct, or abate the violation or to prevent the occupancy of the building or structure involved.

(County: G.S. 153A-372)

NORTH CAROLINA STATE BUILDING CODE

§ 143-138. North Carolina State Building Code.

• • •

(h) Violations. — Any person who shall be adjudged to have violated this Article or the North Carolina State Building Code, except for violations of occupancy limits established by either, shall be guilty of a misdemeanor and shall upon conviction be liable to a fine, not to exceed fifty dollars ($50.00), for each offense. Each 30 days that such violation continues shall constitute a separate and distinct offense. • • •   In case any building or structure is erected, constructed or reconstructed, or its purpose altered, so that it becomes in violation of the North Carolina State Building Code • • •   either the local enforcement officer or the State Commissioner of Insurance or other State official with responsibility under G.S. 143-139 may, in addition to other remedies, institute any appropriate action or proceedings including the civil remedies set out in G.S. 160A-175 and G.S. 153A-123, (i) to prevent such unlawful erection, construction or reconstruction or alteration of purpose, or overcrowding, (ii) to restrain, correct, or abate such violation, or (iii) to prevent the occupancy or use of said building, structure or land until such violation is corrected.

FIRE ESCAPES LAW

§ 69-13. Enforcement by Commissioner of Insurance.

The Commissioner of Insurance is charged with the execution of this Article, and he or the chief of the fire department or the city or county building inspector, electrical inspector, heating inspector, or fire prevention inspector is vested with all privileges, duties, and obligations placed upon them in this Chapter, in regard to the inspection of buildings, for the purpose of enforcing the provisions of this Article in regard to the buildings and requirements herein. Any owner or occupant of premises failing to comply with the provisions of this Article, in accordance with the orders of the authorities above specified, shall be guilty of a misdemeanor and punished by a fine of not less than ten dollars ($10.00) nor more than fifty dollars ($50.00) for each day's neglect.

• • •

HOTEL SAFETY LAW

§ 69-34. Penalty for noncompliance.

Any owner, owners, proprietor or keeper of any hotel or other building of like occupancy who fails to comply with any of the foregoing provisions of this Article shall be guilty of a misdemeanor and punished by a fine of not less than ten dollars ($10.00) nor more than fifty dollars ($50.00). Each day of noncompliance herewith shall constitute a separate offense.

§ 69-36. Penalty for allowing unsafe building to remain occupied.

If any person shall continue to use or occupy or permit the use or occupancy of any hotel or other building of like occupancy which has been condemned as unsafe and dangerous to life by the Commissioner of Insurance or his authorized deputy, after having been notified in writing of the unsafe and dangerous character of said building, and if such use and occupancy shall continue for a period as much as 30 days without remedying the conditions complained of to the satisfaction of the Commissioner of Insurance or the chief of the fire department of the city in which the building is located, such person shall be guilty of a misdemeanor and shall pay a fine of not less than ten dollars ($10.00) nor more than fifty dollars ($50.00) for each day of such continued use and occupancy after the expiration of such 30-day period following such notice. Provided that such 30-day period may be enlarged (for good cause shown) by the Commissioner of Insurance or by the chief of the fire department of the city in which the building is located to such time as in his discretion he may find proper.

LOCAL ORDINANCES (in General)

§ 14-4. Violation of local ordinances misdemeanor.

(a) Except as provided in subsection (b), if any person shall violate an ordinance of a county, city, or town, he shall be guilty of a misdemeanor and shall be fined not more than fifty dollars ($50.00), or imprisoned for not more than 30 days.

(b) If any person shall violate an ordinance of a county, city, or town regulating the operation or parking of vehicles, he shall be responsible for an infraction and shall be required to pay a penalty of not more than fifty dollars ($50.00).

§ 160A-175. (Effective July 1, 1986) Enforcement of ordinances.

(a) A city shall have power to impose fines and penalties for violation of its ordinances, and may secure injunctions and abatement orders to further insure compliance with its ordinances as provided by this section.

(b) Unless the Council shall otherwise provide, violation of a city ordinance is a misdemeanor or infraction as provided by G.S. 14-4. An ordinance may provide by express statement that the maximum fine, term of imprisonment, or infraction penalty to be imposed for a violation is some amount of money or number of days less than the maximum imposed by G.S. 14-4.

(c) An ordinance may provide that violation shall subject the offender to a civil penalty to be recovered by the city in a civil action in the nature of debt if the offender does not pay the penalty within a prescribed period of time after he has been cited for violation of the ordinance.

(d) An ordinance may provide that it may be enforced by an appropriate equitable remedy issuing from a court of competent jurisdiction. In such case, the General Court of Justice shall have jurisdiction to issue such orders as may be appropriate, and it shall not be a defense to the application of the city for equitable relief that there is an adequate remedy at law.

(e) An ordinance that makes unlawful a condition existing upon or use made of real property may be enforced by injunction and order of abatement, and the General Court of Justice shall have jurisdiction to issue such orders. When a violation of such an ordinance occurs the city may apply to the appropriate division of the General Court of Justice for a mandatory or prohibitory injunction and order of abatement commanding the defendant to correct the unlawful condition upon or cease the unlawful use of the property. The action shall be governed in all respects by the laws and rules governing civil proceedings, including the Rules of Civil Procedure in general and Rule 65 in particular.

In addition to an injunction, the court may enter an order of abatement as a part of the judgment in the cause. An order of abatement may direct that buildings or other structures on the property be closed, demolished, or removed; that fixtures, furniture, or other movable property be removed from buildings on the property; that grass and weeds be cut; that improvements or repairs be made; or that any other action be taken that is necessary to bring the property into compliance with the ordinance. If the defendant fails or refuses to comply with an injunction or with an order of abatement within the time allowed by the court, he may be cited for contempt, and the city may execute the order of abatement. The city shall have a lien on the property for the cost of executing an order of abatement in the nature of a mechanic's and materialman's lien. The defendant may secure cancellation of an order of abatement by paying all costs of the proceedings and posting a bond for compliance with the order. The bond shall be given with sureties approved by the clerk of superior court in an amount approved by the judge before whom the matter is heard and shall be conditioned on the defendant's full compliance with the terms of the order of abatement within a time fixed by the judge. Cancellation of an order of abatement shall not suspend or cancel an injunction issued in conjunction therewith.

(f) Subject to the express terms of the ordinance, a city ordinance may be enforced by any one, all, or a combination of the remedies authorized and prescribed by this section.

(g) A city ordinance may provide, when appropriate, that each day's continuing violation shall be a separate and distinct offense.

(County: G.S. 153A-123)

MUNICIPAL ZONING ORDINANCE

§ 160A-389. Remedies.

If a building or structure is erected, constructed, reconstructed, altered, repaired, converted, or maintained, or any building, structure or land is used in violation of this Part or of any ordinance or other regulation made under authority conferred thereby, the city, in addition to other remedies, may institute any appropriate action or proceedings to prevent the unlawful erection, construction, reconstruction, alteration, repair, conversion, maintenance or use, to restrain, correct or abate the violation, to prevent occupancy of the building, structure or land, or to prevent any illegal act, conduct, business or use in or about the premises.

MINIMUM HOUSING STANDARDS ORDINANCE

§ 160A-446. Remedies.

• • •

(g) If any dwelling is erected, constructed, altered, repaired, converted, maintained, or used in violation of this Part or of any ordinance or code adopted under authority of this Part or any valid order or decision of the public officer or board made pursuant to any ordinance or code adopted under authority of this Part, the public officer or board may institute any appropriate action or proceedings to prevent the unlawful erection, construction, reconstruction, alteration or use, to restrain, correct or abate the violation, to prevent the occupancy of the dwelling, or to prevent any illegal act, conduct or use in or about the premises of the dwelling.

11 RECORDS

To carry on an efficient building code enforcement program, an adequate record-keeping system is essential. Neither the statutes nor the State Building Code prescribe the exact contents and organization of such a system, although ordinances governing local records may do so.

The statutes do mandate the keeping of records:

§ 160A-433. Records and reports.

The inspection department shall keep complete and accurate records in convenient form of all applications received, permits issued, inspections and reinspections made, defects found, certificates of compliance granted, and all other work and activities of the department. These records shall be kept in the manner and for the periods prescribed by the North Carolina Department of Cultural Resources. Periodic reports shall be submitted to the city council and to the Commissioner of Insurance as they shall by ordinance, rule, or regulation require.

(County: G.S. 153A-373)

§ 121-2. Definitions.

For the purposes of this Article:
  (1) "Agency" shall mean any State, county, or municipal office, department, division, board, commission or separate unit of government created or established by constitution or law.
  • • •
  (8) "Public record" or "public records" shall mean all documents, papers, letters, maps, books, photographs, films, sound recordings, magnetic or other tapes, electronic data processing records, artifacts, or other documentary material, regardless of physical form or characteristics, made or received pursuant to law or ordinance or in connection with the transaction of official business by any agency.

§ 121-5. Public records and archives.

(a) State Archival Agency Designated. — The Department of Cultural Resources shall be the official archival agency of the State of North Carolina with authority as provided throughout this Chapter and Chapter 132 of the General Statutes of North Carolina in relation to the public records of the State, counties, municipalities, and other subdivisions of government.

(b) Destruction of Records Regulated. — No person may destroy, sell, loan, or otherwise dispose of any public record without the consent of the Department of Cultural Resources. Whoever unlawfully removes a public record from the office where it is usually kept, or alters, mutilates, or destroys it shall be guilty of a misdemeanor and upon conviction fined at the discretion of the court.

When the custodian of any official State records certifies to the Department of Cultural Resources that such records have no further use or value for official and administrative purposes and when

the Department certifies that such records appear to have no further use or value for research or reference, then such records may
be destroyed or otherwise disposed of by the agency having custody
of them.

When the custodian of any official records of any county, city,
municipality, or other subdivision of government certifies to the
Department that such records have no further use or value for
official business and when the Department certifies that such
records appear to have no further use or value for research or reference, then such records may be authorized by the governing body of
said county, city, municipality, or other subdivision of government
to be destroyed or otherwise disposed of by the agency having custody of them. A record of such certification and authorization shall
be entered in the minutes of the governing body granting the authority.

The North Carolina Historical Commission is hereby authorized
and empowered to make such orders, rules, and regulations as may
be necessary and proper to carry into effect the provisions of this
section. When any State, county, municipal, or other governmental
records shall have been destroyed or otherwise disposed of in accordance with the procedure authorized in this subsection, any liability that the custodian of such records might incur for such destruction or other disposal shall cease and determine.

(c) Assistance to Public Officers. — The Department of Cultural
Resources shall have the right to examine into the condition of
public records and shall, subject to the availability of staff and
funds, give advice and assistance to public officials and agencies in
regard to preserving or disposing of the public records in their custody. When requested by the Department of Cultural Resources,
public officials shall assist the Department in the preparation of an
inclusive inventory of records in their custody, to which inventory
shall be attached a schedule, approved by the head of the governmental unit or agency having custody of the records and the Department of Cultural Resources, lishing a time period for the retention or disposal of each series of records. So long as such approved
schedule remains in effect, destruction or disposal of records in
accordance with its provisions shall be deemed to have met the
requirements of G.S. 121-5 (b).

The Department of Cultural Resources is hereby authorized and
directed to conduct a program of inventorying, repairing, and microfilming in the counties for security purposes those official
records of the several counties which the Department determines
have permanent value, and of providing safe storage for microfilm
copies of such records. Subject to the availability of funds, such
program shall be extended to the records of permanent value of the
cities, municipalities, and other subdivisions of government.

(d) Preservation of Permanently Valuable Records. — Public
records certified by the Department of Cultural Resources as being
of permanent value shall be preserved in the custody of the agency
in which the records are normally kept or of the North Carolina
State Archives. Any State, county, municipal, or other public official is hereby authorized and empowered to turn over to the Department of Cultural Resources any State, county, municipal, or other
public records no longer in current official use, and the Department
of Cultural Resources is authorized in its discretion to accept such
records, and having done so shall provide for their administration
and preservation in the North Carolina State Archives. When such
records have been thus surrendered, photocopies, microfilms, type-
scripts, or other copies of them shall be made and certified under

seal of the Department, upon application of any person, which certification shall have the same force and effect as if made by the official or agency by which the records were transferred to the Department of Cultural Resources; and the Department may charge reasonable fees for such copies. The Department may answer written inquiries for nonresidents of North Carolina and for such service charge a search and handling fee not to exceed ten dollars ($10.00), the receipts from which fee shall be used to defray the cost of providing such service.

§ 132-1. "Public records" defined.

"Public record" or "public records" shall mean all documents, papers, letters, maps, books, photographs, films, sound recordings, magnetic or other tapes, electronic data-processing records, artifacts, or other documentary material, regardless of physical form or characteristics, made or received pursuant to law or ordinance in connection with the transaction of public business by any agency of North Carolina government or its subdivisions. Agency of North Carolina government or its subdivisions shall mean and include every public office, public officer or official (State or local, elected or appointed), institution, board, commission, bureau, council, department, authority or other unit of government of the State or of any county, unit, special district or other political subdivision of government.

§ 132-2. Custodian designated.

The public official in charge of an office having public records shall be the custodian thereof.

§ 132-3. Destruction of records regulated.

No public official may destroy, sell, loan, or otherwise dispose of any public record, except in accordance with G.S. 121-5, without the consent of the Department of Cultural Resources. Whoever unlawfully removes a public record from the office where it is usually kept, or alters, defaces, mutilates or destroys it shall be guilty of a misdemeanor and upon conviction fined not less than ten dollars ($10.00) nor more than five hundred dollars ($500.00).

§ 132-4. Disposition of records at end of official's term.

Whoever has the custody of any public records shall, at the expiration of his term of office, deliver to his successor, or, if there be none, to the Department of Cultural Resources, all records, books, writings, letters and documents kept or received by him in the transaction of his official business; and any such person who shall refuse or neglect for the space of 10 days after request made in writing by any citizen of the State to deliver as herein required such public records to the person authorized to receive them shall be guilty of a misdemeanor and upon conviction imprisoned for a term not exceeding two years or fined not exceeding one thousand dollars ($1,000) or both.

§ 132-5. Demanding custody.

Whoever is entitled to the custody of public records shall demand them from any person having illegal possession of them, who shall forthwith deliver the same to him. If the person who unlawfully possesses public records shall without just cause refuse or neglect for 10 days after a request made in writing by any citizen of the State to deliver such records to their lawful custodian, he shall be guilty of a misdemeanor and upon conviction imprisoned for a term not exceeding two years or fined not exceeding one thousand dollars ($1,000) or both.

§ 132-5.1. Regaining custody; civil remedies.

(a) The Secretary of the Department of Cultural Resources or his designated representative or any public official who is the custodian of public records which are in the possession of a person or agency not authorized by the custodian or by law to possess such public records may petition the superior court in the county in which the person holding such records resides or in which the materials in issue, or any part thereof, are located for the return of such public records. The court may order such public records to be delivered to the petitioner upon finding that the materials in issue are public records and that such public records are in the possession of a person not authorized by the custodian of the public records or by law to possess such public records. If the order of delivery does not receive compliance, the petitioner may request that the court enforce such order through its contempt power and procedures.

(b) At any time after the filing of the petition set out in subsection (a) or contemporaneous with such filing, the public official seeking the return of the public records may by ex parte petition request the judge or the court in which the action was filed to grant one of the following provisional remedies:

> (1) An order directed at the sheriff commanding him to seize the materials which are the subject of the action and deliver the same to the court under the circumstances hereinafter set forth; or
>
> (2) A preliminary injunction preventing the sale, removal, disposal or destruction of or damage to such public records pending a final judgment by the court.

(c) The judge or court aforesaid shall issue an order of seizure or grant a preliminary injunction upon receipt of an affidavit from the petitioner which alleges that the materials at issue are public records and that unless one of said provisional remedies is granted, there is a danger that such materials shall be sold, secreted, removed out of the State or otherwise disposed of so as not to be forthcoming to answer the final judgment of the court respecting the same; or that such property may be destroyed or materially damaged or injured if not seized or if injunctive relief is not granted.

(d) The aforementioned order of seizure or preliminary injunction shall issue without notice to the respondent and without the posting of any bond or other security by the petitioner.

§ 132-6. Inspection and examination of records.

Every person having custody of public records shall permit them to be inspected and examined at reasonable times and under his supervision by any person, and he shall furnish certified copies thereof on payment of fees as prescribed by law.

§ 132-7. Keeping records in safe places; copying or repairing; certified copies.

Insofar as possible, custodians of public records shall keep them in fireproof safes, vaults, or rooms fitted with noncombustible materials and in such arrangement as to be easily accessible for convenient use. All public records should be kept in the buildings in which they are ordinarily used. Record books should be copied or repaired, renovated or rebound if worn, mutilated, damaged or difficult to read. Whenever any State, county, or municipal records are in need of repair, restoration, or rebinding, the head of such State agency, department, board, or commission, the board of county commissioners of such county, or the governing body of such municipality may authorize that the records in need of repair, restoration, or rebinding be removed from the building or office in which such records are ordinarily kept, for the length of time required to repair, restore, or rebind them. Any public official who causes a record book to be copied shall attest it and shall certify on oath that it is an accurate copy of the original book. The copy shall then have the force of the original.

§ 132-8. Assistance by and to Department of Cultural Resources.

The Department of Cultural Resources shall have the right to examine into the condition of public records and shall give advice and assistance to public officials in the solution of their problems of preserving, filing and making available the public records in their custody. When requested by the Department of Cultural Resources, public officials shall assist the Department in the preparation of an inclusive inventory of records in their custody, to which shall be attached a schedule, approved by the head of the governmental unit or agency having custody of the records and the Secretary of Cultural Resources, establishing a time period for the retention or disposal of each series of records. Upon the completion of the inventory and schedule, the Department of Cultural Resources shall (subject to the availability of necessary space, staff, and other facilities for such purposes) make available space in its Records Center for the filing of semicurrent records so scheduled and in its archives for noncurrent records of permanent value, and shall render such other assistance as needed, including the microfilming of records so scheduled.

§ 132-8.1. Records management program administered by Department of Cultural Resources; establishment of standards, procedures, etc.; surveys.

A records management program for the application of efficient and economical management methods to the creation, utilization, maintenance, retention, preservation, and disposal of official records shall be administered by the Department of Cultural Resources. It shall be the duty of that Department, in cooperation with and with the approval of the Department of Administration, to establish standards, procedures, and techniques for effective management of public records, to make continuing surveys of paper work operations, and to recommend improvements in current records management practices including the use of space, equipment, and supplies employed in creating, maintaining, and servicing records. It shall be the duty of the head of each State agency and the governing body of each county, municipality and other subdivision of government to cooperate with the Department of Cultural Resources in conducting surveys and to establish and maintain an active, continuing program for the economical and efficient management of the records of said agency, county, municipality, or other subdivision of government.

§ 132-8.2. Selection and preservation of records considered essential; making or designation of preservation duplicates; force and effect of duplicates or copies thereof.

In cooperation with the head of each State agency and the governing body of each county, municipality, and other subdivision of government, the Department of Cultural Resources shall establish and maintain a program for the selection and preservation of public records considered essential to the operation of government and to the protection of the rights and interests of persons, and, within the limitations of funds available for the purpose, shall make or cause to be made preservation duplicates or designate as preservation duplicates existing copies of such essential public records. Preservation duplicates shall be durable, accurate, complete and clear, and such duplicates made by a photographic, photostatic, microfilm, micro card, miniature photographic, or other process which accurately reproduces and forms a durable medium for so reproducing the original shall have the same force and effect for all purposes as the original record whether the original record is in existence or not. A transcript, exemplification, or certified copy of such preservation duplicate shall be deemed for all purposes to be a transcript, exemplification, or certified copy of the original record. Such preservation duplicates shall be preserved in the place and manner of safekeeping prescribed by the Department of Cultural Resources.

§ 132-9. Access to records.

Any person who is denied access to public records for purposes of inspection, examination or copying may apply to the appropriate division of the General Court of Justice for an order compelling disclosure, and the court shall have jurisdiction to issue such orders.

For more detailed information, the code enforcement official should consult the publication titled *The Municipal Records Manual*, available from the Department of Cultural Resources in Raleigh.

12 THE CODE ENFORCEMENT OFFICIAL

The first eleven chapters of this book have focused on the *system* of code enforcement in North Carolina. The final two chapters will focus on the individual code enforcement official and the laws applying to him in his status as a governmental official.

THE OFFICE

The code enforcement official holds a public office and exercises governmental powers. Under what statutory authority can local governments create this office and appoint someone to it? The basic provisions authorizing such actions are found in G.S. 160A-411 (city) and G.S. 153A-351 (county) of the enabling acts for local inspection departments (set forth in the Appendix of this book). More general authority of city councils and boards of county commissioners to organize the governments they head is set forth in G.S. 160A-146 and G.S. 153A-76. In addition, the statutes authorize appointing officials to enforce related regulations; some of these officials may also be members of a local inspection department: G.S. 160A-443 and -448 (city and county housing inspectors), G.S. 153A-234 (county fire marshal), G.S. 153A-235 (county fire prevention inspectors), G.S. 160A-384 and -388 (municipal zoning officers), G.S. 153A-343 and -345 (county zoning officers), and G.S. 143-151.27 (city and county energy and insulation inspectors).

City and county governing boards may also adopt position classification ordinances.[1]

QUALIFICATIONS

Provisions relating to the qualifications of code enforcement officials are to be found in the North Carolina Constitution, the General Statutes, regulations of the North Carolina Code Officials Qualification Board, and local ordinances.

CONSTITUTION

The North Carolina Constitution contains three sections concerning appointees to public office, all in Article VI: Section 9, limiting dual officeholding; Section 8, setting forth factors that disqualify persons for

---

1. N.C. GEN. STAT. Ch. 160A, Art. 7, Part 4 (especially G.S. 160A-162 and -164) for cities; *id.* Ch. 153A, Art. 5, Part 4 (especially G.S. 153A-92 and -94) for counties.

office; and Section 7, setting forth the oath that must be taken before one can enter upon the duties of an office.

In determining the applicability of these provisions, the first question is whether the holder of a particular position holds an "office." If his position is not an office, none of them apply; if it is, all of them apply. Neither the Constitution nor any statute spells out the criteria that go into this determination. However, the Court of Appeals recently decided that a local building inspector is a "public official" for the purpose of determining tort liability, and in reaching this decision it quoted with approval from a standard text:

> The courts have stated certain tests and distinctions [for deciding whether a person is an officer or merely an agent or employee of a municipality] such as that a municipal office is created only by legislation...while the relation of an employee to a municipal corporation is based solely on contract; that an officer is generally required to take an oath of office...while an agent or employee is not required to do so; that an officer performs public functions delegated to him as part of the sovereign power of the state...while no share of the sovereign powers or functions of the government is vested in an employee; that official trust or responsibility is imposed by law on an officer...but not on an employee; that the law prescribes and imposes the duties of an officer ...but not those of an employee; that an officer is charged with fixed, public duties...while the duties of an employee are of nongovernmental nature, and are neither certain nor permanent; that an officer is sometimes vested with a certain measure of discretion...whereas the duties of an employee are purely ministerial; and that an officer is empowered to act in the discharge of a duty or legal authority in official life, whereas an employee does not discharge independent duties, but acts by the direction of others.[2]

It then applied these criteria to the position of the chief building inspector and made a direct ruling that it is an "office."

> In applying these tests to the position of chief building inspector for the city of Wilmington, we find that the position accords with the criteria set forth. First, the position of chief building inspector is "created...by legislation" which authorizes every city in North Carolina to create a building inspection department, to appoint inspectors and to give the inspectors so appointed titles "generally descriptive of the duties assigned." G.S. 160A-411 (Supp. 1979). Second, the chief building inspector is "required to take an oath of office." Wilmington City Charter § 9.6 (Supp. 1979). Third, the chief building inspector performs "public functions delegated to him as part of the sovereign power of the state"; "official trust of responsibility is imposed by law" on him; "the law prescribes and imposes the duties" he must perform; and he is "charged with fixed, public duties" and "empowered to act in the dis-

---

2. Pigott v. City of Wilmington, 50 N.C. App. 401, 403-4 (1981), *quoting* 62 C.J.S., *Municipal Corporations* § 463 at 895-96 (1949).

charge of a duty or legal authority in official life." *See* G.S. 160A-411 to -438; Wilmington City Code § 6-8 (Supp. 1979). Fourth, the chief building inspector is "vested with a certain measure of discretion." North Carolina General Statutes, Chapter 160A, part 5 contains numerous provisions which can only be interpreted as placing discretionary powers in the inspectors designated and appropriately entitled by the cities of this State.

We thus conclude, and so hold, that the chief building inspector for the city of Wilmington is "a public official" of that city. [Footnotes omitted.][3]

Double Officeholding. The North Carolina Constitution of 1868 included a provision that forbade any person from holding two public offices at the same time (with limited exceptions spelled out in the text). This provision was amended in 1970 to allow one person to hold two, but not more, appointive offices if authorized by the General Assembly. The constitutional limitation is still entitled "Dual officeholding," and it is commonly referred to the "double officeholding prohibition."

The current constitutional provisions are as follows:

Article VI, Sec. 9. *Dual officeholding.*

(1) *Prohibitions.* It is salutary that the responsibilities of self-government be widely shared among the citizens of the State and that the potential abuse of authority inherent in the holding of multiple offices by an individual be avoided. Therefore, no person who holds any office or place of trust or profit under the United States or any department thereof, or under any other state or government, shall be eligible to hold any office in this State that is filled by election by the people. No person shall hold concurrently any two offices in this State that are filled by election of the people. No person shall hold concurrently any two or more appointive offices or places of trust or profit, or any combination of elective and appointive offices or places of trust or profit, except as the General Assembly shall provide by general law.

(2) *Exceptions.* The provisions of this Section shall not prohibit any officer of the military forces of the State or of the United States not on active duty for an extensive period of time, any notary public, or any delegate to a Convention of the People from holding concurrently another office or place of trust or profit under this State or the United States or any department thereof.

The statutes effectuating these provisions are as follows:

§ 128-1. No person shall hold more than one office; exception.

No person who shall hold any office or place of trust or profit under the United States, or any department thereof or under this State, or under any other state or government, shall hold or exercise any other office or place of trust or profit under the authority of

---

3. *Id.* at 404-5.

this State, or be eligible to a seat in either house of the General Assembly except as provided in G.S. 128-1.1, or by other General Statute.

§ 128-1.1. Dual-office holding allowed.

(a) Any person who holds an appointive office, place of trust or profit in State or local government is hereby authorized by the General Assembly, pursuant to Article VI, Sec. 9 of the North Carolina Constitution, to hold concurrently one other appointive office, place of trust or profit, or an elective office in either State or local government.

(b) Any person who holds an elective office in State or local government is hereby authorized by the General Assembly, pursuant to Article VI, Sec. 9 of the North Carolina Constitution to hold concurrently one other appointive office, place of trust or profit, in either State or local government.

(c) Any person who holds an office or position in the federal postal system is hereby authorized to hold concurrently therewith one position in State or local government.

(d) The term "elective office," as used herein, shall mean any office filled by election by the people when the election is conducted by a county or municipal board of elections under the supervision of the State Board of Elections.

§ 128-2. Holding office contrary to the Constitution; penalty.

If any person presumes to hold any office, or place of trust or profit, or is elected to a seat in either house of the General Assembly, contrary to Article VI, Sec. 9 of the North Carolina Constitution, he shall forfeit all rights and emoluments incident thereto.

Before the latest constitutional amendment, the State Supreme Court interpreted the double-officeholding prohibition to mean that acceptance of a second office counter to the prohibition automatically vacated any state or local governmental office one might already hold. On the other hand, the holder of a federal office would not lose that office, but his attempted acceptance of a second office was void. Under the new provisions, an appointed officeholder like an inspector may now hold one other appointive or elective office in state or local government without violating the prohibition. But no one knows yet whether a violator of the new rules will lose his first office, his third office, or all three offices.

No one can say with assurance, until the State Supreme Court has ruled, whether a given position is an office. But the danger of forfeiting an office because of this prohibition is great enough that one should be very cautious in accepting additional appointments.

The Supreme Court has outlined one way around the provisions stated above. It has ruled that if a *statute or ordinance* designates the occupant of a particular position (whoever he might be) as an *ex officio* holder of another position, the officeholder does not assume a second office but merely accepts additional duties as the occupant of the first position. For example, until recently the statutes provided that a municipal fire chief was the local building inspector, unless another appointment was made. This provision did not impose a second office, as the court construed it; it simply added additional duties to the fire chief's responsibilities. But if, in the absence of such a provision, a city council appointed (by name) its fire chief, John Jones, to be building inspector, he would hold two offices. The distinction lies in the fact that under the statute *whoever* happened at any given time to be fire chief was *automatically* the building inspector, with no need for appointment, whereas in the second instance an individual was appointed to both posts.

Disqualification for Office.

Article VI, Sec. 8. *Disqualifications for office.* The following persons shall be disqualified for office:

First, any person who shall deny the being of Almighty God.

Second, with respect to any office that is filled by election by the people, any person who is not qualified to vote in an election for that office.

Third, any person who has been adjudged guilty of treason or any other felony against this State or the United States, or any person who has been adjudged guilty of a felony in another state that also would be a felony if it had been committed in this State, or any person who has been adjudged guilty of corruption or malpractice in any office, or any person who has been removed by impeachment from any office, and who has not been restored to the rights of citizenship in the manner prescribed by law.

The provision making atheists ineligible for public office has been held by the U.S. Supreme Court to violate the federal Constitution, so it is ineffective.

Probably the broadest ground of disqualification (in terms of the numbers of people affected) is the one that applies to persons convicted of a felony. The following sections of the General Statutes deal with restoration of citizenship to such persons.

§ 13-1. Restoration of citizenship.

Any person convicted of a crime, whereby the rights of citizenship are forfeited, shall have such rights restored upon the occurrence of any one of the following conditions:

(1) The unconditional discharge of an inmate by the State Department of Correction or the North Carolina Department of Correction, of a probationer by the State Department of Correction, or of a parolee by the Department of Correction; or of a defendant under a suspended sentence by the court.

(2) The unconditional pardon of the offender.

(3) The satisfaction by the offender of all conditions of a conditional pardon.

(4) With regard to any person convicted of a crime against the United States, the unconditional discharge of such person

by the agency of the United States having jurisdiction of such person, the unconditional pardon of such person or the satisfaction by such person of a conditional pardon.

§ 13-2. Issuance and filing of certificate or order of restoration.

The agency, department, or court having jurisdiction over the inmate, probationer, parolee or defendant at the time his rights of citizenship are restored under the provisions of G.S. 13-1(1) shall immediately issue a certificate or order in duplicate evidencing the offender's unconditional discharge and specifying the restoration of his rights of citizenship.

The original of such certificate or order shall be promptly transmitted to the clerk of the General Court of Justice in the county where the official record of the case from which the conviction arose is filed. The clerk shall then file the certificate or order without charge with the official record of the case.

In the case of a person convicted of a crime against the United States, whose rights to citizenship have been restored according to G.S. 13-1, the following provisions shall apply:

(1) It shall be the duty of the clerk of the court in the county where such person resides, upon a showing by such person or his representative that the conditions of G.S. 13-1 have been met, to issue the certificate described in this section. For purposes of this section, the fulfillment of the conditions of G.S. 13-1 shall be considered met upon the presentation to the clerk of any paper writing from the agency of the United States government which had jurisdiction over such person, which shows that the conditions of G.S. 13-1 have been met.

(2) The certificate described in this section shall be filed by the clerk of the General Court of Justice in the county in which such person resides as though it were a civil action bearing such person's name.

(3) The provisions of this section apply equally to conditional and unconditional pardons by the President of the United States, as well as unconditional discharges by the agency of the United States having jurisdiction over said person.

§ 13-3. Issuance, service and filing of warrant of unconditional pardon.

In the event the rights of citizenship are restored by an unconditional pardon as specified in G.S. 13-1(2), the Governor, under the provisions of G.S. 147-23, shall issue his warrant therefor specifying the restoration of rights of citizenship to the offender; and the officer to whom the Governor issues his warrant to effect the release of the offender shall deliver a copy of the warrant to the offender under the provisions of G.S. 147-25. The original warrant bearing the officer's return as specified in G.S. 147-25 shall be filed by the clerk of the General Court of Justice without charge in the county where the official record of the case from which the conviction arose is filed.

§ 13-4. Endorsement of warrant, service and filing of conditional pardon.

When the offender has satified all of the conditions of a conditional pardon, and his rights of citizenship have been restored under the provisions of G.S. 13-1(3), the Governor shall issue an endorsement to the original warrant which specified the conditions of the pardon. Such endorsement shall acknowledge that the offender has satisfied all of the conditions of the pardon.

The Governor shall then deliver the endorsement to the officer specified in G.S. 147-25 for service and delivery to the clerk. Service and delivery to the clerk and filing by the clerk shall be done in accordance with the provisions of G.S. 13-3 so that the endorsement reflecting satisfaction of all conditions of the pardon will be served and recorded as if it were a warrant of unconditional pardon.

Oath-Taking. The State Constitution also contains another requirement that a new officeholder should note:

Article VI, Sec. 7. *Oath.* Before entering upon the duties of an officer, a person elected or appointed to the office shall take and subscribe the following oath:

"I, _____, do solemnly swear (or affirm) that I will support and maintain the Constitution and laws of the United States, and the Constitution and laws of North Carolina not inconsistent therewith, and that I will faithfully discharge the duties of my office as _____, so help me God."

This requirement is also reinforced by statutory provisions:

§ 160A-61. Oath of office.

Every person elected by the people or appointed to any city office shall, before entering upon the duties of the office, take and subscribe the oath of office prescribed in Article VI, § 7 of the Constitution. Oaths of office shall be administered by some person authorized by law to administer oaths, and shall be filed with the city clerk.

§ 153A-26. Oath of office.

Each person elected by the people or appointed to a county office shall, before entering upon the duties of the office, take and subscribe the oath of office prescribed in Article VI, Sec. 7 of the Constitution. The oath of office shall be administered by some person authorized by law to administer oaths and shall be filed with the clerk.

On the first Monday in December following each general election at which county officers are elected, the persons who have been elected to county office in that election shall assemble at the regular meeting place of the board of commissioners. At that time each such officer shall take and subscribe the oath of office. An officer not present at this time may take and subscribe the oath at a later time.

§ 14-229. Acting as officer before qualifying as such.

If any officer shall enter on the duties of his office before he executes and delivers to the authority entitled to receive the same the bonds required by law, and qualifies by taking and subscribing and filing in the proper office the oath of office prescribed, he shall be guilty of a misdemeanor and shall be ejected from his office.

§ 128-5. Oath required before acting; penalty.

Every officer and other person required to take an oath of office, or an oath for the faithful discharge of any duty imposed on him, and also the oath appointed for such as hold any office of trust or profit in the State, shall take all said oaths before entering on the duties of the office, or the duties imposed on such person, on pain of forfeiting five hundred dollars ($500.00) to the use of the poor of the county in or for which the office is to be used, and of being ejected from his office or place by proper proceedings for that purpose.

(Various other oaths and their manner of administration are covered in detail in Chapter 11 of the General Statutes.)

STATUTES

Certification.

§ 153A-351.1. Qualifications of inspectors.

On and after the applicable date set forth in the schedule in G.S. 153A-351, no county shall employ an inspector to enforce the State Building Code as a member of a county or joint inspection department who does not have one of the following types of certificates issued by the North Carolina Code Officials Qualification Board attesting to his qualifications to hold such position: (i) a probationary certificate, valid for one year only; (ii) a standard certificate; or (iii) a limited certificate, which shall be valid only as an authorization for him to continue in the position held on the date specified in G.S. 143-151.10(c) and which shall become invalid if he does not successfully complete in-service training prescribed by the Qualification Board within the period specified in G.S. 143-151.10(c). An inspector holding one of the above certificates can be promoted to a position requiring a higher level certificate only upon issuance by the Board of a standard certificate or probationary certificate appropriate for such new position.

§ 160A-411.1. Qualifications of inspectors.

On and after the applicable date set forth in the schedule in G.S. 160A-411, no city shall employ an inspector to enforce the State Building Code as a member of a city or joint inspection department who does not have one of the following types of certificates issued by the North Carolina Code Officials Qualification Board attesting to his qualifications to hold such position: (i) a probationary certificate, valid for one year only; (ii) a standard certificate; or (iii) a limited certificate which shall be valid only as an authorization for him to continue in the position held on the date specified in G.S. 143-151.13(c) and which shall become invalid if he does not successfully complete in-service training specified by the Qualification Board within the period specified in G.S. 143-151.13(c). An inspector holding one of the above certificates can be promoted to a position requiring a higher level certificate only upon issuance by the Board of a standard certificate or probationary certificate appropriate for such new position.

G.S. Chapter 143, Article 9B, which created and governs the North Carolina Code Officials Qualification Board, is set forth in full in the Appendix. Code enforcement officials will be particularly interested in G.S. 143-151.13 through -151.17, which relate to issuance and denial of certificates.

Illegal Appointment. The statutes make certain actions in connection with appointment to office illegal. These deal, for the most part, with the crime of buying or selling office.

§ 128-3. Bargains for office void.

All bargains, bonds and assurances made or given for the purchase or sale of any office whatsoever, the sale of which is contrary to law, shall be void.

§ 128-4. Receiving compensation of subordinates for appointment or retention; removal.

Any official or employee of this State or any political subdivision thereof, in whose office or under whose supervision are employed one or more subordinate officials or employees who shall, directly or indirectly, receive or demand, for himself or another, any part of the compensation of any such subordinate, as the price of appointment or retention of such subordinate, shall be guilty of a misdemeanor: Provided, that this section shall not apply in cases in which an official or employee is given an allowance for the conduct of his office from which he is to compensate himself and his subordinates in such manner as he sees fit. Any person convicted of violating this section, in addition to the criminal penalties, shall be subject to removal from office. The procedure for removal shall be the same as that provided for removal of certain local officials from office by G.S. 128-16 to 128-20, inclusive.

§ 14-228. Buying and selling offices.

If any person shall bargain away or sell an office or deputation of an office, or any part or parcel thereof, or shall take money, reward or other profit, directly or indirectly, or shall take any promise, covenant, bond or assurance for money, reward or other profit, for an office or the deputation of an office, or any part thereof, which office, or any part thereof, shall touch or concern the administration or execution of justice, or the receipt, collection, control or disbursement of the public revenue, or shall concern or touch any clerkship in any court of record wherein justice is administered; or if any person shall give or pay money, reward or other profit, or shall make any promise, agreement, bond or assurance for any of such offices, or for the deputation of any of them, or for any part of them, the person so offending in any of the cases aforesaid shall be guilty of a misdemeanor, and on conviction thereof shall forfeit all his right, interest and estate in such office, and every part and parcel thereof, and shall be imprisoned and fined at the discretion of the court.

Posting of Bonds. G.S. 14-229 makes it illegal to enter upon duties of an office without posting "the bonds required by law." The following statutory provisions cover this type of requirement, which may affect some code enforcement officials:

§ 159-29. Fidelity bonds.

The finance officer shall give a true accounting and faithful performance bond with sufficient sureties in an amount to be fixed by the governing board, not less than ten thousand dollars ($10,000) nor more than two hundred fifty thousand dollars ($250,000). The premium on the bond shall be paid by the local government or public authority.

(b) Each officer, employee, or agent of a local government or public authority who handles or has in his custody more than one hundred dollars ($100.00) of the unit's or public authority's funds at any time, or who handles or has access to the inventories of the unit or public authority, shall, before being entitled to assume his duties, give a faithful performance bond with sufficient sureties payable to the local government or public authority. The governing board shall determine the amount of the bond, and the unit or public authority may pay the premium on the bond. Each bond, when approved by the governing board, shall be deposited with the clerk to the board.

If another statute requires an officer, employee, or agent to be bonded, this subsection does not require an additional bond for that officer, employee, or agent.

(c) A local government or public authority may adopt a system of blanket faithful performance bonding as an alternative to individual bonds. If such a system is adopted, statutory requirements of individual bonds, except for elected officials and for finance officers and tax collectors by whatever title known, do not apply to an officer, employee, or agent covered by the blanket bond. However, although an individual bond is required for a tax collector or finance officer, such an officer may also be included within the coverage of a blanket bond if the blanket bond protects against risks not protected against by the individual bond.

REGULATIONS OF THE NORTH CAROLINA CODE OFFICIALS QUALIFICATION BOARD

As we have noted earlier, the North Carolina Code Officials Qualification Board was created in 1977 to establish and administer a certification program for all code enforcement officials in the state. The statutory provisions directing and guiding this program are set forth in the Appendix of this book.

Pursuant to these directions, the Board has adopted regulations governing the issuance of limited certificates, probationary certificates, and standard certificates. These contain long lists of qualifications for each type of official.

These regulations have been published in the North Carolina Administrative Code, Title 11, Chapter 8, Sections .0500, .0600, and .0700. Copies of specific regulations have been distributed by the Board to inspection departments and are available to individual code enforcement officials on application to the Board.

LOCAL ORDINANCES

Local units' personnel classification and pay plan ordinances usually contain detailed job qualifications for particular positions, and other personnel ordinances may contain further requirements—most commonly that certain personnel reside within the unit.

13 LEGAL RESTRAINTS ON THE CODE ENFORCEMENT OFFICIAL

Whether or not a code enforcement official is an "officer" in the technical sense of the word, he is a public official. As such, he is subject to criminal and civil penalties for misconduct or negligence in carrying out his duties. Most such penalties are for conduct that almost anyone would realize, on a "common sense" basis, was punishable. But it might be helpful to list some of the specific statutory or court-created rules with which the official must comply.

A basic rule of conduct is that the official should comply with the statutes or ordinances governing his duties. When he does so, he will rarely be subject to penalty. Second, he should accept these guidelines as they are written and not try to second-guess the legislature on whether they are constitutional. When he acts in accordance with a statute, he will not render himself liable, even if the courts later hold that statute to be unconstitutional.

As the North Carolina Supreme Court said in an 1898 case:

> What an anomalous state of things we would have then, if a person believing himself to be a public officer, because of the discharge of the duties which he thought he owed to the public, should afterwards be indicted and punished because the courts had held the act, which created the office and prescribed its duties, to be against the provisions of the Constitution and void. Such a proposition would be equivalent to declaring that the individual officeholder must be wiser than the whole people represented in their General Assembly. Such a proposition to us seems opposed to every idea of justice. It could not be true. The criminal law cannot be invoked to punish one who acts as a public officer ...and who in the discharge of a public duty had obeyed an act of the lawmaking power even though the law be unconstitutional, unless the act itself had required the committal of a crime....[1]

CRIMINAL PENALTIES

Several statutes set forth in Chapter 12 contained criminal penalties. The chief additional statutory provisions imposing penalties of which the official should be aware include these:

---

1. State v. Godwin, 123 N.C. 697, 701 (1898).

GENERAL

§ 160A-416. Failure to perform duties.

If any member of an inspection department shall willfully fail to perform the duties required of him by law, or willfully shall improperly issue a permit, or shall give a certificate of compliance without first making the inspections required by law, or willfully shall improperly give a certificate of compliance, he shall be guilty of a misdemeanor.

(County: G.S. 153A-356)

§ 14-230. Willfully failing to discharge duties.

If any clerk of any court of record, sheriff, magistrate, county commissioner, county surveyor, coroner, treasurer, or official of any of the State institutions, or of any county, city or town, shall willfully omit, neglect or refuse to discharge any of the duties of his office, for default whereof it is not elsewhere provided that he shall be indicted, he shall be guilty of a misdemeanor. If it shall be proved that such officer, after his qualification, willfully and corruptly omitted, neglected or refused to discharge any of the duties of his office, or willfully and corruptly violated his oath of office according to the true intent and meaning thereof, such officer shall be guilty of misbehavior in office, and shall be punished by removal therefrom under the sentence of the court as a part of the punishment for the offense, and shall also be fined or imprisoned in the discretion of the court.

§ 14-231. Failing to make reports and discharge other duties.

If any State or county officer shall fail, neglect or refuse to make, file or publish any report, statement or other paper, or to deliver to his successor all books and other property belonging to his office, or to pay over or deliver to the proper person all moneys which come into his hands by virtue or color of his office, or to discharge any duty devolving upon him by virtue of his office and required of him by law, he shall be guilty of a misdemeanor.

§ 14-232. Swearing falsely to official reports.

If any clerk, sheriff, register of deeds, county commissioner, county treasurer, magistrate or other county officer shall willfully swear falsely to any report or statement required by law to be made or filed, concerning or touching the county, State or school revenue, he shall be guilty of a misdemeanor.

HANDLING OF MONEY

§ 109-36. Summary remedy on official bond. — When a sheriff, coroner, clerk, county or town treasurer, or other officer, collects or receives any money by virtue or under color of his office, and on demand fails to pay the same to the person entitled to require the payment thereof, the person thereby aggrieved may move for judgment in the superior court against such officer and his sureties for any sum demanded; and the court shall try the same and render judgment at the session when the motion shall be made, but 10 days' notice in writing of the motion must have been previously given.

§ 109-37. Officer unlawfully detaining money liable for damages. — When money received as aforesaid is unlawfully detained by any of said officers, and the same is sued for in any mode whatever, the plaintiff is entitled to recover, besides the sum detained, damages at the rate of twelve per centum (12%) per annum from the time of detention until payment.

§ 159-32. Daily deposits.

Except as otherwise provided by law, all taxes and other moneys collected or received by an officer or employee of a local government or public authority shall be deposited in accordance with this section. Each officer and employee of a local government or public authority whose duty it is to collect or receive any taxes or other moneys shall deposit his collections and receipts daily. If the governing board gives its approval, deposits shall be required only when the moneys on hand amount to as much as two hundred fifty dollars ($250.00), but in any event a deposit shall be made on the last business day of the month. All deposits shall be made with the finance officer or in an official depository. Deposits in an official depository shall be immediately reported to the finance officer by means of a duplicate deposit ticket. The finance officer may at any time audit the accounts of any officer or employee collecting or receiving taxes or other moneys, and may prescribe the form and detail of these accounts. The accounts of such an officer or employee shall be audited at least annually.

§ 128-11. Trust funds to be kept separate.

Any sheriff, treasurer or other officer of any county, city, town or other political subdivision of the State, receiving, by virtue of his office, public money or money to be held by him in trust shall keep or deposit such money or the credits or other evidence thereof separate and apart from his own funds and shall not, at any time, apply such money to his own use or benefit or intermingle the same in any manner with credits or funds of his own.

§ 128-12. Violations to be reported; misdemeanors.

It shall be the duty of the director of the Local Government Commission to report to the district attorney of the district any violation of G.S. 128-11 of which he may have knowledge, and any violation of such section shall be unlawful and shall constitute a misdemeanor, punishable by fine or imprisonment, or both, in the discretion of the court.

§ 128-13. Officers compensated from fees in certain counties to render statement; penalty; proceeds to school fund.

Every clerk of the superior court, register of deeds, sheriff, coroner, surveyor, or other county officer, whose compensation or services performed shall be derived from fees, shall render to the board of county commissioners of their respective counties, on the first Monday in December of each year, a statement, verified under oath, showing: first, the total gross amount of all fees collected during the preceding fiscal year; second, the total amount paid out during the preceding fiscal year for clerical or office assistance. Any county officer, subject to this section, who refuses or fails to file such report as above provided, on or before the first Monday in December, shall be subject to a fine of twenty-five dollars ($25.00) and ten dollars ($10.00) additional for each day or fraction of a day such failure shall continue. The board of county commissioners shall assess and collect the penalty above provided for, and supply same to the general school fund of the county. The first report under this section shall be for the fiscal year beginning December 12, 1913.

This section applies only to the Counties of Anson, Bertie, Bladen, Cabarrus, Carteret, Chowan, Currituck, Duplin, Halifax, Harnett, Haywood, Hertford, Johnston, Jones, Moore, Pender, Perquimans, Pitt, Randolph, Richmond, Rowan, Scotland, Union, Vance, Warren, Washington, Wayne, Wilson.

USE OF PUBLICLY OWNED AUTOMOBILES AND RELATED FACILITIES

§ 14-247. Private use of publicly owned vehicle.

It shall be unlawful for any officer, agent or employee of the State of North Carolina, or of any county or of any institution or agency of the State, to use for any private purpose whatsoever any motor vehicle of any type or description whatsoever belonging to the State, or to any county, or to any institution or agency of the State. It is not a private purpose to drive a permanently assigned state-owned motor vehicle between one's official work station and one's home as provided in G.S. 143-341(8)i7a.

It shall be unlawful for any person to violate a rule or regulation adopted by the Department of Administration and approved by the Governor concerning the control of all state-owned passenger motor vehicles as provided in G.S. 143-341(8)i with the intent to defraud the State of North Carolina.

§ 14-248. Obtaining repairs and supplies for private vehicle at expense of State.

It shall be unlawful for any officer, agent or employee to have any privately owned motor vehicle repaired at any garage belonging to the State or to any county, or any institution or agency of the State, or to use any tires, oils, gasoline or other accessories purchased by the State, or any county, or any institution or agency of the State, in or on any such private car.

§ 14-251. Violation made misdemeanor.

Any person, firm or corporation violating any of the provisions of G.S. 14-247 to 14-250 shall be guilty of a misdemeanor punishable by a fine of not less than one hundred dollars ($100.00) and not more than five hundred dollars ($500.00), imprisonment for not more than six months, or both such fine and imprisonment. Nothing in G.S. 14-247 through 14-251 shall apply to the purchase, use or upkeep or expense account of the car for the executive mansion and the Governor.

§ 14-252. Five preceding sections applicable to cities and towns.

General Statutes 14-247 through 14-251 in every respect shall also apply to cities and incorporated towns.

RECEIVING BRIBES

§ 14-217. Bribery of officials.

(a) If any person holding office under the laws of this State who, except in payment of his legal salary, fees or perquisites, shall receive, or consent to receive, directly or indirectly, anything of value or personal advantage, or the promise thereof, for performing or omitting to perform any official act, which lay within the scope of his official authority and was connected with the discharge of his official and legal duties, or with the express or implied understanding that his official action, or omission to act, is to be in any degree influenced thereby, he shall be punished as a Class I felon.

(b) Indictments issued under these provisions shall specify:
  (1) The thing of value or personal advantage sought to be obtained; and
  (2) The specific act or omission sought to be obtained; and
  (3) That the act or omission sought to be obtained lay within the scope of the defendant's official authority and was connected with the discharge of his official and legal duties.

(c) A person commits the offense of conspiracy to commit bribery as defined in subsection (a) when:
  (1) He or she agrees with one or more persons to commit bribery as defined in subsection (a); and
  (2) He or she and at least one other person intend at the time of the agreement that it be carried out; and
  (3) He or she commits at least one overt act to carry out an object of the conspiracy.

A person cannot be convicted of conspiracy to commit bribery as defined in subsection (a) unless all elements of this section are present and are alleged in the bill of indictment including a specific statement setting forth the overt act committed.

UNAUTHORIZED ENTRY UPON, OR DAMAGE TO, PRIVATE PROPERTY

§ 14-126. Forcible entry and detainer.

No one shall make entry into any lands and tenements, or term for years, but in case where entry is given by law; and in such case, not with strong hand nor with multitude of people, but only in a peaceable and easy manner; and if any man do the contrary, he shall be guilty of a misdemeanor.

§ 14-127. Willful and wanton injury to real property.

If any person shall willfully and wantonly damage, injure or destroy any real property whatsoever, either of a public or private nature, he shall be guilty of a misdemeanor and shall be punished by fine or imprisonment or both, in the discretion of the court.

§ 14-134. Trespass on land after being forbidden; license to look for estrays.

If any person after being forbidden to do so, shall go or enter upon the lands of another, without a license therefor, he shall be guilty of a misdemeanor, and on conviction, shall be guilty of a misdemeanor punishable by a fine not to exceed five hundred dollars ($500.00), imprisonment for not more than six months, or both: Provided, that if any person shall make a written affidavit before a magistrate of the county that any of his cattle or other livestock (which shall be specially described in such affidavit) have strayed away, and that he has good reason to believe that they are on the lands of a certain other person, then the magistrate may, in his discretion, allow the affiant to enter on the premises of such person with one or more servants, without firearms, in the daytime (Sunday excepted), between the hours of sunrise and sunset, and make search for his estrays for such limited time as to the magistrate shall appear reasonable. The only effect of such license shall be to protect the persons entering from indictment therefor, and the license shall have this effect only where it is made bona fide and the entry is effected without any damage except such as may be necessary to conduct the search.

§ 14-144. Injuring houses, churches, fences and walls.

If any person shall, by any other means than burning or attempting to burn, unlawfully and willfully demolish, destroy, deface, injure or damage any of the houses or other buildings mentioned in this Chapter in the Article entitled Arson and Other Burnings; or shall by any other means than burning or attempting to burn unlawfully and willfully demolish, pull down, destroy, deface, damage or injure any church, uninhabitated house, outhouse or other house or building not mentioned in such article; or shall unlawfully and willfully burn, destroy, pull down, injure or remove any fence, wall or other inclosure, or any part thereof, surrounding or about any yard, garden, cultivated field or pasture, or about any church or graveyard, or about any factory or other house in which machinery is used, every person so offending shall be guilty of a misdemeanor punishable by a fine not to exceed five hundred dollars ($500.00), imprisonment for not more than six months, or both.

§ 14-159. Injuring buildings or fences; taking possession of house without consent.

If any person shall deface, injure or damage any house, uninhabited house or other building belonging to another; or deface, damage, pull down, injure, remove or destroy any fence or wall enclosing, in whole or in part, the premises belonging to another; or shall move into, take possession of and/or occupy any house, uninhabited house or other building situated on the premises belonging to another, without having first obtained authority so to do and consent of the owner or agent thereof, he shall be guilty of a misdemeanor and shall be fined not exceeding fifty dollars ($50.00), or imprisoned not exceeding 30 days.

While the above provisions are undoubtedly aimed primarily at private violators and not public officials, G.S. 1-52(13) fixes a statutory period of three years within which an action or proceeding may be brought against "a public officer, for a trespass under color of his office"—which indicates the legislative intent that public officers also be subject to such provisions.

Another type of punishment, a so-called "civil penalty," was added to the statutes in 1985.

§ 58-9.7. Civil penalties or restitution for violations.

(a) This section applies to any person who is subject to licensure or certification under the provisions of this Chapter, General Statutes Chapters 57, 57B or 85C, Articles 9B or 9C of General Statutes Chapter 66, or Articles 9A or 9B of General Statutes Chapter 143.

(b) Whenever the Commissioner has reason to believe that any person has violated any of the provisions of the statutes cited in subsection (a) of this section, and the violation subjects the license or certification of that person to suspension or revocation, or whenever the Commissioner has reason to believe that any person has violated Article 3A of this Chapter, the Commissioner may issue and serve upon that person a written statement of charges and a written notice of hearing, to be held at a time and place fixed in the notice. The date for the hearing shall not be less than 10 days after the date of service. It shall be sufficient to give such notice either by delivering it to the person charged or by sending the notice to the last known address of that person by certified mail, return receipt requested. At the time and place fixed for the hearing the person charged shall have an opportunity to answer the charges against him and present evidence on his behalf. Upon good cause shown, the Commissioner may permit any adversely affected person to intervene, appear, and be heard at the hearing by counsel or in person. The Commissioner may consolidate a hearing under this section with a hearing allowed under G.S. 58-54.6 where there is common subject matter involved and subject to procedural requirements set out in both sections being followed.

(c) In any case where a hearing pursuant to subsection (b) of this section results in the findings by the Commissioner of a knowing violation of any of the provisions of the statutes cited in subsection (a) of this section, and the violation subjects the license or certification of that person to suspension or revocation, or findings by the Commissioner of a knowing violation of Article 3A of this Chapter, the Commissioner may, in addition to or in lieu of suspending or revoking the license or certification, apply to a court of competent jurisdiction for an order directing payment of a monetary penalty as provided in subsection (d) of this section or an order directing payment of restitution as provided in subsection (e) of this section, or both. Each day during which a violation occurs shall constitute a separate offense.

(d) Upon application by the Commissioner and a finding by the court of a knowing violation as specified in subsection (c) of this section, the court shall direct the payment of a penalty of not less than five hundred dollars ($500.00) nor more than forty thousand dollars ($40,000), in the discretion of the court. The penalty shall be payable to the Commissioner, who shall then forward the clear proceeds of which to the State Treasurer for deposit in the General Fund of the State. Payment of the civil penalty under this section shall be in addition to payment off any other penalty for a violation of the penal laws of this State.

(e) Upon application of the Commissioner and a finding by the court of a knowing violation as specified in subsection (c) of this section, the court may order the person who committed the violation to make restitution in an amount that would make whole any person harmed by the violation.

(f) Restitution to any State agency for extraordinary administrative expenses incurred in the investigation and hearing of the violation may also be ordered by the court in such amount that would reimburse the agency for the expenses.

(g) Nothing in this section shall prevent the Commissioner from negotiating a mutually acceptable agreement with any person as to the status of the person's license or certificate or as to any civil penalty or restitution; and to submit such agreement with respect to any civil penalty or restitution to the court pursuant to subsections (d) and (e) of this section for the court's adoption and approval.

As will be noted, it could produce much heavier costs than most of the criminal penalties noted above.

CIVIL LIABILITY

NORTH CAROLINA LAW

Besides possibly incurring criminal penalties, the code official may by his conduct subject himself to a civil lawsuit brought by a private citizen. Normally the governmental unit for which he works (the city or county) enjoys governmental immunity for any damage done in the course of his duties, so the property owner's only recourse will be a suit against the inspector himself.

Apart from the liabilities that any citizen might accrue from such action as punching someone in the nose or smashing the windshield of his car with a rock, the official can be sued for damages for many actions in the course of his normal duties. For example, a property owner might sue him for his refusal to issue a building permit. A property owner's neighbor might sue the official, alleging that he improperly issued a permit. A property owner might sue him for trespassing on private property in order to make an inspection. A property owner or contractor might sue for damages resulting from his having issued a "stop order" to halt work on a construction project. A property owner might sue for his loss of rental income resulting from a condemnation order that prevents occupancy of a building. A property owner might sue the official for having demolished as substandard an allegedly "standard" building.

To say that someone can "sue" does not necessarily mean that he can recover damages. No one need fear being sued; the fear should be whether there is any likelihood that one will be liable for damages. Depending on the circumstances, the code official might or might not have to pay damages in the cases listed above. What are the general rules that govern his liability if he loses a suit?

First, if the official *intentionally* damages someone's person or property, he is liable to the same extent that any private citizen would be for committing such an action.

The situation is more complex, however, if the harm results from *negligence* or *failure to act.*

The first factor that the courts will consider is whether the duties being exercised by the officer involve the exercise of judgment and discretion or are purely "ministerial." The North Carolina Supreme Court has stated:

> It is the established law in this jurisdiction that public officers, in the performance of their official and governmental duties involving the exercise of judgment and discretion, may not be held liable as individuals for breach of such duty unless they act corruptly and of malice. *Templeton v. Beard,* 159 N.C., 63, 74 S.E., 735. It is also a recognized principle with us that in case of duties plainly ministerial in character the individual liability of public officers for a negligent breach thereof does not attach where the duties are of a public nature, imposed entirely for public benefit, unless the statute creating the office or imposing the duties makes provision for such liability. *Hudson v. McArthur,* 152 N.C., 445, 67 S.E., 995; *Hipp v. Ferrall,* 173 N.C., 167, 91 S.E., 831.[2]

Elaborating on this distinction, the State Supreme Court in another case quoted with approval from a legal textbook:

> The liability of a public officer to an individual for his negligent acts or omissions in the discharge of an official duty depends altogether upon the nature of the duty to which the neglect is alleged. Where his duty is absolute, certain, and imperative, involving merely the execution of a set task—in other words, is simply ministerial—he is liable in damages to anyone specially injured, either by his omitting to perform the task, or by performing it negligently or unskillfully. On the other hand, where his powers are discretionary, to be exerted or withheld according to his own judgment as to what is necessary or proper, he is not liable to any private person for neglect to exercise those powers, nor for the consequence of a lawful exercise of them where no corruption or malice can be imputed, and he keeps within the scope of his authority.[3]

Whether a court would regard particular duties as "discretionary" or "ministerial" is not easy to determine. It appears probable that some of a code official's duties are "discretionary"—for example, the issuance of a building permit or the determination that a building is unsafe. Other duties undoubtedly are routine enough to be regarded as "ministerial."[4]

---

2. Old Fort v. Harmon, 219 N.C. 241, 243 (1940).

3. Hipp v. Farrell, 169 N.C. 551, 556 (1915).

4. In Pigott v. City of Wilmington, 50 N.C. App. 401 (1981), the Court of Appeals broadly concluded that the duties of a building inspector involve the exercise of judgment and discretion. However, driving an automobile to the site of an inspection is an example of a duty the court might rule was ministerial if an accident occurred.

Let us assume that the duties involved in a particular case can be classified as "discretionary." In this event the officer is protected unless it is shown that "corruption" or "malice" influenced his actions. The North Carolina Supreme Court has defined these terms:

> Malice in law, as distinguished from malice in fact, is presumed from tortious acts, deliberately done without just cause, excuse, or justification, which are reasonably calculated to injure another or others. 18 R.C.L., 4; 38 C.J., 348.

> Speaking to the subject in *Brown v. Brown*, 124 N.C., 19, 32 S.E., 320, *Montgomery, J.*, delivering the opinion of the Court, quoted with approval the following: "The term 'malice,' as applied to torts, does not necessarily mean that which must proceed from a spiteful, malignant, or revengeful disposition, but a conduct injurious to another, though proceeding from an ill-regulated mind not sufficiently cautious before it occasions an injury to another. 11 Serg. & R., 39, 40. If the conduct of the defendant was unjustifiable and actually caused the injury complained of by the plaintiff, which was a question for the jury, malice in law would be implied from such conduct, and the court should have so charged."

> Corruption is more nearly akin to malignancy, hatred, ill-will, or spite and flows from improper motives. *Downing v. Stone*, 152 N.C., 525, 68 S.E., 9.[5]

Suppose, on the other hand, that the duties involved were classed as "ministerial." In this event, the Court has said that "where the duty is plain and certain, if it be negligently performed or not performed at all, the officer is liable at the suit of a private individual especially injured thereby.[6]

In a 1945 case a merchant sued several State Highway Commission employees for damages suffered when they ran a sweeper and blower past his store, with no previous warning, and blew an accumulation of dust, dirt, and other filth onto his store of goods. The State Supreme Court held that the defendants were "mere employees," not engaged in "discretionary" activities, and the question of their negligence must go to the jury:

> The mere fact that a person charged with negligence is an employee of others to whom immunity from liability is extended on grounds of public policy does not thereby excuse him from liability for negligence in the manner in which his duties are performed, or for performing a lawful act in an unlawful manner. The authorities generally hold the employee individually liable for negligence in the performance of his duties, notwithstanding the immunity of his employer. . . . The State of North Carolina has adopted this view. . . and any extension of this immunity is a matter of legislative action.

---

5. Betts v. Jones, 208 N.C. 410, 411-12 (1935).
6. Hipp v. Farrell, 169 N.C. 551, 555 (1915).

> It is proper to say...that it is a broad general rule that any person who violates a legal duty he owes to another is liable for the natural and probable consequences of his act or omission, and exceptions to that rule should not, by mere judicial rationalization, be extended beyond the recognized public policy out of which they may spring.[7]

Nevertheless, as the quotation from *Old Fort v. Harmon* earlier in this chapter noted, even though the duties are ministerial the officer will be immune from liability where "the duties are of a public nature, imposed entirely for public benefit, unless the statute creating the office or imposing the duties makes provision for such liability." This view has been reaffirmed in two more recent cases.[8]

Finally, even if the official had no governmental immunity to protect him in a particular suit, he would still have all the defenses available to a private citizen. In other words, the person harmed would have to prove that his injuries were "proximately caused" (that is, directly caused) by the officer's negligence, that they were reasonably foreseeable when the negligent actions or omissions took place, and that he was not contributorily negligent.

Two other rules should be mentioned. Occasionally someone threatens that if an officer brings legal action against him, he will sue the officer for "malicious prosecution." It is true that if the person should be found innocent in such an action, he could sue on that basis. But the officer will not be found liable if (a) he acted in good faith (not out of spite, out of malice, or for personal gain); and (b) after making a reasonable investigation, he has acted in a reasonable belief that there had been a violation.[9]

Second, in some circumstances the officer might be personally liable for his deputies' actions, even though he himself directly harmed no one. Such liability would result, however, only if (a) he directed the actions that caused harm, or (b) he negligently hired someone who was obviously unqualified to handle the job and harm resulted from this lack of qualification.[10]

Summing up, under North Carolina law the building official who deliberately sets out to use his powers to harm someone will always be liable. The officer who is exercising "discretionary" powers and negligently harms someone will normally be found liable only if he has been malicious or corrupt. The officer who is exercising mere "ministerial" or routine powers may also be immune if he is engaged in public duties; if not, he may be found liable for negligence, but it must be shown that the damage resulted directly from his negligence and was reasonably foreseeable. He is immune from liability for malicious prosecution if he proceeds out of proper motives, on the basis of a reasonable investigation and a reasonable

---

7. Miller v. Jones, 224 N.C. 783, 787-8 (1945).

8. Seibold v. Kinston-Lenoir County Pub. Library, 264 N.C. 360, 141 S.E.2d 519 (1965); Robinson v. Nash County, 43 N.C. App. 33, 257 S.E.2d 679 (1979).

9. Perry v. Hurdle, 229 N.C. 216 (1948).

10. *See, e.g.,* Betts v. Jones, 208 N.C. 410 (1935).

belief that there has been a violation. And it is possible that in some circumstances he may be liable for the actions of his subordinates, particularly if he hired obviously unsuitable persons.

FEDERAL LAW

In recent years a new element has been thrust into the area of civil liability. Section 1983 of the United States Code, Title 42, Chapter 21, is a provision originally enacted as part of the Civil Rights Act of 1871, which gave a person the right to sue for damages anyone who, under color of law, deprives him of "any rights, privileges, or immunities secured by the Constitution and laws." For years it was believed that that right applied only to deprivation of "civil rights" (right to vote, free speech, freedom of religion, freedom of assembly, etc.). But within the past decade courts have begun to apply it to *all* constitutional rights, including property rights, and lawsuits against local officials for alleged infringement of those rights have increased.

Building officials have not escaped suits of this type. However, in general the courts' decisions in these suits have not been too far different from North Carolina's common law concerning liability of public officials. In such cases as *Monroe v. Pape*,[11] *Wood v. Strickland*,[12] *Procunier v. Navarette*,[13] and *Owen v. Independence*,[14] the courts have generally concluded that public officials, as individuals, will be immune from liability if they were acting under appropriate authorization and in good faith (without malice and in accordance with settled law).

DEFENSE BY LOCAL GOVERNMENTS

Code enforcement officials, faced with possible lawsuits for injuries resulting from their official actions or omissions, should be aware of the following statutory provisions, together with any policies adopted by their local governing boards pursuant to the authority granted in these statutes:

§ 153A-97. Defense of officers, employees and others.

A county may, pursuant to G.S. 160A-167, provide for the defense of any county officer or employee, including the county board of elections or any county election official, and of any member of a volunteer fire department or rescue squad which receives public funds.

§ 160A-167. Defense of employees and officers; payment of judgments.

(a) Upon request made by or in behalf of any member or former member of the governing body of any authority, or any city, county, or authority em-

11. 365 U.S. 167 (1967).
12. 420 U.S. 308 (1975).
13. 434 U.S. 555 (1978).
14. 445 U.S. 622 (1981).

ployee or officer, or former employee or officer, or any member of a volunteer fire department or rescue squad which receives public funds, any city, authority, county or county alcoholic beverage control board may provide for the defense of any civil or criminal action or proceeding brought against him either in his official or in his individual capacity, or both, on account of any act done or omission made, or any act allegedly done or omission allegedly made, in the scope and course of his employment or duty as an employee or officer of the city, authority, county or county alcoholic beverage control board. The defense may be provided by the city, authority, county or county alcoholic beverage control board by its own counsel, or by employing other counsel, or by purchasing insurance which requires that the insurer provide the defense. Providing for a defense pursuant to this section is hereby declared to be for a public purpose, and the expenditure of funds therefor is hereby declared to be a necessary expense. Nothing in this section shall be deemed to require any city, authority, county or county alcoholic beverage control board to provide for the defense of any action or proceeding of any nature.

(b) Any city council or board of county commissioners may appropriate funds for the purpose of paying all or part of a claim made or any civil judgment entered against any of its members or former members of the governing body of any authority, or any city, county, or authority employees or officers, or former employees or officers, when such claim is made or such judgment is rendered as damages on account of any act done or omission made, or any act allegedly done or omission allegedly made, in the scope and course of his employment or duty as an members or former members [a member or former member] of the governing body of any authority, or any city, county, or authority employee or officer of the city, authority, or county; provided, however, that nothing in this section shall authorize any city, authority, or county to appropriate funds for the purpose of paying any claim made or civil judgment entered against any of its members or former members of the governing body of any authority, or any city, county, or authority employees or officers or former employees or officers if the city council or board of county commissioners finds that such members or former members of the governing body of any authority, or any city, county, or authority employee or officer acted or failed to act because of actual fraud, corruption or actual malice on his part. Any city, authority, or county may purchase insurance coverage for payment of claims or judgments pursuant to this section. Nothing in this section shall be deemed to require any city, authority, or county to pay any claim or judgment referred to herein, and the purchase of insurance coverage for payment of any such claim or judgment shall not be deemed an assumption of any liability not covered by such insurance contract, and shall not be deemed an assumption of liability for payment of any claim or judgment in excess of the limits of coverage in such insurance contract.

(c) Subsection (b) shall not authorize any city, authority, or county to pay all or part of a claim made or civil judgment entered unless (1) notice of the claim or litigation is given to the city council, authority governing board, or board of county commissioners as the case may be prior to the time that the claim is settled or civil judgment is entered, and (2) the city council, authority governing board, or board of county commissioners as the case may be shall have adopted, and made available for public inspection, uniform standards under which claims made or civil judgments entered against members or former members of the governing body of any authority, or any city, county, or authority employees or officers, or former employees or officers, shall be paid.

(d) For the purposes of this section, "authority" means an authority organized under Article 1 of Chapter 162A of the General Statutes, the North Carolina Water and Sewer Authorities Act.

MISCELLANEOUS RESTRAINTS

§ 153A-355. Conflicts of interest.

Unless he is the owner of the building, no member of an inspection department may be financially interested in furnishing labor, material, or appliances for the construction, alteration, or maintenance of any building within the county's territorial jurisdiction or any part or system thereof, or in making plans or specifications therefor. No member of any inspection department may engage in any work that is inconsistent with his duties or with the interest of the county.

§ 160A-415. Conflicts of interest.

No member of an inspection department shall be financially interested in the furnishing of labor, material, or appliances for the construction, alteration, or maintenance of any building within the city's jurisdiction or any part or system thereof, or in the making of plans or specifications therefor, unless he is the owner of the building. No member of an inspection department shall engage in any work that is inconsistent with his duties or with the interest of the city.

The following section authorizes disciplinary actions by the North Carolina Code Officials Qualification Board. Regulations adopted by the Board to effectuate these provisions are codified in the North Carolina Administrative Code, Title 11, Chapter 8, Section .0800.

§ 143-151.17. Grounds for disciplinary actions; investigation; administrative procedures.

(a) The Board shall have the power to suspend, revoke or refuse to grant any certificate issued under the provisions of this Article to any person who:

(1) Has been convicted of a felony against this State or the United States, or convicted of a felony in another state that would also be a felony if it had been committed in this State;

(2) Has obtained certification through fraud, deceit, or perjury;

(3) Has knowingly aided or abetted any person practicing contrary to the provisions of this Article or the State Building Code;

(4) Has defrauded the public or attempted to do so;

(5) Has affixed his signature to a report of inspection or other instrument of service if no inspection has been made by him or under his immediate and responsible direction; or,

(6) Has been guilty of willful misconduct, gross negligence or gross incompetence.

(b) The Board may investigate the actions of any qualified Code-enforcement official or applicant upon the verified complaint in writing of any person alleging a violation of subsection (a). The Board may suspend or revoke the certification of any qualified Code-enforcement official and refuse to grant a certificate to any applicant, whom it finds to have been guilty of one or more of the actions set out in subsection (a) as grounds for disciplinary action.

(c) The Board shall establish administrative rules and regulations for actions under this section which shall be in accordance with the requirements of Chapter 150A. Such rules and regulations shall include provisions for the removal of suspensions, the reissuance of certificates, and the conditions for these actions.

APPENDIX

STATE BUILDING CODE AND BUILDING CODE COUNCIL ENABLING ACT

Chapter 143.

State Departments, Institutions and Commissions.

ARTICLE 9.

Building Code Council and Building Code.

§ 143-136. Building Code Council created; membership.

(a) Creation; Membership; Terms. — There is hereby created a Building Code Council, which shall be composed of 12 members appointed by the Governor, consisting of one registered architect, one licensed general contractor, one registered architect or licensed general contractor specializing in residential design or construction, one registered engineer practicing structural engineering, one registered engineer practicing mechanical engineering, one registered engineer practicing electrical engineering, one licensed plumbing and heating contractor, one municipal or county building inspector, a representative of the public who is not a member of the building construction industry, a licensed electrical contractor, a registered engineer on the engineering staff of a State agency charged with approval of plans of state-owned buildings, and an active member of the North Carolina fire service with expertise in fire safety. Of the members initially appointed by the Governor, three shall serve for terms of two years each, three shall serve for terms of four years each, and three shall serve for terms of six years each. Thereafter, all appointments shall be for terms of six years. The Governor may remove appointive members at any time. Neither the architect nor any of the above named engineers shall be engaged in the manufacture, promotion or sale of any building material, and any member who shall, during his term, cease to meet the qualifications for original appointment (through ceasing to be a practicing member of the profession indicated or otherwise) shall thereby forfeit his membership on the Council.

The Governor may make appointments to fill the unexpired portions of any terms vacated by reason of death, resignation, or removal from office. In making such appointment, he shall preserve the composition of the Council required above.

(b) Compensation. — Members of the Building Code Council other than any who are employees of the State shall receive seven dollars ($7.00) per day, including necessary time spent in traveling to and from their place of residence within the State to any place of meeting or while traveling on official business of the Council. In addition, all members shall receive mileage and subsistence according to State practice while going to and from any place of meeting, or when on official business of the Council.

§ 143-137. Organization of Council; rules and regulations; meetings; staff; fiscal affairs.

(a) First Meeting; Organization; Rules and Regulations. — Within 30 days after its appointment, the Building Code Council shall meet on call of the Commissioner of Insurance. The Council shall elect from its appointive members a chairman and such other officers as it may choose, for such terms as it may designate in its rules and regulations. The Council shall adopt such rules and regulations not inconsistent herewith as it may deem necessary for the proper discharge of its duties. The chairman may appoint members to such committees as the work of the Council may require.

(b) Meetings. — The Council shall meet regularly, at least once every six months, at places and dates to be determined by the Council. Special meetings may be called by the chairman on his own initiative and must be called by him at the request of two or more members of the Council. All members shall be notified by the chairman in writing of the time and place of regular and special meetings at least seven days in advance of such meeting. Five members shall constitute a quorum. All meetings shall be open to the public.

(c) Staff. — Personnel of the Division of Engineering of the Department of Insurance shall serve as a staff for the Council. Such staff shall have the duties of

(1) Keeping an accurate and complete record of all meetings, hearings, correspondence, laboratory studies, and technical work performed by or for the Council, and making these records available for public inspection at all reasonable times;

(2) Handling correspondence for the Council.

(d) Fiscal Affairs of the Council. — All funds for the operations of the Council and its staff shall be appropriated to the Department of Insurance for the use of the Council. All such funds shall be held in a separate or special account on the books of the Department of Insurance, with a separate financial designation or code number to be assigned by the Department of Administration or its agent. Expenditures for staff salaries and operating expenses shall be made in the same manner as the expenditure of any other Department of Insurance funds. The Department of Insurance may hire such additional personnel as may be necessary to handle the work of the Building Code Council, within the limits of funds appropriated for the Council and with the approval of the Council.

§ 143-138. North Carolina State Building Code.

(a) Preparation and Adoption. — The Building Code Council is hereby empowered to prepare and adopt, in accordance with the provisions of this Article, a North Carolina State Building Code. Prior to the adoption of this Code, or any part thereof, the Council shall hold at least one public hearing in the City of Raleigh. A notice of such public hearing shall be given once a week for two successive calendar weeks in a newspaper published in Raleigh, said notice to be published the first time not less than 15 days prior to the date fixed for said hearing. The Council may hold such other public hearings and give such other notice as it may deem necessary.

(b) Contents of the Code. — The North Carolina State Building Code, as adopted by the Building Code Council, may include reasonable and suitable classifications of buildings and structures, both as to use and occupancy; general building restrictions as to location, height, and floor areas; rules for the lighting and ventilation of buildings and structures; requirements concerning means of egress from buildings and structures; requirements concerning means of ingress in buildings and structures; regulations governing construction and precautions to be taken during construction; regulations as to permissible materials, loads, and stresses; regulations of chimneys, heating appliances, elevators, and other facilities connected with the buildings and structures; regulations governing plumbing, heating, air conditioning for the purpose of comfort cooling by the lowering of temperature, and electrical systems; and such other reasonable rules and regulations pertaining to the construction of buildings and structures and the installation of particular facilities therein as may be found reasonably necessary for the protection of the occupants of the building or structure, its neighbors, and members of the public at large.

The Code may contain provisions regulating every type of building or structure, wherever it might be situated in the State.

Provided further, that nothing in this Article shall be construed to make any building regulations applicable to farm buildings located outside the building-regulation jurisdiction of any municipality.

Provided further, that no building permit shall be required under the Code or any local variance thereof approved under subsection (e) for any construction, installation, repair, replacement, or alteration costing five thousand dollars ($5,000) or less in any single family residence or farm building unless the work involves: the addition, repair, or replacement of load bearing structures; the addition (excluding replacement of same size and capacity) or change in the design of plumbing; the addition, replacement or change in the design of heating, air conditioning, or electrical wiring, devices, appliances, or equipment, the use of materials not permitted by the North Carolina Uniform Residential Building Code; or the addition (excluding replacement of like grade of fire resistance) of roofing.

Provided further, that no building permit shall be required under such Code from any State agency for the construction of any building or structure, the total cost of which is less than twenty thousand dollars ($20,000), except public or institutional buildings.

For the information of users thereof, the Code shall include as appendices
   (1) Any boiler regulations adopted by the Board of Boiler Rules,
   (2) Any elevator regulations relating to safe operation adopted by the Commissioner of Labor, and
   (3) Any regulations relating to sanitation adopted by the Department of Human Resources which the Building Code Council believes pertinent.

In addition, the Code may include references to such other regulations of special types, such as those of the Medical Care Commission and the Department of Public Instruction as may be useful to persons using the Code. No regulations issued by other agencies than the Building Code Council shall be construed as a part of the Code, nor supersede that Code, it being intended that they be presented with the Code for information only.

Nothing in this Article shall extend to or be construed as being applicable to the regulation of the design, construction, location, installation, or operation of (1) equipment for storing, handling, transporting, and utilizing liquefied petroleum gases for fuel purposes or anhydrous ammonia or other liquid fertilizers, or (2) equipment or facilities, other than buildings, of a public utility, as defined in G.S. 62-3, or an electric or telephone membership corporation, including without limitation poles, towers, and other structures supporting electric or communication lines.

(c) Standards to Be Followed in Adopting the Code. — All regulations contained in the North Carolina State Building Code shall have a reasonable and substantial connection with the public health, safety, morals, or general welfare, and their provisions shall be construed liberally to those ends. Requirements of the Code shall conform to good engineering practice, as evidenced generally by the requirements of the National Building Code of the American Insurance Association, formerly the National Board of Fire Underwriters, the Southern Standard Building Code of the Southern Building Code Congress, the Uniform Building Code of the Pacific Coast Building Officials Conference, the Basic Building Code of the Building Officials Conference of America, Inc., the National Electric Code, the Life Safety Code, formerly Building Exits Code of the National Fire Protection Association, the American Standard Safety Code for Elevators, Dumbwaiters, and Escalators, the Boiler Code of the American Society of Mechanical Engineers, Standards of the American Insurance Association for the Installation of Gas Piping and Gas Appliances in Buildings, and standards promulgated by the United States of America Standards Institute, formerly the American Standards Association, Underwriters' Laboratories, Inc., and similar national agencies engaged in research concerning strength of materials, safe design, and other factors bearing upon health and safety.

(d) Amendments of the Code. — The Building Code Council may from time to time revise and amend the North Carolina State Building Code, either on its own motion or upon application from any citizen, State agency, or political subdivision of the State. In adopting any amendment, the Council shall comply with the same procedural requirements and the same standards set forth above for adoption of the Code.

(e) Effect upon Local Building Codes. — The North Carolina State Building Code shall apply throughout the State, from the time of its adoption. However, any political subdivision of the State may adopt a building code or building rules and regulations governing construction within its jurisdiction. The territorial jurisdiction of any municipality or county for this purpose, unless otherwise specified by the General Assembly, shall be as follows: Municipal jurisdiction shall include all areas within the corporate limits of the municipality; county jurisdiction shall include all other areas of the county. No such building code or regulations shall be effective until they have been officially approved by the Building Code Council as providing adequate minimum standards to preserve and protect health and safety, in accordance with the provisions of subsection (c) above. While it remains effective, such approval shall be taken as conclusive evidence that a local code or local regulations supersede the State Building Code in its particular political subdivision. Whenever the Building Code Council adopts an amendment to the State Building Code, it shall consider any previously approved local regulations dealing with the same general matters, and it shall have authority to withdraw its approval of any such local code or regulations unless the local governing body makes such appropriate amendments to that local code or regulations as it may direct. In the absence of approval by the Building Code Council, or in the event that approval is withdrawn, local codes and regulations shall have no force and effect.

(f) Effect upon Existing Laws. — Until such time as the North Carolina State Building Code has been legally adopted by the Building Code Council pursuant to this Article, the North Carolina Building Code adopted by the Council and the Commissioner of Insurance in 1953 shall remain in full force and effect. Such Code is hereby ratified and adopted.

(g) Publication and Distribution of Code. — The Building Code Council shall cause to be printed, after adoption by the Council, the North Carolina State Building Code and each amendment thereto. It shall, at the State's expense, distribute copies of the Code and each amendment to State and local governmental officials, departments, agencies, and educational institutions, as is set out in the table below. (Those marked by an asterisk will receive copies only on written request to the Council.)

OFFICIAL OR AGENCY	NUMBER OF COPIES
State Departments and Officials	
Governor	
Lieutenant Governor	1
Auditor	1
Treasurer	1
Secretary of State	1
Superintendent of Public Instruction	3
State Board of Education	2
Attorney General	5

OFFICIAL OR AGENCY	NUMBER OF COPIES
Commissioner of Agriculture	1
Commissioner of Labor	3
Commissioner of Insurance	5
Department of Human Resources [Commission for Health Services]	10
Department of Human Resources [Commission for Medical Facility Services and Licensure]	3
Board of Transportation	3
Adjutant General	1
Utilities Commission	1
Department of Administration	3
Department of Conservation and Development	3
Department of Human Resources [Social Services Commission]	7
Justices of the Supreme Court	1 each
Clerk of the Supreme Court	1
Judges of the Court of Appeals	1 each
Clerk of the Court of Appeals	1
Judges of the Superior Court	* 1 each
Emergency Judges of the Superior Court	* 1 each
Special Judges of the Superior Court	* 1 each
Solicitors of the Superior Court	* 1 each
Department of Cultural Resources [State Library]	2
Supreme Court Library	2
State Senators	* 1 each
Representatives of General Assembly	* 1 each
Legislative Building Library	1
Other state-supported institutions, at the discretion of the Council	* 1 each
Schools	
University of North Carolina at Chapel Hill	* 25
North Carolina State University at Raleigh	* 15
North Carolina Agricultural and Technical State University	* 5
All other state-supported colleges and universities in the State of North Carolina	* 1 each
Local Officials	
Clerks of the Superior Courts	1 each
Registers of Deeds of the Counties	* 1 each
Chairman of the Boards of County Commissioners	* 1 each
City Clerks of each incorporated municipality	1 each
Chief Building Inspector of each incorporated municipality or county	* 1

In addition, the Building Code Council shall make additional copies available at such price as it shall deem reasonable to members of the general public.

(h) Violations. — Any person who shall be adjudged to have violated this Article or the North Carolina State Building Code, except for violations of occupancy limits established by either, shall be guilty of a misdemeanor and shall upon conviction be liable to a fine, not to exceed fifty dollars ($50.00), for each offense. Each 30 days that such violation continues shall constitute a separate and distinct offense. Violation of occupancy limits established pursuant to the North Carolina State Building Code shall be a misdemeanor subject to a one hundred dollar ($100.00) fine for a first offense, a two hundred fifty dollar ($250.00) fine for a second offense, and a five hundred dollar ($500.00) fine and up to 30 days imprisonment for a third and any subsequent offenses. Any violation incurred more than one year after another conviction for violation of the occupancy limits shall be treated as a first offense for purposes of establishing and imposing penalties. In case any building or structure is erected, constructed or reconstructed, or its purpose altered, so that it becomes in violation of the North Carolina State Building Code or if the occupancy limits established pursuant to the North Carolina State Building Code are exceeded, either the local enforcement officer or the State Commissioner of Insurance or other State official with responsibility under G.S. 143-139 may, in addition to other remedies, institute any appropriate action or proceedings including the civil remedies set out in G.S. 160A-175 and G.S. 153A-123, (i) to prevent such unlawful erection, construction or reconstruction or alteration of purpose, or overcrowding, (ii) to restrain, correct, or abate such violation, or (iii) to prevent the occupancy or use of said building, structure or land until such violation is corrected.

(*l*) When any question arises as to any provision of the Code, judicial notice shall be taken of that provision of the Code.

(i) Section 1008 of Chapter X of Volume 1 of the North Carolina State Building Code, Title "Special Safety to Life Requirements Applicable to Existing High-Rise Buildings" as adopted by the North Carolina State Building Code Council on March 9, 1976, as ratified and adopted as follows:

SECTION 1008-SPECIAL SAFETY TO LIFE REQUIREMENTS APPLICABLE TO EXISTING HIGH-RISE BUILDINGS

1008 — GENERAL.

(a) *Applicability.* — Within a reasonable time, as fixed by "written order" of the building official, and except as otherwise provided in subsection (j) of this section every building the [then] existing, that qualifies for classification under Table 1008.1 shall be considered to be a high-rise building and shall be provided with safety to life facilities as hereinafter specified. All other buildings shall be considered as low-rise. NOTE: The requirements of Section 1008 shall be considered as minimum requirements to provide for reasonable safety to life requirements for existing buildings and where possible, the owner and designer should consider the provisions of Section 506 applicable to new high-rise buildings.

(b) *Notification of Building Owner.* — The Department of Insurance will send copies of amendments adopted to all local building officials with the suggestion that all local building officials transmit to applicable building owners in their jurisdiction copies of adopted amendments, within six months from the date the amendments are adopted, with the request that each building owner respond to the local building official how he plans to comply with these requirements within a reasonable time.

NOTE: Suggested reasonable time and procedures for owners to respond to the building official's request is as follows:

(1) The building owner shall, upon receipt of written request from the building official on compliance procedures within a reasonable time, submit an overall plan required by 1008(c) below within one year and within the time period specified in the approved overall plan, but not to exceed five years after the overall plan is approved, accomplish compliance with this section, as evidenced by completion of the work in accordance with approved working drawings and specifications and by issuance of a new Certificate of Compliance by the building official covering the work. Upon approval of building owner's overall plan, the building official shall issue a "written order", as per 1008(a) above, to

comply with Section 1008 in accordance with the approved overall plan.

(2) The building official may permit time extensions beyond five years to accomplish compliance in accordance with the overall plan when the owner can show just cause for such extension of time at the time the overall plan is approved.

(3) The local building official shall send second request notices as per 1008(b) to building owners who have made no response to the request at the end of six months and a third request notice to no response building owners at the end of nine months.

(4) If the building owner makes no response to any of the three requests for information on how the owner plans to comply with Section 1008 within 12 months from the first request, the building official shall issue a "written order" to the building owner to provide his building with the safety to life facilities as required by this section and to submit an overall plan specified by (1) above within six months with the five-year time period starting on the date of the "written order".

(5) For purposes of this section, the Construction Section of the Division of Facility Services, Department of Human Resources, will notify all non-State owned I-Institutional buildings requiring licensure by the Division of Facility Services and coordinate compliance requirements with the Department of Insurance and the local building official.

(c) Submission of Plans and Time Schedule for Completing Work. — Plans and specifications, but not necessarily working drawings covering the work necessary to bring the building into compliance with this section shall be submitted to the building official within a reasonable time. (See suggested time in NOTE of Section 1008(b) above). A time schedule for accomplishing the work, including the preparation of working drawings and specifications shall be included. Some of the work may require longer periods of time to accomplish than others, and this shall be reflected in the plan and schedule.

NOTE: Suggested Time Period For Compliance:

SUGGESTED TIME PERIOD FOR COMPLIANCE

ITEM	CLASS I (SECTION)	CLASS II (SECTION)	CLASS III (SECTION)	TIME FOR COMPLETION
Signs in Elevator Lobbies and Elevator Cabs	1008.2(h)	1008.3(h)	1008.4(h)	180 days
Emergency Evacuation Plan	1008(b)	NOTE:		180 days
Corridor Smoke Detectors (Includes alternative door closers)	1008.2(c)	1008.3(c)	1008.4(c)	1 year
Manual Fire Alarm	1008.2(a)	1008.3(a)	1008.4(a)	1 year
Voice Communication System Required	1008.2(b)	1008.3(b)	1008.4(b)	2 years
Smoke Detectors Required	1008.2(c)	1008.3(c)	1008.4(c)	1 year
Protection and Fire Stopping for Vertical Shafts	1008.2(f)	1008.3(f)	1008.4(f)	3 years
Special Exit Requirements-Number, Location and Illumination to be in accordance with Section 1007	1008.2(e)	1008.3(e)	1008.4(e)	3 years
Emergency Electrical Power Supply	1008.2(d)	1008.3(d)	1008.4(d)	4 years

ITEM	CLASS I (SECTION)	CLASS II (SECTION)	CLASS III (SECTION)	TIME FOR COMPLETION
Special Exit Facilities Required	1008.2(e)	1008.3(e)	1008.4(e)	5 years
Compartmentation for Institutional Buildings	1008.2(f)	1008.3(f)	1008.4(f)	5 years
Emergency Elevator Requirements	1008.2(h)	1008.3(h)	1008.4(h)	5 years
Central Alarm Facility Required		1008.3(i)	1008.4(i)	5 years
Areas of Refuge Required on Every Eighth Floor			1008.4(j)	5 years
Smoke Venting			1008.4(k)	5 years
Fire Protection of Electrical Conductors			1008.4(l)	5 years
Sprinkler System Required			1008.4(m)	5 years

(d) Building Official Notification of Department of Insurance. — The building official shall send copies of written notices he sends to building owners to the Engineering and Building Codes Division for their files and also shall file an annual report by August 15th of each year covering the past fiscal year setting forth the work accomplished under the provisions of this section.

(e) Construction Changes and Design of Life Safety Equipment. — Plans and specifications which contain construction changes and design of life safety equipment requirements to comply with provisions of this section shall be prepared by a registered architect in accordance with provisions of Chapter 83 of the General Statutes or by a registered engineer in accordance with provisions of Chapter 89 of the General Statutes or by both an architect and engineer particularly qualified by training and experience for the type of work involved. Such plans and specifications shall be submitted to the Engineering and Building Codes Division of the Department of Insurance for approval. Plans and specifications for I-Institutional buildings licensed by the Division of Facility Services as noted in (b) above shall be submitted to the Construction Section of that Division for review and approval.

(f) Filing of Test Reports and Maintenance on Life Safety Equipment. — The engineer performing the design for the electrical and mechanical equipment, including sprinkler systems, must file the test results with the Engineering and Building Codes Division of the Department of Insurance, or to the agency designated by the Department of Insurance, that such systems have been tested to indicate that they function in accordance with the standards specified in this section and according to design criteria. These test results shall be a prerequisite for the Certificate of Compliance required by (b) above. Test results for I-Institutional shall be filed with the Construction Section, Division of Facility Services. It shall be the duty and responsibility of the owners of Class I, II and III buildings to maintain smoke detection, fire detection, fire control, smoke removal and venting as required by this section and similar emergency systems in proper operating condition at all times. Certification of full tests and inspections of all emergency systems shall be provided by the owner annually to the fire department.

(g) Applicability of Chapter X and Conflicts with Other Sections. — The requirements of this section shall be in addition to those of Sections 1001 through 1007; and in case of conflict, the requirements affording the higher degree of safety to life shall apply, as determined by the building official.

(h) Classes of Buildings and Occupancy Classifications. — Buildings shall be classified as Class I, II or III according to Table 1008.1. In the case of mixed occupancies, for this purpose, the classification shall be the most restrictive one resulting from the application of the most prevalent occupancies to Table 1008.1.

FOOTNOTE: Emergency Plan. — Owners, operators, tenants, administrators or managers of high-rise buildings should consult with the fire authority having jurisdiction and establish procedures which shall include but not necessarily be limited to the following:

(1) Assignment of a responsible person to work with the fire authority in the establishment, implementation and maintenance of the emergency pre-fire plan.

(2) Emergency plan procedures shall be supplied to all tenants and shall be posted conspicuously in each hotel guest room, each office area, and each schoolroom.

(3) Submission to the local fire authority of an annual renewal or amended emergency plan.

(4) Plan should be completed as soon as possible.

1008.1 — ALL EXISTING BUILDINGS SHALL BE CLASSIFIED AS CLASS I, II AND III ACCORDING TO TABLE 1008.1.

TABLE 1008.1

Scope

CLASS (1)	OCCUPANCY GROUP (3)(4)	OCCUPIED FLOOR ABOVE AVERAGE GRADE EXCEEDING HEIGHT (2)
CLASS I	Group R-Residential Group B-Business Group E-Educational Group A-Assembly Group H-Hazardous Group I-Institutional-Restrained	60' but less than 120' above average grade or 6 but less than 12 stories above average grade.
	Group I-Institutional-Unrestrained	36' but less than 60' above average grade or 3 but less than 6 stories above average grade.
CLASS II	Group R-Residential Group B-Business Group E-Educational Group A-Assembly Group H-Hazardous Group I-Institutional-Restrained	120' but less than 250' above average grade or 12 but less than 25 stories above average grade.
	Group I-Institutional-Unrestrained	60' but less than 250' above average grade or 6 but less than 25 stories above average grade.
CLASS III	Group R-Residential Group B-Business Group E-Educational Group I-Institutional Group A-Assembly	250' or 25 stories above average grade.

Group H-Hazardous

NOTE 1: The entire building shall comply with this section when the building has an occupied floor above the height specified, except that portions of the buildings which do not exceed the height specified are exempt from this section, subject to the following provisions:

(a) Low-rise portions of Class I buildings must be separated from high-rise portions by one-hour construction.

(b) Low-rise portions of Class II and III buildings must be separated from high-rise portions by two-hour construction.

(c) Any required exit from the high-rise portion which passes through the low-rise portions must be separated from the low-rise portion by the two-hour construction.

NOTE 2: The height described in Table 1008.1 shall be measured between the average grade outside the building and the finished floor of the top occupied story.

NOTE 3: Public parking decks meeting the requirements of Section 412.7 and less than 75 feet in height are exempt from the requirements of this section when there is no other occupancy above or below such deck.

NOTE 4: Special purpose equipment buildings, such as telephone equipment buildings housing the equipment only, with personnel occupant load limited to persons required to maintain the equipment may be exempt from any or all of these requirements at the discretion of the Engineering and Building Codes Division provided such special purpose equipment building is separated from other portions of the building by two-hour fire rated construction.

1008.2—REQUIREMENTS FOR EXISTING CLASS I BUILDINGS.

All Class I buildings shall be provided with the following:

(a) An approved manual fire alarm system, meeting the requirements of Section 1125 and applicable portions of NFPA 71, 72A, 72B, 72C or 72D, shall be provided unless the building is fully sprinklered or equipped with an approved automatic fire detection system connected to the fire department.

(b) All Class I buildings shall meet the requirements of Sections 1001-1007.

(c) *Smoke Detectors Required.* — At least one approved listed smoke detector tested in accordance with UL-167, capable of detecting visible and invisible particles of combustion shall be installed as follows:

   (1) All buildings classified as institutional, residential and assembly occupancies shall be provided with listed smoke detectors in all required exit corridors spaced no further than 60' on center or more than 15' from any wall. Exterior corridors open to the outside are not required to comply with this requirement. If the corridor walls have one-hour fire resistance rating with all openings protected with 1-¾ inch solid wood core or hollow metal door or equivalent and all corridor doors are equipped with approved self-closing devices, the smoke detectors in the corridor may be omitted. Detectors in corridors may be omitted when each dwelling unit is equipped with smoke detectors which activate the alarm system.

   (2) In every mechanical equipment, boiler, electrical equipment, elevator equipment or similar room unless the room is sprinklered or the room is separated from other areas by two-hour fire resistance construction with all openings therein protected with approved fire dampers and Class B fire doors. (Approved listed fire (heat) detectors may be submitted for these rooms.)

   (3) In the return air portion of every air conditioning and mechanical ventilation system that serves more than one floor.

   (4) The activation of any detector shall activate the alarm system, and shall cause such other operations as required by this Code.

   (5) The annuciator shall be located near the main entrance or in a central alarm and control facility.

NOTE 1: Limited area sprinklers may be supplied from the domestic water system provided the domestic water system is designed to support the design flow of the largest number of sprinklers in any one of the enclosed areas. When supplied by the domestic water system, the maximum number of sprinklers in any one enclosed room or area shall not exceed 20 sprinklers which must totally protect the room or area.

(d) Emergency Electrical Power Supply. — An emergency electrical power supply shall be provided to supply the following for a period of not less than two hours. An emergency electrical power supply may consist of generators, batteries, a minimum of two remote connections to the public utility grid supplied by multiple generating stations, a combination of the above.

(1) Emergency, exit and elevator cab lighting.

(2) Emergency illumination for corridors, stairs, etc.

(3) Emergency Alarms and Detection Systems. — Power supply for fire alarm and fire detection. Emergency power does not need to be connected to fire alarm or detection systems when they are equipped with their own emergency power supply from float or trickle charge battery in accordance with NFPA standards.

(e) Special Exit Requirements. — Exits and exitways shall meet the following requirements:

(1) Protection of Stairways Required. — All required exit stairways shall be enclosed with noncombustible one-hour fire rated construction with a minimum of 1-¾ inch solid core wood door or hollow metal door or 20 minute UL listed doors as entrance thereto. (See Section 1007.5).

(2) Number and Location of Exits. — All required exit stairways shall meet the requirements of Section 1007 to provide for proper number and location and proper fire rated enclosures and illumination of and designation for means of egress.

(3) Exit Outlets. — Each required exit stair shall exit directly outside or through a separate one-hour fire rated corridor with no openings except the necessary openings to exit into the fire rated corridor and from the fire rated corridor and such openings shall be protected with 1-¾ inch solid wood core or hollow metal door or equivalent unless the exit floor level and all floors below are equipped with an approved automatic sprinkler system meeting the requirements of NFPA No. 13.

(f) Smoke Compartments Required for I-Institutional Buildings. — Each occupied floor shall be divided into at least two compartments with each compartment containing not more than 30 institutional occupants. Such compartments shall be subdivided with one-half hour fire rated partitions which shall extend from outside wall to outside wall and from floor to and through any concealed space to the floor slab or roof above and meet the following requirements:

(1) Maximum area of any smoke compartment shall be not more than 22,500 square feet in area with both length and width limited to 150 feet.

(2) At least one smoke partition per floor regardless of building size forming two smoke zones of approximately equal size.

(3) All doors located in smoke partitions shall be properly gasketed to insure a substantial barrier to the passage of smoke and gases.

(4) All doors located in smoke partitions shall be no less than 1-¾ inch thick solid core wood doors with UL, ¼ inch wire glass panel in metal frames. This glass panel shall be a minimum of 100 square inches and a maximum of 720 square inches.

(5) Every door located in a smoke partition shall be equipped with an automatic closer. Doors that are normally held in the open position shall be equipped with an electrical device that shall, upon actuation of the fire alarm or smoke detection system in an adjacent zone, close the doors in that smoke partition.

(6) Glass in all corridor walls shall be ¼", UL approved, wire glass in metal frames in pieces not to exceed 1296 square inches.

(7) Doors to all patient rooms and treatment areas shall be a minimum of 1-¾ inch solid core wood doors except in fully sprinklered buildings.

(g) Protection and Fire Stopping for Vertical Shafts. — All vertical shafts extending more than one floor including elevator shafts, plumbing shafts, electrical shafts and other vertical openings shall be protected with noncombustible one-hour fire rated construction with shaft wall openings protected with 1-¾ inch solid core wood door or hollow metal door. Vertical shafts (such as electrical wiring shafts) which have openings such as ventilated doors on each floor must be fire stopped at the floor slab level with noncombustible materials having a fire resistance rating not less than one hour to provide an effective barrier to the passage of smoke, heat and gases from floor to floor through such shafts.

EXCEPTION: Shaft wall openings protected in accordance with NFPA No. 90A and openings connected to metal ducts equipped with approved fire dampers within the shaft wall openings do not need any additional protection.

(h) Signs in Elevator Lobbies and Elevator Cabs. — Each elevator lobby call station on each floor shall have an emergency sign located adjacent to the call button and each elevator cab shall have an emergency sign located adjacent to the floor status indicator. The required emergency sign shall be readable at all times and shall be a minimum of ½" high block letters with the words: "IN CASE OF FIRE DO NOT USE ELEVATOR — USE THE EXIT STAIRS" or other words to this effect.

1008.3 — REQUIREMENTS FOR EXISTING CLASS II BUILDINGS.

All Class II buildings must meet the following requirements:

(a) Manual Fire Alarm. — Provide manual fire alarm system in accordance with Section 1008.2(a). In addition, buildings so equipped with sprinkler alarm system or automatic fire detection system must have at least one manual fire alarm station near an exit on each floor as a part of such sprinkler or automatic fire detection and alarm system. Such manual fire alarm systems shall report a fire by floor.

(b) Voice Communication System Required. — An approved voice communication system or systems operated from the central alarm and control facilities shall be provided and shall consist of the following:

   (1) One-Way Voice Communication Public Address System Required. — A one-way voice communication system shall be established on a selective basis which can be heard clearly by all occupants in all exit stairways, elevators, elevator lobbies, corridors, assembly rooms and tenant spaces.

NOTE 1: This system shall function so that in the event of one circuit or speaker being damaged or out of service, the remainder of the system shall continue to be operable.

NOTE 2: This system shall include provisions for silencing the fire alarm devices when the loud speakers are in use, but only after the fire alarm devices have operated initially for not less than 15 seconds.

(c) Smoke Detectors Required. — Smoke detectors are required as per Section 1008.2(c). The following are additional requirements:

   (1) Storage rooms larger than 24 square feet or having a maximum dimension of over eight feet shall be provided with approved fire detectors or smoke detectors installed in an approved manner unless the room is sprinklered.

   (2) The actuation of any detectors shall activate the fire alarm system.

(d) Emergency Electrical Power Supply. — An emergency electrical power supply shall be provided to supply the following for a period of not less than two hours. An emergency electrical power supply may consist of generators, batteries, a minimum of two remote connections to the public utility grid supplied by multiple generating stations, a combination of the above. Power supply shall furnish power for items listed in Section 1008.2(d) and the following:

   (1) Pressurization Fans. — Fans to provide required pressurization, smoke venting or smoke control for stairways.

   (2) Elevators. — The designated emergency elevator.

(e) Special Exit Facilities Required. — The following exit facilities are required:

(1) The special exit facilities required in 1008.2(e) are required. All required exit stairways shall be enclosed with noncombustible two-hour fire rated construction with a minimum of 1-½ hour Class B-labeled doors as entrance thereto: (See Section 1007.5).

(2) Smoke-Free Stairways Required. — At least one stairway shall be a smoke free stairway in accordance with Section 1104.2 or at least one stairway shall be pressurized to between 0.15 inch and 0.35 inch water column pressure with all doors closed. Smoke-free stairs and pressurized stairs shall be identified with signs containing letters a minimum of ½ inch high containing the words "PRIMARY EXIT STAIRS" unless all stairs are smoke free or pressurized. Approved exterior stairways meeting the requirements of Chapter XI or approved existing fire escapes meeting the requirements of Chapter X with all openings within 10 feet protected with wire glass or other properly designed stairs protected to assure similar smoke-free vertical egress may be permitted. All required exit stairways shall also meet the requirements of Section 1008.2(e).

(3) If stairway doors are locked from the stairway side, keys shall be provided to unlock all stairway doors on every eighth floor leading into the remainder of the building and the key shall be located in a glass enclosure adjacent to the door at each floor level (which may sound an alarm when the glass is broken). When the key unlocks the door, the hardware shall be of the type that remains unlocked after the key is removed. Other means, approved by the building official may be approved to enable occupants and fire fighters to readily unlock stairway doors on every eighth floor that may be locked from the stairwell side. The requirements of this section may be eliminated in smoke-free stairs and pressurized stairs provided fire department access keys are provided in locations acceptable to the local fire authority.

(f) Compartmentation for I-Institutional Buildings Required. — See Section 1008.2(f).

(g) Protection and Fire Stopping for Vertical Shafts. — All vertical shafts extending more than one floor including elevator shafts, plumbing shafts, electrical shafts and other vertical openings shall be protected with noncombustible two-hour fire rated construction with Class B-labeled door except for elevator doors which shall be hollow metal or equivalent. All vertical shafts which are not so enclosed must be fire stopped at each floor slab with noncombustible materials having a fire resistance rating of not less than two hours to provide an effective barrier to the passage of smoke, heat and gases from floor to floor through such shaft.

EXCEPTION: Shaft wall openings protected in accordance with NFPA No. 90A and openings connected to metal ducts equipped with approved fire dampers within the shaft wall opening do not need any additional protection.

(h) Emergency Elevator Requirements.

(1) Elevator Recall. — Each elevator shall be provided with an approved manual return. When actuated, all cars taking a minimum of one car at a time, in each group of elevators having common lobby, shall return directly at normal car speed to the main floor lobby, or to a smoke-free lobby leading most directly to the outside. Cars that are out of service are exempt from this requirement. The manual return shall be located at the main floor lobby.

NOTE: Manually operated cars are considered to be in compliance with this provision if each car is equipped with an audible or visual alarm to signal the operator to return to the designated level.

(2) Identification of Emergency Elevator. — At least one elevator shall be identified as the emergency elevator and shall serve all floor levels.

NOTE: This elevator will have a manual control in the cab which will override all other controls including floor call buttons and door controls.

(3) Signs in Elevator Lobbies and Elevator Cabs. — Each elevator lobby call station on each floor shall have an emergency sign located adjacent to the call button and each elevator cab shall have an emergency sign located adjacent to the floor status indicator. These required emergency signs shall be readable at all times and shall be a minimum of ½ inch high block letters with the words: "IN CASE OF FIRE DO NOT USE ELEVATOR — USE THE EXIT STAIRS" or other words to this effect.

(i) *Central Alarm Facility Required.* — A central alarm facility accessible at all times to fire department personnel or attended 24 hours a day, shall be provided and shall contain the following:

(1) Facilities to automatically transmit manual and automatic alarm signals to the fire department either directly or through a signal monitoring service.

(2) Public service telephone.

(3) Fire detection and alarm systems annunciator panels to indicate the type of signal and the floor or zone from which the fire alarm is received. These signals shall be both audible and visual with a silence switch for the audible.

NOTE: Detectors in HVAC systems used for fan shut down need not be annunciated.

(4) Master keys for access from all stairways to all floors.

(5) One-way voice emergency communications system controls.

1008.4 — REQUIREMENTS FOR EXISTING CLASS III BUILDINGS.

All Class III Buildings shall be provided with the following:

(a) *Manual Fire Alarm System.* — A manual fire alarm system meeting the requirements of Section 1008.3(a).

(b) *Voice Communication System Required.* — An approved voice communication system or systems operated from the central alarm and control facilities shall be provided and shall consist of the following:

(1) One-Way Voice Communication Public Address System Required. — A one-way voice communication system shall be established on a selective or general basis which can be heard clearly by all occupants in all elevators, elevator lobbies, corridors, and rooms or tenant spaces exceeding 1,000 sq. ft. in area.

NOTE 1: This system shall be designed so that in the event of one circuit or speaker being damaged or out of service the remainder of the system shall continue to be operable.

NOTE 2: This system shall include provisions for silencing the fire alarm devices when the loud speakers are in use, but only after the fire alarm devices have operated initially for not less than 15 seconds.

(2) Two-way system for use by both fire fighters and occupants at every fifth level in stairways and in all elevators.

(3) Within the stairs at levels not equipped with two-way voice communications, signs indicating the location of the nearest two-way device shall be provided.

NOTE: The one-way and two-way voice communication systems may be combined.

(c) *Smoke Detectors Required.* — Approved listed smoke detectors shall be installed in accordance with Section 1008.3(c) and in addition, such detectors shall terminate at the central alarm and control facility and be so designed that it will indicate the fire floor or the zone on the fire floor.

(d) *Emergency Electrical Power Supply.* — Emergency electrical power supply meeting the requirements of Section 1008.3(d) to supply all emergency equipment required by Section 1008.3(d) shall be provided and in addition, provisions shall be made for automatic transfer to emergency power in not more than ten seconds for emergency illumination, emergency lighting and emergency communication systems. Provisions shall be provided to transfer power to a second designated elevator located in a separate shaft from the primary emergency elevator. Any standpipe or sprinkler system serving occupied floor areas 400 feet or more above grade shall be provided with on-site generated power or diesel driven pump.

(e) Special Exit Requirements. — All exits and exitways shall meet the requirements of Section 1008.3(e).

(f) Compartmentation of Institutional Buildings Required. — See Section 1008.2(f).

(g) Protection and Fire Stopping for Vertical Shafts. — Same as Class II buildings. See Section 1008.3(g).

(h) Emergency Elevator Requirements.

(1) Primary Emergency Elevator. — At least one elevator serving all floors shall be identified as the emergency elevator with identification signs both outside and inside the elevator and shall be provided with emergency power to meet the requirements of Section 1008.3(c).
NOTE: This elevator will have a manual control in the cab which will override all other controls including floor call buttons and door controls.

(2) Elevator Recall. — Each elevator shall be provided with an approved manual return. When actuated, all cars taking a minimum of one car at a time, in each group of elevators having common lobby, shall return directly at normal car speed to the main floor lobby or to a smoke-free lobby leading most directly to the outside. Cars that are out of service are exempt from this requirement. The manual return shall be located at the main floor lobby.
NOTE: Manually operated cars are considered to be in compliance with this provision if each car is equipped with an audible or visual alarm to signal the operator to return to the designated level.

(3) Signs in Elevator Lobbies and Elevator Cabs. — Each elevator lobby call station on each floor shall have an emergency sign located adjacent to the call button and each elevator cab shall have an emergency sign located adjacent to the floor status indicator. These required emergency signs shall be readable at all times and have a minimum of ½" high block letters with the words: "IN CASE OF FIRE, UNLESS OTHERWISE INSTRUCTED, DO NOT USE THE ELEVATOR — USE THE EXIT STAIRS" or other words to this effect.

(4) Machine Room Protection. — When elevator equipment located above the hoistway is subject to damage from smoke particulate matter, cable slots entering the machine room shall be sleeved beneath the machine room floor to inhibit the passage of smoke into the machine room.

(5) Secondary Emergency Elevator. — At least one elevator located in separate shaft from the Primary Emergency Elevator shall be identified as the "Secondary Emergency Elevator" with identification signs both outside and inside the elevator. It will serve all occupied floors above 250 feet and shall have all the same facilities as the primary elevator and will be capable of being transferred to the emergency power system.
NOTE: Emergency power supply can be sized for nonsimultaneous use of the primary and secondary emergency elevators.

(i) Central Alarm and Control Facilities Required.

(1) A central alarm facility accessible at all times to Fire Department personnel or attended 24 hours a day, shall be provided. The facility shall be located on a completely sprinklered floor or shall be enclosed in two-hour fire resistive construction. Openings are permitted if protected by listed 1-½ hour Class B-labeled closures or water curtain devices capable of a minimum discharge of three gpm per lineal foot of opening. The facility shall contain the following:

(i) Facilities to automatically transmit manual and automatic alarm signals to the fire department either directly or through a signal monitoring service.

(ii) Public service telephone.

(iii) Direct communication to the control facility.

(iv) Controls for the voice communication systems.

(v) Fire detection and alarm system annunciator panels to indicate the type of signal and the floor or zone from which the fire alarm is received, those signals, shall be both audible and visual with a silence switch for the audible.

NOTE: Detectors in HVAC systems used for fan shut down need not be annunciated.

(2) A control facility (fire department command station) shall be provided at or near the fire department response point and shall contain the following:

(i) Elevator status indicator.

NOTE: Not required in buildings where there is a status indicator at the main elevator lobby.

(ii) Master keys for access from all stairways to all floors.

(iii) Controls for the two-way communication system.

(iv) Fire detection and alarm system annunciator panels to indicate the type of signal and the floor or zone from which the fire alarm is received.

(v) Direct communication to the central alarm facility.

(3) The central alarm and control facilities may be combined in a single approved location. If combined, the duplication of facilities and the direct communication system between the two may be deleted.

(j) Areas of Refuge Required. — Class III buildings shall be provided with a designated "area of refuge" at the 250 ft. level and on at least every eighth floor or fraction thereof above that level to be designed so that occupants above the 250 ft. level can enter at all times and be safely accommodated in floor areas meeting the following requirements unless the building is completely sprinklered:

(1) Identification and Size. — These areas of refuge shall be identified on the plans and in the building as necessary. The area of refuge shall provide not less than 3 sq. ft. per occupant for the total number of occupants served by the area based on the occupancy content calculated by Section 1105. A minimum of two percent (2%) of the number of occupants on each floor shall be assumed to be handicapped and no less than 16 sq. ft. per handicapped occupant shall be provided. Smoke proof stairways meeting the requirements of Section 1104.2 and pressurized stairways meeting the requirements of Section 1108.3(e)(2) may be used for ambulatory occupants at the rate of 3 sq. ft. of area of treads and landings per person, but in no case shall the stairs count for more than one-third of the total occupants. Doors leading to designated areas of refuge from stairways or other areas of the building shall not have locking hardware or shall be automatically unlocked upon receipt of any manual or automatic fire alarm signal.

(2) Pressurized. — The area of refuge shall be pressurized with 100% fresh air utilizing the maximum capacity of existing mechanical building air conditioning system without recirculation from other areas or other acceptable means of providing fresh air into the area.

(3) Fire Resistive Separation. — Walls, partitions, floor assemblies and roof assemblies separating the area of refuge from the remainder of the building shall be noncombustible and have a fire resistance rating of not less than one hour. Duct penetrations shall be protected as required for penetrations of shafts. Metallic piping and metallic conduit may penetrate or pass through the separation only if the openings around the piping or conduit are sealed on each side of the

penetrations with impervious noncombustible materials to prevent the transfer of smoke or combustion gases from one side of the separation to the other. The fire door serving as a horizontal exit between compartments shall be so installed, fitted and gasketed to provide a barrier to the passage of smoke.

(4) Access Corridors. — Any corridor leading to each designated area of refuge shall be protected as required by Sections 1104 and 702. The capacity of an access corridor leading to an area of refuge shall be based on 150 persons per unit width as defined in Section 1105.2. An access corridor may not be less than 44 inches in width. The width shall be determined by the occupant content of the most densely populated floor served. Corridors with one-hour fire resistive separation may be utilized for area of refuge at the rate of three sq. ft. per ambulatory occupant provided a minimum of one cubic ft. per minute of outside air per square foot of floor area is introduced by the air conditioning system.

(5) Penetrations. — The continuity of the fire resistance at the juncture of exterior walls and floors must be maintained.

(k) Smoke Venting. — Smoke venting shall be accomplished by one of the following methods in nonsprinklered buildings:

(1) In a nonsprinklered building, the heating, ventilating and air conditioning system shall be arranged to exhaust the floor of alarm origin at its maximum exhausting capacity without recirculating air from the floor of alarm origin to any other floor. The system may be arranged to accomplish this either automatically or manually. If the air conditioning system is also used to pressurize the areas of refuge, this function shall not be compromised by using the system for smoke removal.

(2) Venting facilities shall be provided at the rate of 20 square feet per 100 lineal feet or 10 square feet per 50 lineal feet of exterior wall in each story and distributed around the perimeter at not more than 50 or 100 foot intervals openable from within the fire floor. Such panels and their controls shall be clearly identified.

(3) Any combination of the above two methods or other approved designs which will produce equivalent results and which is acceptable to the building official.

(l) Fire Protection of Electrical Conductors. — New electrical conductors furnishing power for pressurization fans for stairways, power for emergency elevators and fire pumps required by Section 1008.4(d) shall be protected by a two-hour fire rated horizontal or vertical enclosure or structural element which does not contain any combustible materials. Such protection shall begin at the source of the electrical power and extend to the floor level on which the emergency equipment is located. It shall also extend to the emergency equipment to the extent that the construction of the building components on that floor permits. New electrical conductors in metal raceways located within a two-hour fire rated assembly without any combustible therein are exempt from this requirement.

(m) Automatic Sprinkler Systems Required.

(1) All areas which are classified as Group M-mercantile and Group H-hazardous shall be completely protected with an automatic sprinkler system.

(2) All areas used for commercial or institutional food preparation and storage facilities adjacent thereto shall be provided with an automatic sprinkler system.

(3) An area used for storage or handling of hazardous substances shall be provided with an automatic sprinkler system.

(4) All laboratories and vocational shops in Group E, Educational shall be provided with an automatic sprinkler system.

(5) Sprinkler systems shall be in strict accordance with NFPA No. 13 and the following requirements:

The sprinkler system must be equipped with a water flow and supervisory signal system that will transmit automatically a water flow signal directly to the fire department or to an independent signal monitoring service satisfactory to the fire department.

(j) Subsection (i) of this section does not apply to business occupancy buildings as defined in the North Carolina State Building Code except that evacuation plans as required on page 8, lines 2 through 16 [Section 1008, footnote following subsection (h)], and smoke detectors as required for Class I Buildings as required by Section 1008.2, page 11, lines 5 through 21 [Section 1008.2, subdivision (c)(1)]; Class II Buildings as required by Section 1008.3, page 17, lines 17 through 28 and page 18, lines 1 through 10 [Section 1008.3, subsections (c) and (d)]; and Class III Buildings, as required by Section 1008.4, lines 21 through 25 [Section 1008.4, subsection (c)] shall not be exempted from operation of this act as applied to business occupancy buildings.

(k) For purposes of use in the Code, the term "Family Care Home" shall mean a domicilary home having two to six residents.

§ 143-139. Enforcement of Building Code.

(a) Procedural Requirements. — Subject to the provisions set forth herein, the Building Code Council shall adopt such procedural requirements in the North Carolina State Building Code as shall appear reasonably necessary for adequate enforcement of the Code while safeguarding the rights of persons subject to the Code.

(b) General Building Regulations. — The Insurance Commissioner shall have general supervision, through the Division of Engineering of the Department of Insurance, of the administration and enforcement of all sections of the North Carolina State Building Code pertaining to plumbing, electrical systems, general building restrictions and regulations, heating and air conditioning, fire protection, and the construction of buildings generally, except those sections of the Code, the enforcement of which is specifically allocated to other agencies by subsections (c) and (d) below. The Insurance Commissioner, by means of the Division of Engineering, shall exercise his duties in the enforcement of the North Carolina State Building Code (including local building codes which have superseded the State Building Code in a particular political subdivision pursuant to G.S. 143-138(e)) in cooperation with local officials and local inspectors duly appointed by the governing body of any municipality or board of county commissioners pursuant to Article 11, Chapter 160 of the General Statutes of North Carolina, or G.S. 160-200(29), or G.S. 153-9(47) and (52), or any other applicable statutory authority.

(c) Boilers. — The Bureau of Boiler Inspection of the Department of Labor shall have general supervision of the administration and enforcement of those sections of the North Carolina State Building Code which pertain to boilers of the types enumerated in Article 7 of Chapter 95 of the General Statutes.

(d) Elevators. — The Department of Labor shall have general supervision of the administration and enforcement of those sections of the North Carolina State Building Code which pertain to elevators, moving stairways, and amusement devices such as merry-go-rounds, roller coasters, Ferris wheels, etc.

§ 143-139.1. Certification of manufactured buildings, structures or components by recognized independent testing laboratory.

The State Building Code may provide, in circumstances deemed appropriate by the Building Code Council, for testing, evaluation, inspection, and certification of buildings, structures or components manufactured off the site on which they are to be erected, by a recognized independent testing laboratory having follow-up inspection services approved by the Building Code Council. Approval of such buildings, structures or components shall be evidenced by labels or seals acceptable to the Council. All building units, structures or components bearing such labels or seals shall be deemed to meet the requirements of the State Building Code and this Article without further inspection or payment of fees, except as may be required for the enforcement of the Code relative to the connection of units and components and enforcement of local ordinances governing zoning, utility connections, and foundations permits. The Building Code Council shall adopt and may amend from time to time such reasonable and appropriate rules and regulations as it deems necessary for approval of agencies offering such testing, evaluation, inspection, and certification services and for overseeing their operations. Such rules and regulations shall include provisions to insure that such agencies are independent and free of any potential conflicts of interest which might influence their judgment in exercising their functions under the Code. Such rules and regulations may include a schedule of reasonable fees to cover administrative expenses in approving and overseeing operations of such agencies and may require the posting of a bond or other security satisfactory to the Council guaranteeing faithful performance of duties under the Code.

§ 143-139.2. Enforcement of insulation requirements; certificate for occupancy; no electric service without compliance.

(a) In addition to other enforcement provisions set forth in this Chapter, no single family or multi-unit residential building on which construction is begun in North Carolina on or after January 1, 1978, shall be occupied until it has been certified as being in compliance with the minimum insulation standards for residential construction, as prescribed in the North Carolina State Building Code or as approved by the Building Code Council as provided in G.S. 143-138(e). It shall be the duty of each county government and each municipality to provide for a building inspection program for certification of compliance with this section, either through a person in the county, city or joint inspection department who is responsible for enforcement of the insulation and energy utilization standards of the State Building Code or in any county or city which does not have an inspection department, through a person designated as the energy and insulation inspector.

(b) No public supplier of electric service, including regulated public utilities, municipal electric service and electric membership corporations, shall connect for electric service to an occupant any residential building on which construction is begun on or after January 1, 1978, unless said building complies with the insulation requirements of the North Carolina State Building Code or of local building codes approved by the Building Codes Council as provided in G.S. 143-138(e), and has been certified for occupancy in compliance with the minimum insulation standards of the North Carolina State Building Code or of any local modification approved as provided in G.S. 143-138(e), by a person designated as an inspector pursuant to subsection (a) of this section.

§ 143-140. Hearings before enforcement agencies as to questions under Building Code.

Any person desiring to raise any question under this Article or under the North Carolina State Building Code shall be entitled to a full hearing before the appropriate enforcement agency, as designated in the preceding section. Upon request in writing by any such person, the enforcement agency shall appoint a time for the hearing, giving such person reasonable notice thereof. The enforcement agency, through an appropriate official, shall conduct a full and complete hearing of the matters in controversy and make a determination thereof within a reasonable time thereafter. The person requesting the hearing shall, upon request, be furnished a written statement of the decision, setting forth the facts found, the decision reached, and the reasons therefor. In the event of dissatisfaction with such decision, the person affected shall have the options of

    (1) Appealing to the Building Code Council or

    (2) Appealing directly to the superior court, as provided in G.S. 143-141.

§ 143-141. Appeals to Building Code Council.

(a) Method of Appeal. — Whenever any person desires to take an appeal to the Building Code Council from the decision of a State enforcement agency relating to any matter under this Article or under the North Carolina State Building Code, he shall within 30 days after such decision give written notice to the Building Code Council through the Division of Engineering of the Department of Insurance that he desires to take an appeal. A copy of such notice shall be filed at the same time with the enforcement agency from which the appeal is taken. The chairman of the Building Code Council shall fix a reasonable time and place for a hearing, giving reasonable notice to the appellant and to the enforcement agency. Such hearing shall be not later than the next regular meeting of the Council. The Building Code Council shall thereupon conduct a full and complete hearing as to the matters in controversy, after which it shall within a reasonable time give a written decision setting forth its findings of fact and its conclusions.

(b) Interpretations of the Code. — The Building Code Council shall have the duty, in hearing appeals, to give interpretations of such provisions of the Building Code as shall be pertinent to the matter at issue. Where the Council finds that an enforcement agency was in error in its interpretation of the Code, it shall remand the case to the agency with instructions to take such action as it directs.

(c) Variations of the Code. — Where the Building Code Council finds on appeal that materials or methods of construction proposed to be used are as good as those required by the Code, it shall remand the case to the enforcement agency with instructions to permit the use of such materials or methods of construction. The Council shall thereupon immediately initiate procedures for amending the Code as necessary to permit the use of such materials or methods of construction.

(d) Further Appeals to the Courts. — Whenever any person desires to take an appeal from a decision of the Building Code Council or from the decision of an enforcement agency (with or without an appeal to the Building Code Council), he may take an appeal either to the Wake County Superior Court or to the superior court of the county in which the proposed building is to be situated, in accordance with the provisions of Chapter 150A of the General Statutes.

§ 143-142. Further duties of the Building Code Council.

(a) Recommended Statutory Changes. — It shall be the duty of the Building Code Council to make a thorough study of the building laws of the State, including both the statutes enacted by the General Assembly and the rules and regulations adopted by State and local agencies. On the basis of such study, the Council shall recommend to the 1959 and subsequent General Assemblies desirable statutory changes to simplify and improve such laws.

(b) Recommend Changes in Enforcement Procedures. — It shall be the duty of the Building Code Council to make a thorough and continuing study of the manner in which the building laws of the State are enforced by State, local, and private agencies. On the basis of such studies, the Council may recommend to the General Assembly any statutory changes necessary to improve and simplify the enforcement machinery. The Council may also advise State agencies as to any changes in administrative practices which could be made to improve the enforcement of building laws without statutory changes.

§ 143-143. Effect on certain existing laws.

Nothing in this Article shall be construed as abrogating or otherwise affecting the power of any State department or agency to promulgate regulations, make inspections, or approve plans in accordance with any other applicable provisions of law not in conflict with the provisions herein.

§ 143-143.2. Electric wiring of houses.

The electric wiring of houses or buildings for lighting or for other purposes shall conform to the requirements of the State Building Code, which includes the National Electric Code and any amendments and supplements thereto as adopted and approved by the State Building Code Council, and any other applicable State and local laws. In order to protect the property of citizens from the dangers incident to defective electric wiring of buildings, it shall be unlawful for any firm or corporation to allow any electric current for use in any newly erected building to be turned on without first having had an inspection made of the wiring by the appropriate official electrical inspector or inspection department and having received from that inspector or department a certificate approving the wiring of such building. It shall be unlawful for any person, firm, or corporation engaged in the business of selling electricity to furnish initially any electric current for use in any building, unless said building shall have first been inspected by the appropriate official electrical inspector or inspection department and a certificate given as above provided. In the event that there is no legally appointed inspector or inspection department with jurisdiction over the property involved, the two preceding sentences shall have no force or effect.

NORTH CAROLINA CODE OFFICIALS QUALIFICATION BOARD ENABLING ACT

Chapter 143.

State Departments, Institutions and Commissions.

ARTICLE 9B.

North Carolina Code Officials Qualifications Board.

§ 143-151.8. Definitions.

(a) As used in this Article, unless the context otherwise requires:
  (1) "Board" means the North Carolina Code Officials Qualification Board.
  (2) "Code" means the North Carolina State Building Code and related local building rules and regulations approved by the Building Code Council heretofore or hereinafter enacted, adopted or approved pursuant to G.S. 143-138.
  (3) "Code enforcement" means the examination and approval of plans and specifications, or the inspection of the manner of construction, workmanship, and materials for construction of buildings and structures and components thereof as an employee of the State or local government, except an employee of the State Department of Labor engaged in the administration and enforcement of those sections of the Code which pertain to boilers and elevators, to assure compliance with the State Building Code and related local building rules and regulations.
  (4) "Local inspection department" means the agency or agencies of local government with authority to make inspections of buildings and to enforce the Code and other laws, ordinances, and regulations enacted by the State and the local government which establish standards and requirements applicable to the construction, alteration, repair, or demolition of buildings.
  (5) "Qualified Code-enforcement official" means a person qualified under this Article to engage in the practice of Code enforcement.

(b) For purposes of this Article, the population of a city or county shall be determined according to the most current federal census, unless otherwise specified.

§ 143-151.9. North Carolina Code Officials Qualification Board established; members; terms; vacancies.

(a) There is hereby established the North Carolina Code Officials Qualification Board in the Department of Insurance. The Board shall be composed of 20 members appointed as follows:

(1) One member who is a city or county manager;

(2) Two members, one of whom is an elected official representing a city over 5,000 population and one of whom is an elected official representing a city under 5,000 population;

(3) Two members, one of whom is an elected official representing a county over 40,000 population and one of whom is an elected official representing a county under 40,000 population;

(4) Two members serving as building officials with the responsibility for administering building, plumbing, electrical and heating codes, one of whom serves a county and one of whom serves a city;

(5) One member who is a registered architect;

(6) One member who is a registered engineer;

(7) Two members who are licensed general contractors, at least one of whom specializes in residential construction;

(8) One member who is a licensed electrical contractor;

(9) One member who is a licensed plumbing or heating contractor;

(10) One member selected from the faculty of the North Carolina State University School of Engineering and one member selected from the faculty of the School of Engineering of the North Carolina Agricultural and Technical State University;

(11) One member selected from the faculty of the Institute of Government;

(12) One member selected from the Department of Community Colleges;

(13) One member selected from the Division of Engineering and Building Codes in the Department of Insurance; and,

(14) Two members who are citizens of the State.

The various categories shall be appointed as follows: (1), (2), (3), and (14) by the Governor; (4), (5), and (6) by the Lieutenant Governor; (7), (8), and (9) by the Speaker of the House of Representatives; (10) by the deans of the respective schools of engineering of the named universities; (11) by the Director of the Institute of Government; (12) by the President of the Division of Community Colleges; and (13) by the Commissioner of Insurance.

(b) The members shall be appointed for staggered terms and the initial appointments shall be made prior to September 1, 1977, and the appointees shall hold office until July 1 of the year in which their respective terms expire and until their successors are appointed and qualified as provided hereafter:

For the terms of one year: the members from subdivisions (1), (6) and (10) of subsection (a), and one member from subdivision (3).

For the terms of two years: the member from subdivision (11) of subsection (a), one member from subdivision (2), one member from subdivision (4), one member from subdivision (7), and one member from subdivision (14).

For the terms of three years: the members from subdivisions (8) and (12) of subsection (a), one member from subdivision (2), one member from subdivision (4), and one member from subdivision (14).

For the terms of four years: the members from subdivision (5), (9) and (13) of subsection (a), one member from subdivision (3), and one member from subdivision (7).

Thereafter, as the term of each member expires, his successor shall be appointed for a term of four years. Notwithstanding the appointments for a term of years, each member shall serve at the will of the Governor.

Members of the Board who are public officers shall serve ex officio and shall perform their duties on the Board in addition to the duties of their office.

(c) Vacancies in the Board occurring for any reason shall be filled for the unexpired term by the person making the appointment.

§ 143-151.10. Compensation.

Members of the Board who are State officers or employees shall receive no salary for serving on the Board, but shall be reimbursed for their expenses in accordance with G.S. 138-6. Members of the Board who are full-time salaried public officers or employees other than State officers or employees shall receive no salary for serving on the Board, but shall be reimbursed for subsistence and travel expenses in accordance with G.S. 138-5(a)(2) and (3). All other members of the Board shall receive compensation and reimbursement for expenses in accordance with G.S. 138-5(a).

§ 143-151.11. Chairman; vice-chairman; other officers; meetings; reports.

(a) The members of the Board shall select one of their members as chairman upon its creation, and shall select the chairman each July 1 thereafter.

(b) The Board shall select a vice-chairman and such other officers and committee chairmen from among its members, as it deems desirable, at the first regular meeting of the Board after its creation and at the first regular meeting after July 1 of each year thereafter. Provided, nothing in this subsection shall prevent the creation or abolition of committees or offices of the Board, other than the office of vice-chairman, as the need may arise at any time during the year.

(c) The Board shall hold at least four regular meetings per year upon the call of the chairman. Special meetings shall be held upon the call of the chairman or the vice-chairman, or upon the written request of four members of the Board.

(d) The activities and recommendations of the Board with respect to standards for Code officials training and certification shall be set forth in regular and special reports made by the Board. Additionally, the Board shall present special reports and recommendations to the Governor or the General Assembly, or both, as the need may arise or as the Governor or the General Assembly may request.

§ 143-151.12. Powers.

In addition to powers conferred upon the Board elsewhere in this Article, the Board shall have the power to:

(1) Promulgate rules and regulations for the administration of this Article including the authority to require the submission of reports and information by State agencies, local inspection departments, and local governing bodies within this State relating to the employment, education and training of Code-enforcement officials;

(2) Establish minimum standards for employment as a Code-enforcement official: (i) in probationary or temporary status, and (ii) in permanent positions;

(3) Certify persons as being qualified under the provisions of this Article to be Code-enforcement officials;

(4) Consult and cooperate with counties, municipalities, agencies of this State, other governmental agencies, and with universities, colleges, junior colleges, community colleges, technical institutes, and other institutions concerning the development of Code-enforcement training schools and programs or courses of instruction;

(5) Establish minimum standards and levels of education or equivalent experience for all Code-enforcement instructors, teachers or professors;

(6) Conduct and encourage research by public and private agencies which shall be designed to improve education and training in the administration of Code enforcement;

(7) Adopt and amend bylaws, consistent with law, for its internal management and control; appoint such advisory committees as it may deem necessary; and enter into contracts and do such other things as may be necessary and incidental to the exercise of its authority pursuant to this Article; and,

(8) Make recommendations concerning any matters within its purview pursuant to this Article.

§ 143-151.13. Required standards and certificates for Code-enforcement officials.

(a) The Board shall provide by regulation that on and after July 1, 1979, no person may engage in Code enforcement pursuant to this Article unless he possesses one of the following types of certificates, currently valid, issued by the Board attesting to his qualifications to hold such position: (i) a standard certificate; (ii) a limited certificate provided for in subsection (c); or (iii) a probationary certificate provided for in subsection (d). To obtain a standard certificate, a person must pass an examination, as prescribed by the Board, which is based on the North Carolina State Building Code and administrative procedures required to enforce the Code. The Board shall issue a standard certificate of qualification to each person who successfully completes the examination authorizing the person named therein to practice as a qualified Code-enforcement official in North Carolina. The certificate of qualification shall bear the signatures of the chairman and secretary of the Board.

(b) The Board shall establish by regulation appropriate performance levels, including designation of territory and type and size of buildings and structures, and classes of qualified Code-enforcement officials and may develop examinations and prescribe course of instruction for the various levels and classes. The certificate of qualification shall set forth the performance level for which the Code-enforcement official is qualified. The Board may by regulation limit the jurisdiction of Code-enforcement officials based on the performance level for which they have qualified; provided, a person who receives a certificate of qualification at the highest performance level established by the Board shall be entitled to serve anywhere in North Carolina.

(c) A Code-enforcement official holding office as of the date specified in this subsection for the county or municipality by which he is employed, shall not be required to possess a standard certificate as a condition of tenure or continued employment but shall be required to complete such in-service training as may be prescribed by the Board. At the earliest practicable date, such official shall receive from the Board a limited certificate qualifying him to engage in Code enforcement at the performance level and within the governmental jurisdiction in which he is employed. The limited certificate shall be valid only as an authorization for the official to continue in the position he held on the applicable date and shall become invalid if he does not complete in-service training within two years following the applicable date in the schedule below, according to the governmental jurisdiction's population as published in the 1970 U.S. Census:

Counties and Municipalities over 75,000 population — July 1, 1979
Counties and Municipalities between 50,001 and 75,000 — July 1, 1981
Counties and Municipalities between 25,001 and 50,000 — July 1, 1983
Counties and Municipalities 25,000 and under — July 1, 1985.

An official holding a limited certificate can be promoted to a position requiring a higher level certificate only upon issuance by the Board of a standard certificate or probationary certificate appropriate for such new position.

(d) The Board may provide for the issuance of probationary or temporary certificates valid for such period (not less than one year nor more than three years) as specified by the Board's regulations, or until June 30, 1983, whichever is later, to any Code-enforcement official newly employed or newly promoted who lacks the qualifications prescribed by the Board as prerequisite to applying for a standard certificate under subsection (a). No official may have his probationary or temporary certificate extended beyond the specified period by renewal or otherwise. The Board may by regulation provide for appropriate levels of probationary or temporary certificates and may issue these certificates with such special conditions or requirements relating to the place of employment of the person holding the certificate, his supervision on a consulting or advisory basis, or other matters as the Board may deem necessary to protect the public safety and health.

(e) The Board shall, without requiring an examination, issue a standard certificate to any person who is currently certified as a county electrical inspector pursuant to G.S. 153A-351. The certificate issued by the Board shall authorize the person to serve at the electrical inspector level approved by the Commissioner of Insurance in G.S. 153A-351.

(f) The Board shall issue a standard certificate to any person who is currently licensed to practice as a(n):

(1) Architect, registered pursuant to Chapter 83;
(2) General contractor, licensed pursuant to Article 1 of Chapter 87;
(3) Plumbing or heating contractor, licensed pursuant to Article 2 of Chapter 87;
(4) Electrical contractor, licensed pursuant to Article 4 of Chapter 87; or,
(5) Professional engineer, registered pursuant to Chapter 89;

provided the person successfully completes a short course, as prescribed by the Board, relating to the State Building Code regulations and Code-enforcement administration. The standard certificate shall authorize the person to practice as a qualified Code-enforcement official at the performance level determined by the Board, based on the type of license or registration held in any profession specified above.

§ 143-151.14. Comity.

The Board may, without requiring an examination, grant a standard certificate as a qualified Code-enforcement official to any person who, at the time of application, is certified as a qualified Code-enforcement official by a similar board of another state, district or territory where standards are acceptable to the Board and not lower than those required by this Article. A fee of not more than twenty dollars ($20.00), as determined by the Board, must be paid by the applicant to the Board for the issuance of a certificate under the provisions of this section. The provisions of G.S. 143-151.16(b) relating to renewal fees and late renewals shall apply to every person granted a standard certificate in accordance with this section.

§ 143-151.15. Return of certificate to Board; reissuance by Board.

A certificate issued by the Board pursuant to this Article shall remain valid only so long as the person certified is employed by the State of North Carolina or any political subdivision thereof as a Code-enforcement official. When the person certified leaves such employment for any reason, he shall return the certificate to the Board. If the person subsequently obtains employment as a Code-enforcement official in any governmental jurisdiction described above, the Board shall reissue the certificate to him. The provisions of G.S. 143-151.16(b) relating to renewal fees and late renewals shall apply, if appropriate. The provisions of G.S. 143-151.16(c) shall not apply. The provisions of this section shall not affect the Board's power to suspend or revoke any certificate pursuant to G.S. 143-151.17

§ 143-151.16. Certification fees; renewal of certificates.

(a) The Board shall establish a schedule of fees to be paid by each applicant for certification as a qualified Code-enforcement official. Such fee shall not exceed twenty dollars ($20.00) for each applicant.

(b) A certificate, other than a probationary certificate, as a qualified Code-enforcement official issued pursuant to the provisions of this Article must be renewed annually on or before the first day of July. Each application for renewal must be accompanied by a renewal fee to be determined by the Board, but not to exceed ten dollars ($10.00). The Board is authorized to charge an extra two dollar ($2.00) late renewal fee for renewals made after the first day of July each year.

(c) Any person who fails to renew his certificate for a period of two consecutive years may be required by the Board to take and pass the same examination as unlicensed applicants before allowing such person to renew his certificate.

§ 143-151.17. Grounds for disciplinary actions; investigation; administrative procedures.

(a) The Board shall have the power to suspend, revoke or refuse to grant any certificate issued under the provisions of this Article to any person who:
  (1) Has been convicted of a felony against this State or the United States, or convicted of a felony in another state that would also be a felony if it had been committed in this State;
  (2) Has obtained certification through fraud, deceit, or perjury;
  (3) Has knowingly aided or abetted any person practicing contrary to the provisions of this Article or the State Building Code;
  (4) Has defrauded the public or attempted to do so;
  (5) Has affixed his signature to a report of inspection or other instrument of service if no inspection has been made by him or under his immediate and responsible direction; or,
  (6) Has been guilty of willful misconduct, gross negligence or gross incompetence.

(b) The Board may investigate the actions of any qualified Code-enforcement official or applicant upon the verified complaint in writing of any person alleging a violation of subsection (a). The Board may suspend or revoke the certification of any qualified Code-enforcement official and refuse to grant a certificate to any applicant, whom it finds to have been guilty of one or more of the actions set out in subsection (a) as grounds for disciplinary action.

(c) The Board shall establish administrative rules and regulations for actions under this section which shall be in accordance with the requirements of Chapter 150A. Such rules and regulations shall include provisions for the removal of suspensions, the reissuance of certificates, and the conditions for these actions.

§ 143-151.18. Violations; penalty; injunction.

On and after July 1, 1979, it shall be unlawful for any person to represent himself as a qualified Code-enforcement official who does not hold a currently valid certificate of qualification issued by the Board. Any person violating any of the provisions of this Article shall be guilty of a misdemeanor and punishable in the discretion of the court. The Board is authorized to apply to any judge of the superior court for an injunction in order to prevent any violation or threatened violation of the provisions of this Article.

§ 143-151.19. Administration.

(a) The Division of Engineering and Building Codes in the Department of Insurance shall provide clerical and other staff services required by the Board, and shall administer and enforce all provisions of this Article and all rules and regulations promulgated pursuant to this Article, subject to the direction of the Board, except as delegated by this Article to local units of government, other State agencies, corporations, or individuals.

(b) A certified copy of this Article and all rules and regulations promulgated pursuant thereto shall be filed with the Attorney General in accordance with Article 5 of Chapter 150A. The Board shall have printed additional copies of this Article and all rules and regulations promulgated pursuant thereto which shall be available to the public at a price determined by the Board.

(c) The Board shall keep current a record of the names and addresses of all qualified Code-enforcement officials and additional personal data as the Board deems necessary. The Board annually shall publish a list of all currently certified Code-enforcement officials.

(d) Each certificate issued by the Board shall contain such identifying information as the Board requires.

(e) The Board shall issue a duplicate certificate to practice as a qualified Code-enforcement official in place of one which has been lost, destroyed, or mutilated upon proper application and payment of a fee to be determined by the Board.

§ 143-151.20. Donations and appropriations.

(a) In addition to appropriations made by the General Assembly, the Board may accept for any of its purposes and functions under this Article any and all donations, both real and personal, and grants of money from any governmental unit or public agency, or from any institution, person, firm or corporation, and may receive, utilize, disburse and transfer the same, subject to the approval of the Council of State. Any arrangements pursuant to this section shall be detailed in the next regular report of the Board. Such report shall include the identity of the donor, the nature of the transaction, and the conditions, if any. Any moneys received by the Board pursuant to this section shall be deposited in the State treasury to the account of the Board.

(b) The Board may provide grants as a reimbursement for actual expenses incurred by the State or political subdivision thereof for the provisions of training programs of officials from other jurisdictions within the State. The Board, by rules and regulations, shall provide for the administration of the grant program authorized herein. In promulgating such rules, the Board shall promote the most efficient and economical program of Code-enforcement training, including the maximum utilization of existing facilities and programs for the purpose of avoiding duplication.

MUNICIPAL PLANNING AND ZONING ENABLING ACTS

Chapter 160A.

Cities and Towns.

ARTICLE 19.

Planning and Regulation of Development.

Part. 1. General Provisions.

§ 160A-360. Territorial jurisdiction.

(a) All of the powers granted by this Article may be exercised by any city within its corporate limits. In addition, any city may exercise these powers within a defined area extending not more than one mile beyond its limits. With the approval of the board or boards of county commissioners with jurisdiction over the area, a city of 10,000 or more population but less than 25,000 may exercise these powers over an area extending not more than two miles beyond its limits and a city of 25,000 or more population may exercise these powers over an area extending not more than three miles beyond its limits. The boundaries of the city's extraterritorial jurisdiction shall be the same for all powers conferred in this Article. No city may exercise extraterritorially any power conferred by this Article that it is not exercising within its corporate limits. In determining the population of a city for the purposes of this Article, the city council and the board of county commissioners may use the most recent annual estimate of population as certified by the Secretary of the North Carolina Department of Administration.

(b) Any council wishing to exercise extraterritorial jurisdiction under this Article shall adopt, and may amend from time to time, an ordinance specifying the areas to be included based upon existing or projected urban development and areas of critical concern to the city, as evidenced by officially adopted plans for its development. Boundaries shall be defined, to the extent feasible, in terms of geographical features identifiable on the ground. A council may, in its discretion, exclude from its extraterritorial jurisdiction areas lying in another county, areas separated from the city by barriers to urban growth, or areas whose projected development will have minimal impact on the city. The boundaries specified in the ordinance shall at all times be drawn on a map, set forth in a written description, or shown by a combination of these techniques. This delineation shall be maintained in the manner provided in G.S. 160A-22 for the delineation of the corporate limits, and shall be recorded in the office of the register of deeds of each county in which any portion of the area lies.

(c) Where the extraterritorial jurisdiction of two or more cities overlaps, the jurisdictional boundary between them shall be a line connecting the midway points of the overlapping area unless the city councils agree to another boundary line within the overlapping area based upon existing or projected patterns of development.

(d) If a city fails to adopt an ordinance specifying the boundaries of its extraterritorial jurisdiction, the county of which it is a part shall be authorized to exercise the powers granted by this Article in any area beyond the city's corporate limits. The county may also, on request of the city council, exercise any or all these powers in any or all areas lying within the city's corporate limits or within the city's specified area of extraterritorial jurisdiction.

(e) No city may hereafter extend its extraterritorial powers under this Article into any area for which the county at that time has adopted and is enforcing a zoning ordinance and subdivision regulations and within which it is enforcing the State Building Code. However, the city may do so where the county is not exercising all three of these powers, or when the city and the county have agreed upon the area within which each will exercise the powers conferred by this Article.

(f) When a city annexes, or a new city is incorporated in, or a city extends its jurisdiction to include, an area that is currently being regulated by the county, the county regulations and powers of enforcement shall remain in effect until (i) the city has adopted such regulations, or (ii) a period of 60 days has elapsed following the annexation, extension or incorporation, whichever is sooner. During this period the city may hold hearings and take any other measures that may be required in order to adopt its regulations for the area.

(f1) When a city relinquishes jurisdiction over an area that it is regulating under this Article to a county, the city regulations and powers of enforcement shall remain in effect until (i) the county has adopted this regulation or (ii) a period of 60 days has elapsed following the action by which the city relinquished jurisdiction, whichever is sooner. During this period the county may hold hearings and take other measures that may be required in order to adopt its regulations for the area.

(g) When a local government is granted powers by this section subject to the request, approval, or agreement of another local government, the request, approval, or agreement shall be evidenced by a formally adopted resolution of that government's legislative body. Any such request, approval, or agreement can be rescinded upon two years' written notice to the other legislative bodies concerned by repealing the resolution. The resolution may be modified at any time by mutual agreement of the legislative bodies concerned.

(h) Nothing in this section shall repeal, modify, or amend any local act which defines the boundaries of a city's extraterritorial jurisdiction by metes and bounds or courses and distances.

(i) Whenever a city or county, pursuant to this section, acquires jurisdiction over a territory that theretofore has been subject to the jurisdiction of another local government, any person who has acquired vested rights under a permit, certificate, or other evidence of compliance issued by the local government surrendering jurisdiction may exercise those rights as if no change of jurisdiction had occurred. The city or county acquiring jurisdiction may take any action regarding such a permit, certificate, or other evidence of compliance that could have been taken by the local government surrendering jurisdiction pursuant to its ordinances and regulations. Except as provided in this subsection, any building, structure, or other land use in a territory over which a city or county has acquired jurisdiction is subject to the ordinances and regulations of the city or county.

(j) Repealed by Session Laws 1973, c. 669, s. 1.

§ 160A-361. Planning agency.

Any city may by ordinance create or designate one or more agencies to perform the following duties:

(1) Make studies of the area within its jurisdiction and surrounding areas;
(2) Determine objectives to be sought in the development of the study area;
(3) Prepare and adopt plans for achieving these objectives;

(4) Develop and recommend policies, ordinances, administrative procedures, and other means for carrying out plans in a coordinated and efficient manner;

(5) Advise the council concerning the use and amendment of means for carrying out plans;

(6) Exercise any functions in the administration and enforcement of various means for carrying out plans that the council may direct;

(7) Perform any other related duties that the council may direct.

An agency created or designated pursuant to this section may include, but shall not be limited to, one or more of the following, with such staff as the council may deem appropriate:

(1) A planning board or commission of any size (not less than three members) or composition deemed appropriate, organized in any manner deemed appropriate;

(2) A joint planning board created by two or more local governments pursuant to Article 20, Part 1, of this Chapter.

§ 160A-362. Extraterritorial representation.

When a city elects to exercise extraterritorial zoning or subdivision-regulation powers under G.S. 160A-360, it shall in the ordinance creating or designating its planning agency or agencies provide a means of representation for residents of the extraterritorial area to be regulated. Representation shall be provided by appointing residents of the area to the planning agency and the board of adjustment that makes recommendations or grants relief in these matters. Any advisory board established prior to July 1, 1983, to provide the required extraterritorial representation shall constitute compliance with this section until the board is abolished by ordinance of the city. The representatives on the planning agency and the board of adjustment shall be appointed by the board of county commissioners with jurisdiction over the area. If there is an insufficient number of qualified residents of the area to meet membership requirements, the board of county commissioners may appoint as many other residents of the county as necessary to make up the requisite number. When the extraterritorial area extends into two or more counties, each board of county commissioners concerned shall appoint representatives from its portion of the area, as specified in the ordinance. If a board of county commissioners fails to make these appointments within 90 days after receiving a resolution from the city council requesting that they be made, the city council may make them. If the ordinance so provides, the outside representatives may have equal rights, privileges, and duties with the other members of the agency to which they are appointed, regardless of whether the matters at issue arise within the city or within the extraterritorial area; otherwise they shall function only with respect to matters within the extraterritorial area.

§ 160A-363. Supplemental powers.

A city or its designated planning agency may accept, receive, and disburse in furtherance of its functions any funds, grants, and services made available by the federal government and its agencies, the State government and its agencies, any local government and its agencies, and any private and civic sources. Any city, or its designated planning agency with the concurrence of the council, may enter into and carry out contracts with the State and federal governments or any agencies thereof under which financial or other planning assistance is made available to the city and may agree to and comply with any reasonable conditions that are imposed upon such assistance.

Any city, or its designated planning agency with the concurrence of the council, may enter into and carry out contracts with any other city, county, or regional council or planning agency under which it agrees to furnish technical planning assistance to the other local government or planning agency. Any city, or its designated planning agency with the concurrence of its council, may enter into and carry out contracts with any other city, county, or regional council or planning agency under which it agrees to pay the other local government or planning agency for technical planning assistance.

Any city council is authorized to make any appropriations that may be necessary to carry out any activities or contracts authorized by this Article or to support, and compensate members of, any planning agency that it may create pursuant to this Article, and to levy taxes for these purposes as a necessary expense.

§ 160A-364. Procedure for adopting or amending ordinances under Article.

Before adopting or amending any ordinance authorized by this Article, the city council shall hold a public hearing on it. A notice of the public hearing shall be given once a week for two successive calendar weeks in a newspaper having general circulation in the area. The notice shall be published the first time not less than 10 days nor more than 25 days before the date fixed for the hearing. In computing such period, the day of publication is not to be included but the day of the hearing shall be included.

§ 160A-364.1. Statute of limitations.

A cause of action as to the validity of any zoning ordinance, or amendment thereto, adopted under this Article or other applicable law shall accrue upon adoption of the ordinance, or amendment thereto, and shall be brought within nine months as provided in G.S. 1-54.1.

§ 160A-365. Enforcement of ordinances.

Subject to the provisions of the ordinance, any ordinance adopted pursuant to authority conferred by this Article may be enforced by any remedy provided by G.S. 160A-175.

§ 160A-366. Validation of ordinance.

Any city ordinance regularly adopted before January 1, 1972, under authority of general laws revised and reenacted in Chapter 160A, Article 19, or under authority of any city charter or local act concerning the same subject matter, is validated with respect to its application within the corporate limits of the city and as to its application within the extraterritorial jurisdiction of the city. Such an ordinance, and any city ordinance adopted since January 1, 1972, under authority of general laws revised and reenacted in Chapter 160A, Article 19, are hereby validated, notwithstanding the fact that such ordinances were not recorded pursuant to G.S. 160A-360(b) or 160A-364 and notwithstanding the fact that the adopting city council did not also adopt an ordinance defining or delineating by specific description the areas within its extraterritorial jurisdiction pursuant to G.S. 160A-360; provided that this act shall be deemed to validate ordinances of cities in Mecklenburg County only with respect to their application within the corporate limits of such cities.

Part 3. Zoning

§ 160A-381. Grant of power.

For the purpose of promoting health, safety, morals, or the general welfare of the community, any city is hereby empowered to regulate and restrict the height, number of stories and size of buildings and other structures, the percentage of lots that may be occupied, the size of yards, courts and other open spaces, the density of population, and the location and use of buildings, structures and land for trade, industry, residence or other purposes. These regulations may provide that a board of adjustment may determine and vary their application in harmony with their general purpose and intent and in accordance with general or specific rules therein contained. The regulations may also provide that the board of adjustment or the city council may issue special use permits or conditional use permits in the classes of cases or situations and in accordance with the principles, conditions, safeguards, and procedures specified therein and may impose reasonable and appropriate conditions and safeguards upon these permits. Where appropriate, such conditions may include requirements that street and utility rights-of-way be dedicated to the public and that provision be made of recreational space and facilities. When issuing or denying special use permits or conditional use permits, the city council shall follow the procedures for boards of adjustment except that no vote greater than a majority vote shall be required for the city council to issue such permits, and every such decision of the city council shall be subject to review by the superior court by proceedings in the nature of certiorari. Any petition for review by the superior court shall be filed with the clerk of superior court within 30 days after the decision of the city council is filed in such office as the ordinance specifies, or after a written copy thereof is delivered to every aggrieved party who has filed a written request for such copy with the clerk at the time of the hearing of the case, whichever is later. The decision of the city council may be delivered to the aggrieved party either by personal service or by registered mail or certified mail return receipt requested.

§ 160A-382. Districts.

For any or all these purposes, the city may divide its territorial jurisdiction into districts of any number, shape, and area that may be deemed best suited to carry out the purposes of this Part; and within those districts it may regulate and restrict the erection, construction, reconstruction, alteration, repair or use of buildings, structures, or land. Such districts may include, but shall not be limited to, general use districts, in which a variety of uses are permissible in accordance with general standards; overlay districts, in which additional requirements are imposed on certain properties within one or more underlying general or special use districts; and special use districts or conditional use districts, in which uses are permitted only upon the issuance of a special use permit or a conditional use permit. Property may be placed in a special use district or conditional use district only in response to a petition by the owners of all the property to be included. Except as authorized by the foregoing, all regulations shall be uniform for each class or kind of building throughout each district, but the regulations in one district may differ from those in other districts.

§ 160A-383. Purposes in view.

Zoning regulations shall be made in accordance with a comprehensive plan and designed to lessen congestion in the streets; to secure safety from fire, panic and other dangers; to promote health and the general welfare; to provide adequate light and air; to prevent the overcrowding of land; to avoid undue concentration of population; and to facilitate the adequate provision of transportation, water, sewerage, schools, parks, and other public requirements. The regulations shall be made with reasonable consideration, among other things, as to the character of the district and its peculiar suitability for particular uses, and with a view to conserving the value of buildings and encouraging the most appropriate use of land throughout such city.

§ 160A-384. Method of procedure.

The city council shall provide for the manner in which zoning regulations and restrictions and the boundaries of zoning districts shall be determined, established and enforced, and from time to time amended, supplemented or changed, in accordance with the provisions of this Article. The procedures adopted pursuant to this section shall provide that whenever there is a zoning classification action involving a parcel of land, the owner of that parcel of land as shown on the county tax listing, and the owners of all parcels of land abutting that parcel of land as shown on the county tax listing, shall be mailed a notice of the proposed classification by first class mail at the last addresses listed for such owners on the county tax abstracts. The person or persons mailing such notices shall certify to the City Council that fact, and such certificate shall be deemed conclusive in the absence of fraud.

§ 160A-385. Changes.

(a) Zoning regulations and restrictions and zone boundaries may from time to time be amended, supplemented, changed, modified or repealed. In case, however, of a protest against such change, signed by the owners of twenty percent (20%) or more either of the area of the lots included in a proposed change, or of those immediately adjacent thereto either in the rear thereof or on either side thereof, extending 100 feet therefrom, or of those directly opposite thereto extending 100 feet from the street frontage of the opposite lots, an amendment shall not become effective except by favorable vote of three fourths of all the members of the city council. The foregoing provisions concerning protests shall not be applicable to any amendment which initially zones property added to the territorial coverage of the ordinance as a result of annexation or otherwise.

(b) Amendments, modifications, supplements, repeal or other changes in zoning regulations and restrictions and zone boundaries shall not be applicable or enforceable without consent of the owner with regard to lots for which building permits have been issued pursuant to G.S. 160A-417 prior to the enactment of the ordinance making the change or changes so long as the permits remain valid and unexpired pursuant to G.S. 160A-418 and unrevoked pursuant to G.S. 160A-422.

§ 160A-386. Protest petition; form; requirements; time for filing.

No protest against any change in or amendment to a zoning ordinance or zoning map shall be valid or effective for the purposes of G.S. 160A-385 unless it be in the form of a written petition actually bearing the signatures of the requisite number of property owners and stating that the signers do protest the proposed change or amendment, and unless it shall have been received by the city clerk in sufficient time to allow the city at least two normal work days, excluding Saturdays, Sundays and legal holidays, before the date established for a public hearing on the proposed change or amendment to determine the sufficiency and accuracy of the petition. The city council may by ordinance require that all protest petitions be on a form prescribed and furnished by the city, and such form may prescribe any reasonable information deemed necessary to permit the city to determine the sufficiency and accuracy of the petition.

§ 160A-387. Planning agency; zoning plan; certification to city council.

In order to exercise the powers conferred by this Part, a city council shall create or designate a planning agency under the provisions of this Article or of a special act of the General Assembly. The planning agency shall prepare a proposed zoning ordinance, including both the full text of such ordinance and maps showing proposed district boundaries. The planning agency may hold public hearings in the course of preparing the ordinance. Upon completion, the planning agency shall certify the ordinance to the city council. The city council shall not hold its required public hearing or take action until it has received a certified ordinance from the planning agency. Following its required public hearing, the city council may refer the ordinance back to the planning agency for any further recommendations that the agency may wish to make prior to final action by the city council in adopting, modifying and adopting, or rejecting the ordinance.

§ 160A-388. Board of adjustment.

(a) The city council may provide for the appointment and compensation of a board of adjustment consisting of five or more members, each to be appointed for three years. In appointing the original members of such board, or in the filling of vacancies caused by the expiration of the terms of existing members, the council may appoint certain members for less than three years to the end that thereafter the terms of all members shall not expire at the same time. The council may, in its discretion, appoint and provide compensation for alternate members to serve on the board in the absence of any regular member. Alternate members shall be appointed for the same term, at the same time, and in the same manner as regular members. Each alternate member, while attending any regular or special meeting of the board and serving in the absence of any regular member, shall have and may exercise all the powers and duties of a regular member. A city may designate a planning agency to perform any or all of the duties of a board of adjustment in addition to its other duties.

(b) The board of adjustment shall hear and decide appeals from and review any order, requirement, decision, or determination made by an administrative official charged with the enforcement of any ordinance adopted pursuant to this Part. An appeal may be taken by any person aggrieved or by an officer, department, board, or bureau of the city. Appeals shall be taken within times prescribed by the board of adjustment by general rule, by filing with the officer from whom the appeal is taken and with the board of adjustment a notice of appeal, specifying the grounds thereof. The officer from whom the appeal is taken shall forthwith transmit to the board all the papers constituting the record upon which the action appealed from was taken. An appeal stays all proceedings in furtherance of the action appealed from, unless the officer from whom the appeal is taken certifies to the board of adjustment, after notice of appeal has been filed with him, that because of facts stated in the certificate a stay would, in his opinion, cause imminent peril to life or property or that because the violation charged is transitory in nature a stay would seriously interfere with enforcement of the ordinance. In that case proceedings shall not be stayed except by a restraining order, which may be granted by the board of adjustment or by a court of record on application, on notice to the officer from whom the appeal is taken and on due cause shown. The board of adjustment shall fix a reasonable time for the hearing of the appeal, give due notice thereof to the parties, and decide it within a reasonable time. The board of adjustment may reverse or affirm, wholly or partly, or may modify the order, requirement, decision, or determination appealed from, and shall make any order, requirement, decision, or determination that in its opinion ought to be made in the premises. To this end the board shall have all the powers of the officer from whom the appeal is taken.

(c) The zoning ordinance may provide that the board of adjustment may permit special exceptions to the zoning regulations in classes of cases or situations and in accordance with the principles, conditions, safeguards, and procedures specified in the ordinance. The ordinance may also authorize the board to interpret zoning maps and pass upon disputed questions of lot lines or district boundary lines and similar questions as they arise in the administration of the ordinance. The board shall hear and decide all matters referred to it or upon which it is required to pass under any zoning ordinance.

(d) When practical difficulties or unnecessary hardships would result from carrying out the strict letter of a zoning ordinance, the board of adjustment shall have the power, in passing upon appeals, to vary or modify any of the regulations or provisions of the ordinance relating to the use, construction or alteration of buildings or structures or the use of land, so that the spirit of the ordinance shall be observed, public safety and welfare secured, and substantial justice done.

(e) The concurring vote of four-fifths of the members of the board shall be necessary to reverse any order, requirement, decision, or determination of any administrative official charged with the enforcement of an ordinance adopted pursuant to this Part, or to decide in favor of the applicant any matter upon which it is required to pass under any ordinance, or to grant a variance from the provisions of the ordinance. Every decision of the board shall be subject to review by the superior court by proceedings in the nature of certiorari. Any petition for review by the superior court shall be filed with the clerk of superior court within 30 days after the decision of the board is filed in such office as the ordinance specifies, or after a written copy thereof is delivered to every aggrieved party who has filed a written request for such copy with the secretary or chairman of the board at the time of its hearing of the case, whichever is later. The decision of the board may be delivered to the aggrieved party either by personal service or by registered mail or certified mail return receipt requested.

(f) The chairman of the board of adjustment or any member temporarily acting as chairman, is authorized in his official capacity to administer oaths to witnesses in any matter coming before the board.

§ 160A-389. Remedies.

If a building or structure is erected, constructed, reconstructed, altered, repaired, converted, or maintained, or any building, structure or land is used in violation of this Part or of any ordinance or other regulation made under authority conferred thereby, the city, in addition to other remedies, may institute any appropriate action or proceedings to prevent the unlawful erection, construction, reconstruction, alteration, repair, conversion, maintenance or use, to restrain, correct or abate the violation, to prevent occupancy of the building, structure or land, or to prevent any illegal act, conduct, business or use in or about the premises.

§ 160A-390. Conflict with other laws.

When regulations made under authority of this Part require a greater width or size of yards or courts, or require a lower height of a building or fewer number of stories, or require a greater percentage of a lot to be left unoccupied, or impose other higher standards than are required in any other statute or local ordinance or regulation, regulations made under authority of this Part shall govern. When the provisions of any other statute or local ordinance or regulation require a greater width or size of yards or courts, or require a lower height of a building or a fewer number of stories, or require a greater percentage of a lot to be left unoccupied, or impose other higher standards than are required by the regulations made under authority of this Part, the provisions of that statute or local ordinance or regulation shall govern.

§ 160A-391. Other statutes not repealed.

This Part shall not repeal any zoning act or city planning act, local or general, now in force, except those that are repugnant to or inconsistent herewith. This Part shall be construed to be an enlargement of the duties, powers, and authority contained in other laws authorizing the appointment and proper functioning of city planning commissions or zoning commissions by any city or town in the State of North Carolina.

§ 160A-392. Part applicable to buildings constructed by State and its subdivisions; exception.

All of the provisions of this Part are hereby made applicable to the erection, construction, and use of buildings by the State of North Carolina and its political subdivisions.

Notwithstanding the provisions of any general or local law or ordinance, no land owned by the State of North Carolina may be included within an overlay district or a special use or conditional use district without approval of the Council of State.

COUNTY PLANNING AND ZONING ENABLING ACTS

Chapter 153A.
Counties.
ARTICLE 18.
Planning and Regulation of Development.
Part 1. General Provisions.

§ 153A-320. Territorial jurisdiction.

Each of the powers granted to counties by this Article, by Chapter 157A, and by Chapter 160A, Article 19 may be exercised throughout the county except as otherwise provided in G.S. 160A-360.

§ 153A-321. Planning agency.

A county may by ordinance create or designate one or more agencies to perform the following duties:

(1) Make studies of the county and surrounding areas;

(2) Determine objectives to be sought in the development of the study area;

(3) Prepare and adopt plans for achieving these objectives;

(4) Develop and recommend policies, ordinances, administrative procedures, and other means for carrying out plans in a coordinated and efficient manner;

(5) Advise the board of commissioners concerning the use and amendment of means for carrying out plans;

(6) Exercise any functions in the administration and enforcement of various means for carrying out plans that the board of commissioners may direct;

(7) Perform any other related duties that the board of commissioners may direct.

An agency created or designated pursuant to this section may include but shall not be limited to one or more of the following, with any staff that the board of commissioners considers appropriate:

(1) A planning board or commission of any size (not less than three members) or composition considered appropriate, organized in any manner considered appropriate;

(2) A joint planning board created by two or more local governments according to the procedures and provisions of Chapter 160A, Article 20, Part 1.

§ 153A-322. Supplemental powers.

A county or its designated planning agency may accept, receive, and disburse in furtherance of its functions funds, grants, and services made available by the federal government or its agencies, the State government or its agencies, any local government or its agencies, and private or civic sources. A county, or its designated planning agency with the concurrence of the board of commissioners, may enter into and carry out contracts with the State or federal governments or any agencies of either under which financial or other planning assistance is made available to the county and may agree to and comply with any reasonable conditions that are imposed upon the assistance.

A county, or its designated planning agency with the concurrence of the board of commissioners, may enter into and carry out contracts with any other county, city, regional council, or planning agency under which it agrees to furnish technical planning assistance to the other local government or planning agency. A county, or its designated planning agency with the concurrence of the board of commissioners, may enter into and carry out contracts with any other county, city, regional council, or planning agency under which it agrees to pay the other local government or planning agency for technical planning assistance.

A county may make any appropriations that may be necessary to carry out an activity or contract authorized by this Article, by Chapter 157A, or by Chapter 160A, Article 19 or to support, and compensate members of, any planning agency that it may create or designate pursuant to this Article.

§ 153A-323. Procedure for adopting or amending ordinances under this Article and Chapter 160A, Article 19.

Before adopting or amending any ordinance authorized by this Article or Chapter 160A, Article 19, the board of commissioners shall hold a public hearing on the ordinance or amendment. The board shall cause notice of the hearing to be published once a week for two successive calendar weeks. The notice shall be published the first time not less than 10 days nor more than 25 days before the date fixed for the hearing. In computing such period, the day of publication is not to be included but the day of the hearing shall be included.

§ 153A-324. Enforcement of ordinances.

In addition to the enforcement provisions of this Article and subject to the provisions of the ordinance, any ordinance adopted pursuant to this Article, to Chapter 157A, or to Chapter 160A, Article 19 may be enforced by any remedy provided by G.S. 153A-123.

§ 153A-325. Submission of statement concerning improvements.

A county may by ordinance require that when a property owner improves property at a cost of more than twenty-five hundred dollars ($2500) but less than five thousand dollars ($5,000), the property owner must, within 14 days after the completion of the work, submit to the county tax supervisor a statement setting forth the nature of the improvement and the total cost thereof.

Part 3. Zoning.

§ 153A-340. Grant of power.

For the purpose of promoting health, safety, morals, or the general welfare, a county may regulate and restrict

(1) The height, number of stories, and size of buildings and other structures,

(2) The percentage of lot that may be occupied,

(3) The size of yards, courts, and other open spaces,

(4) The density of population, and

(5) The location and use of buildings, structures, and land for trade, industry, residence, or other purposes, except farming.

These regulations may not affect bona fide farms, but any use of farm property for nonfarm purposes is subject to the regulations. The regulations may provide that a board of adjustment may determine and vary their application in harmony with their general purpose and intent and in accordance with general or specific rules therein contained. The regulations may also provide that the board of adjustment or the board of commissioners may issue special use permits or conditional use permits in the classes of cases or situations and in accordance with the principles, conditions, safeguards, and procedures specified therein and may impose reasonable and appropriate conditions and safeguards upon these permits. Where appropriate, the conditions may include requirements that street and utility rights-of-way be dedicated to the public and that recreational space be provided. When issuing or denying special use permits or conditional use permits, the board of commissioners shall follow the procedures for boards of adjustment except that no vote greater than a majority vote shall be required for the board of commissioners to issue such permits, and every such decision of the board of commissioners shall be subject to review by the superior court by proceedings in the nature of certiorari.

A county may regulate the development over estuarine waters and over lands covered by navigable waters owned by the State pursuant to G.S. 146-12, within the bounds of that county.

For the purpose of this section, the term "structures" shall include floating homes. Any petition for review by the superior court shall be filed with the clerk of superior court within 30 days after the decision of the board of commissioners is filed in such office as the ordinance specifies, or after a written copy thereof is delivered to every aggrieved party who has filed a written request for such copy with the clerk at the time of the hearing of the case, whichever is later. The decision of the board of commissioners may be delivered to the aggrieved party either by personal service or by registered mail or certified mail return receipt requested.

§ 153A-341. Purposes in view.

Zoning regulations shall be made in accordance with a comprehensive plan and designed to lessen congestion in the streets; to secure safety from fire, panic, and other dangers; to promote health and the general welfare; to provide adequate light and air; to prevent the overcrowding of land; to avoid undue concentration of population; and to facilitate the adequate provision of transportation, water, sewerage, schools, parks, and other public requirements. The regulations shall be made with reasonable consideration as to, among other things, the character of the district and its peculiar suitability for particular uses, and with a view to conserving the value of buildings and encouraging the most appropriate use of land throughout the county. In addition, the regulations shall be made with reasonable consideration to expansion and development of any cities within the county, so as to provide for their orderly growth and development.

§ 153A-342. Districts; zoning less than entire jurisdiction.

A county may divide its territorial jurisdiction into districts of any number, shape, and area that it may consider best suited to carry out the purposes of this Part. Within these districts a county may regulate and restrict the erection, construction, reconstruction, alteration, repair, or use of buildings, structures, or land. Such districts may include, but shall not be limited to, general use districts, in which a variety of uses are permissible in accordance with general standards; overlay districts, in which additional requirements are imposed on certain properties within one or more underlying general or special use districts; and special use districts or conditional use districts, in which uses are permitted only upon the issuance of a special use permit or a conditional use permit. Property may be placed in a special use district or conditional use district only in response to a petition by the owners of all the property to be included. Except as authorized by the foregoing, all regulations shall be uniform for each class or kind of building throughout each district, but the regulations in one district may differ from those in other districts.

A county may determine that the public interest does not require that the entire territorial jurisdiction of the county be zoned and may designate one or more portions of that jurisdiction as a zoning area or areas. A zoning area must originally contain at least 640 acres and at least 10 separate tracts of land in separate ownership and may thereafter be expanded by the addition of any amount of territory. A zoning area may be regulated in the same manner as if the entire county were zoned, and the remainder of the county need not be regulated.

§ 153A-343. Method of procedure.

The board of commissioners shall, in accordance with the provisions of this Article, provide for the manner in which zoning regulations and restrictions and the boundaries of zoning districts shall be determined, established, and enforced, and from time to time amended, supplemented, or changed. The procedures adopted pursuant to this section shall provide that whenever there is a zoning classification action involving a parcel of land, the owner of that parcel of land as shown on the county tax listing, and the owners of all parcels of land abutting that parcel of land as shown on the county tax listing, shall be mailed a notice of the proposed classification by first class mail at the last addresses listed for such owners on the county tax abstracts. The person or persons mailing such notices shall certify to the Board of Commissioners that fact, and such certificate shall be deemed conclusive in the absence of fraud.

§ 153A-344. Planning agency; zoning plan; certification to board of commissioners; amendments.

(a) To exercise the powers conferred by this Part, a county shall create or designate a planning agency under the provisions of this

Article or of a local act. The planning agency shall prepare a proposed zoning ordinance, including both the full text of such ordinance and maps showing proposed district boundaries. The planning agency may hold public hearings in the course of preparing the ordinance. Upon completion, the planning agency shall certify the ordinance to the board of commissioners. The board of commissioners shall not hold the public hearing required by G.S. 153A-323 or take action until it has received a certified ordinance from the planning agency. Following its required public hearing, the board of commissioners may refer the ordinance back to the planning agency for any further recommendations that the agency may wish to make prior to final action by the board in adopting, modifying and adopting, or rejecting the ordinance.

Zoning regulations and restrictions and zone boundaries may from time to time be amended, supplemented, changed, modified, or repealed. Whenever territory is added to an existing designated zoning area, it shall be treated as an amendment to the zoning ordinance for that area. Before an amendment may be adopted, it must be referred to the planning agency for the agency's recommendation. The agency shall be given at least 30 days in which to make a recommendation. The board of commissioners is not bound by the recommendations, if any, of the planning agency.

(b) Amendments, modifications, supplements, repeal or other changes in zoning regulations and restrictions and zone boundaries shall not be applicable or enforceable without consent of the owner with regard to lots for which building permits have been issued pursuant to G.S. 153A-357 prior to the enactment of the ordinance making the change or changes so long as the permits remain valid and unexpired pursuant to G.S. 153A-358 and unrevoked pursuant to G.S. 153A-362.

§ 153A-345. Board of adjustment.

(a) The board of commissioners may provide for the appointment and compensation, if any, of a board of adjustment consisting of at least five members, each to be appointed for three years. In appointing the original members of the board, or in filling vacancies caused by the expiration of the terms of existing members, the board of commissioners may appoint some members for less than three years to the end that thereafter the terms of all members do not expire at the same time. The board of commissioners may provide for the appointment and compensation, if any, of alternate members to serve on the board in the absence of any regular member. Alternate members shall be appointed for the same term, at the same time, and in the same manner as regular members. Each alternate member, while attending any regular or special meeting of the board and serving in the absence of a regular member, has and may exercise all the powers and duties of a regular member. If the board of commissioners does not zone the entire territorial jurisdiction of the county, each designated zoning area shall have at least one resident as a member of the board of adjustment.

A county may designate a planning agency to perform any or all of the duties of a board of adjustment in addition to its other duties.

(b) The board of adjustment shall hear and decide appeals from and review any order, requirement, decision, or determination made by an administrative official charged with enforcing an ordinance adopted pursuant to this Part.

Any person aggrieved or any officer, department, board, or bureau of the county may take an appeal. Appeals shall be taken within times prescribed by the board of adjustment by general rule, by filing with the officer from whom the appeal is taken and with the board of adjustment a notice of appeal, specifying the grounds thereof. The officer from whom the appeal is taken shall forthwith transmit to the board all the papers constituting the record upon which action appealed from was taken. An appeal stays all proceedings in furtherance of the action appealed from, unless the officer from whom the appeal is taken certifies to the board of adjustment, after notice of appeal has been filed with him, that because of facts stated in the certificate a stay would, in his opinion, cause imminent peril to life or property or that because the violation charged is transitory in nature a stay would seriously interfere with enforcement of the ordinance. In that case proceedings may not be stayed except by a restraining order, which may be granted by the board of adjustment or by a court of record on application, on notice to the officer from whom the appeal is taken and on due cause shown. The board of adjustment shall fix a reasonable time for the hearing of the appeal, give due notice of the appeal to the parties, and decide the appeal within a reasonable time. The board of adjustment may reverse or affirm, in whole or in part, or may modify the order, requirement, decision, or determination appealed from, and shall make any order, requirement, decision, or determination that in its opinion ought to be made in the circumstances. To this end the board has all of the powers of the officer from whom the appeal is taken.

(c) The zoning ordinance may provide that the board of adjustment may permit special exceptions to the zoning regulations in classes of cases or situations and in accordance with the principles, conditions, safeguards, and procedures specified in the ordinance. The ordinance may also authorize the board to interpret zoning maps and pass upon disputed questions of lot lines or district boundary lines and similar questions that may arise in the administration of the ordinance. The board shall hear and decide all matters referred to it or upon which it is required to pass under the zoning ordinance.

(d) When practical difficulties or unnecessary hardships would result from carrying out the strict letter of a zoning ordinance, the board of adjustment may, in passing upon appeals, vary or modify any regulation or provision of the ordinance relating to the use, construction, or alteration of buildings or structures or the use of land, so that the spirit of the ordinance is observed, public safety and welfare secured, and substantial justice done.

(e) The board of adjustment, by a vote of four-fifths of its members, may reverse any order, requirement, decision, or determination of an administrative officer charged with enforcing an ordinance adopted pursuant to this Part, or may decide in favor of the applicant a matter upon which the board is required to pass under the ordinance, or may grant a variance from the provisions of the ordinance. Each decision of the board is subject to review by the superior court by proceedings in the nature of certiorari. Any petition for review by the superior court shall be filed with the clerk of superior court within 30 days after the decision of the board is filed in such office as the ordinance specifies, or after a written copy thereof is delivered to every aggrieved party who has filed a written request for such copy with the secretary or chairman of the board at the time of its hearing of the case, whichever is later. The decision of the board may be delivered to the aggrieved party either by personal service or by registered mail or certified mail return receipt requested.

(f) The chairman of the board of adjustment or any member temporarily acting as chairman may in his official capacity administer oaths to witnesses in any matter coming before the board.

§ 153A-346. Conflict with other laws.

When regulations made under authority of this Part require a greater width or size of yards or courts, or require a lower height of a building or fewer number of stories, or require a greater percentage of a lot to be left unoccupied, or impose other higher standards than are required in any other statute or local ordinance or regulation, the regulations made under authority of this Part govern. When the provisions of any other statute or local ordinance or regulation require a greater width or size of yards or courts, or require a lower height of a building or a fewer number of stories, or require a greater percentage of a lot to be left unoccupied, or impose other higher standards than are required by regulations made under authority of this Part, the provisions of the other statute or local ordinance or regulation govern.

§ 153A-347. Part applicable to buildings constructed by the State and its subdivisions; exception.

Each provision of this Part is applicable to the erection, construction, and use of buildings by the State of North Carolina and its political subdivisions.

Notwithstanding the provisions of any general or local law or ordinance, no land owned by the State of North Carolina may be included within an overlay district or a special use or conditional use district without approval of the Council of State.

§ 153A-348. Statute of limitations.

A cause of action as to the validity of any zoning ordinance, or amendment thereto, adopted under this Part or other applicable law shall accrue upon adoption of the ordinance, or amendment thereto, and shall be brought within nine months as provided in G.S. 1-54.1.

ENABLING ACT FOR HISTORIC DISTRICT ZONING BY MUNICIPALITIES AND COUNTIES

Chapter 160A.

Cities and Towns.

ARTICLE 19.

Planning and Regulation of Development.

Part 3A. Historic Districts.

§ 160A-395. Exercise of powers under this Part by counties as well as cities; designation of historic districts.

The term "municipality" or "municipal" as used in G.S. 160A-395 through 160A-399 shall be deemed to include the governing board or legislative board of a county, to the end that counties may exercise the same powers as cities with respect to the establishment of historic districts.

Any such legislative body may, as part of a zoning ordinance enacted or amended pursuant to this Article, designate and from time to time amend one or more historic districts within the area subject to the ordinance. Such ordinance may treat historic districts either as a separate use-district classification or as districts which overlay other zoning districts. Where historic districts are designated as separate-use districts, the zoning ordinance may include as uses by right or as conditional uses those uses found by the historic district commission to have existed during the period sought to be restored or preserved, or to be compatible with the restoration or preservation of the district. No historic district or districts shall be designated until:

    (1) An investigation and report describing the significance of the buildings, structures, features, sites or surroundings included in any such proposed district, and a description of the boundaries of such district has been prepared; and

    (2) The Department of Cultural Resources, acting through an agent or employee designated by its Secretary, shall have made an analysis of and recommendations concerning such report and description of proposed boundaries. Failure of the Department to submit its written analysis and recommendations to the municipal governing body within 30 calendar days after a written request for such analysis has been mailed to it shall relieve the municipality of any responsibility for awaiting such analysis, and said body may at any time thereafter take any necessary action to adopt or amend its zoning ordinance.

The municipal governing body may also, in its discretion, refer the report and proposed boundaries to any local historic properties commission or other interested body for its recommendations prior to taking action to amend the zoning ordinance. With respect to any changes in the boundaries of such districts subsequent to its initial establishment, or the creation of additional districts within the jurisdiction, the investigative studies and reports required by subdivision (1) of this section shall be prepared by the historic district commission, and shall be referred to the local planning agency for its review and comment according to procedures set forth in the zoning ordinance. Changes in the boundaries of an initial district or proposals for additional districts shall also be submitted to the Department of Cultural Resources in accordance with the provisions of subdivision (2) of this section.

On receipt of these reports and recommendations, the municipality may proceed in the same manner as would otherwise be required for the adoption or amendment of any appropriate zoning ordinance provisions.

§ 160A-395.1. Character of historic district defined.

Historic districts established pursuant to this Part shall consist of areas which are deemed to be of special significance in terms of their history, architecture and/or culture, and to possess integrity of design, setting, materials, feeling and association.

§ 160A-396. Historic district commission.

Before it may designate one or more historic districts, a municipality shall establish or designate a historic district commission. The municipal governing board shall determine the number of members of the commission, which shall be at least three, and the length of their terms, which shall be no greater than four years. A majority of the members of such a commission shall have demonstrated special interest, experience, or education in history or architecture; and all the members shall reside within the territorial jurisdiction of the municipality as established pursuant to G.S. 160A-360.

In lieu of establishing a separate historic district commission, a municipality may designate as its historic district commission, (i) a historic properties commission established pursuant to G.S. 160A-399.2, (ii) a planning agency established pursuant to G.S. 160A-361, or (iii) a community appearance commission established pursuant to Part 7 of this Article. In order for a commission or board other than the historic district commission to be designated, at least two of its members shall have demonstrated special interest, experience, or education in history or architecture. At the discretion of the municipality the ordinance may also provide that the historic district commission may exercise within a historic district any or all of the powers of a planning agency or a community appearance commission.

A county and one or more cities in the county may establish or designate a joint historic district commission. If a joint commission is established or designated, the county and cities involved shall determine the residence requirements of members of the joint historic district commission.

§ 160A-397. Certificate of appropriateness required.

From and after the designation of a historic district, no exterior portion of any building or other structure (including masonry walls, fences, light fixtures, steps and pavement, or other appurtenant features) nor above-ground utility structure nor any type of outdoor advertising sign shall be erected, altered, restored, moved or demolished within such district until after an application for a certificate of appropriateness as to exterior features has been submitted to and approved by the historic district commission. The municipality shall require such a certificate to be issued by the commission prior to the issuance of a building permit or other permit granted for the purposes of constructing, altering, moving or demolishing structures, which certificate may be issued subject to reasonable conditions necessary to carry out the purposes of this Part. A certificate of appropriateness shall be required whether or not a building or other permit is required.

For purposes of this Part, "exterior features" shall include the architecture style, general design, and general arrangement of the exterior of a building or other structure, including the kind and texture of the building material, the size and scale of the building, and the type and style of all windows, doors, light fixtures, signs, and other appurtenant fixtures. In the case of outdoor advertising signs, "exterior features" shall be construed to mean the style, material, size, and location of all such signs. Such "exterior features" may, in the discretion of the local governing board, include color and important landscape and natural features of the area.

The commission shall have no jurisdiction over interior arrangement and shall take no action under this section except for the purpose of preventing the construction, reconstruction, alteration, restoration, moving or demolition of buildings, structures, appurtenant fixtures, outdoor advertising signs, or other significant features in the district which would be incongruous with the special character of the district.

Prior to any action to enforce a historic district ordinance, the commission shall (i) prepare and adopt rules of procedure, and (ii) prepare and adopt principles and guidelines not inconsistent with this Part for new construction, alterations, additions, moving and demolition. The ordinance may provide, subject to prior adoption by the historic district commission of detailed standards, for the review and approval by an administrative official, of minor works as defined by ordinance; provided, however, that no application for a certificate of appropriateness may be denied without formal action by the historic district commission.

Prior to issuance or denial of a certificate of appropriateness the commission shall take such steps as may be reasonably required in the ordinance and/or rules of procedure to inform the owners of any property likely to be materially affected by the application, and shall give the applicant and such owners an opportunity to be heard. In cases where the commission deems it necessary, it may hold a public hearing concerning the application. All meetings of the commission shall be open to the public, in accordance with the North Carolina Open Meetings Law, Chapter 143, Article 33B. An appeal may be taken to the Board of Adjustment from the commission's action in granting or denying any certificate, which appeals (i) may be taken by any aggrieved party, (ii) shall be taken within times prescribed by the historic district commission by general rule, and (iii) shall be in the nature of certiorari. Any appeal from the Board of Adjustment's decision in any such case shall be heard by the superior court of the county in which the municipality is located.

All applications for certificates of appropriateness shall be reviewed and acted upon within a reasonable time, as defined by the ordinance or the commission's rules of procedure. As part of its review procedure, the commission may view the premises and seek the advice of the Department of Cultural Resources or such other expert advice as it may deem necessary under the circumstances.

§ 160A-398. Certain changes not prohibited.

Nothing in this Part shall be construed to prevent the ordinary maintenance or repair of any exterior architectural feature in a historic district which does not involve a change in design, material or outer appearance thereof, nor to prevent the construction, reconstruction, alteration, restoration, moving or demolition of any such feature which the building inspector or similar official shall certify is required by the public safety because of an unsafe or dangerous condition.

§ 160A-398.1. Applicability of Part.

All of the provisions of this Part are hereby made applicable to the construction, alteration, moving and demolition of buildings by the State of North Carolina, its political subdivisions, agencies and instrumentalities.

The State shall have a right of appeal to the North Carolina Historical Commission from any decision of a local historic district commission. The North Carolina Historical Commission shall render its decision within 30 days from the date that the notice of appeal by the State is received by the Commission. The decision of the Commission shall be final and binding upon both the State and the historic district commission.

The Secretary of the Interior's Standards for Rehabilitation and Guideline for Rehabilitating Historic Buildings shall be the sole principles and guidelines used in reviewing applications of the State for certificates of appropriateness.

No provision of this Part shall be applicable to the construction, use, alteration, moving or demolition of buildings of the University of North Carolina, or any of its constituent institutions or agencies.

§ 160A-399. Delay in demolition of buildings within historic district.

An application for a certificate of appropriateness authorizing the demolition of a building or structure within the district may not be denied. However, the effective date of such a certificate may be delayed for a period of up to 180 days from the date of approval. The maximum period of delay authorized by this section shall be reduced by the commission where it finds that the owner would suffer extreme hardship or be permanently deprived of all beneficial use of or return from such property by virtue of the delay. During such period the historic district commission may negotiate with the owner and with any other parties in an effort to find a means of preserving the building. If the historic district commission finds that the building has no particular significance or value toward maintaining the character of the district, it shall waive all or part of such period and authorize earlier demolition or removal.

MUNICIPAL INSPECTION DEPARTMENT ENABLING ACT

Chapter 160A.

Cities and Towns.

ARTICLE 19.

Planning and Regulation of Development.

Part 5. Building Inspection.

§ 160A-411. Inspection department.

Every city in the State is hereby authorized to create an inspection department, and may appoint one or more inspectors who may be given the titles of building inspector, electrical inspector, plumbing inspector, housing inspector, zoning inspector, heating and air-conditioning inspector, fire prevention inspector, or deputy or assistant inspector, or such other titles as may be generally descriptive of the duties assigned. The department may be headed by a superintendent or director of inspections. Every city shall perform the duties and responsibilities set forth in G.S. 160A-412 either by: (i) creating its own inspection department; (ii) creating a joint inspection department in cooperation with one or more other units of local government, pursuant to G.S. 160A-413 or Part 1 of Article 20 of this Chapter; (iii) contracting with another unit of local government for the provision of inspection services pursuant to Part 1 of Article 20 of this Chapter; or (iv) arranging for the county in which it is located to perform inspection services within the city's jurisdiction as authorized by G.S. 160A-413 and G.S. 160A-360. Such action shall be taken no later than the applicable date in the schedule below, according to the city's population as published in the 1970 United States Census:

Cities over 75,000 population — July 1, 1979
Cities between 50,001 and 75,000 — July 1, 1981
Cities between 25,001 and 50,000 — July 1, 1983
Cities 25,000 and under — July 1, 1985.

In the event that any city shall fail to provide inspection services by the date specified above or shall cease to provide such services at any time thereafter, the Commissioner of Insurance shall arrange for the provision of such services, either through personnel employed by his department or through an arrangement with other units of government. In either event, the Commissioner shall have and may exercise within the city's jurisdiction all powers made available to the city council with respect to building inspection under Part 5 of Article 19, and Part 1 of Article 20 of this Chapter. Whenever the Commissioner has intervened in this manner, the city may assume provision of inspection services only after giving the Commissioner two years' written notice of its intention to do so; provided, however, that the Commissioner may waive this requirement or permit assumption at an earlier date if he finds that such earlier assumption will not unduly interfere with arrangements he has made for the provision of those services.

§ 160A-411.1. Qualifications of inspectors.

On and after the applicable date set forth in the schedule in G.S. 160A-411, no city shall employ an inspector to enforce the State Building Code as a member of a city or joint inspection department who does not have one of the following types of certificates issued by the North Carolina Code Officials Qualification Board attesting to his qualifications to hold such position: (i) a probationary certificate, valid for one year only; (ii) a standard certificate; or (iii) a limited certificate which shall be valid only as an authorization for him to continue in the position held on the date specified in G.S. 143-151.13(c) and which shall become invalid if he does not successfully complete in-service training specified by the Qualification Board within the period specified in G.S. 143-151.13(c). An inspector holding one of the above certificates can be promoted to a position requiring a higher level certificate only upon issuance by the Board of a standard certificate or probationary certificate appropriate for such new position.

§ 160A-412. Duties and responsibilities.

The duties and responsibilities of an inspection department and of the inspectors therein shall be to enforce within their territorial jurisdiction State and local laws relating to

(1) The construction of buildings and other structures;
(2) The installation of such facilities as plumbing systems, electrical systems, heating systems, refrigeration systems, and air-conditioning systems;
(3) The maintenance of buildings and other structures in a safe, sanitary, and healthful condition;
(4) Other matters that may be specified by the city council.

These duties shall include the receipt of applications for permits and the issuance or denial of permits, the making of any necessary inspections, the issuance or denial of certificates of compliance, the issuance of orders to correct violations, the bringing of judicial actions against actual or threatened violations, the keeping of adequate records, and any other actions that may be required in order adequately to enforce those laws. The city council shall have the authority to enact reasonable and appropriate provisions governing the enforcement of those laws.

§ 160A-413. Joint inspection department; other arrangements.

A city council may enter into and carry out contracts with another city, county, or combination thereof under which the parties agree to create and support a joint inspection department for the enforcement of State and local laws specified in the agreement. The governing boards of the contracting parties are authorized to make any necessary appropriations for this purpose.

In lieu of a joint inspection department, a city council may designate an inspector from any other city or county to serve as a member of its inspection department with the approval of the governing body of the other city or county. The inspector shall, while exercising the duties of the position, be considered a municipal employee.

The city council of any city may request the board of county commissioners of the county in which the city is located to direct one or more county building inspectors to exercise their powers within part or all of the city's jurisdiction, and they shall thereupon be empowered to do so until the city council officially withdraws its request in the manner provided in G.S. 160A-360(g).

§ 160A-414. Financial support.

The city council may appropriate for the support of the inspection department any funds that it deems necessary. It may provide for paying inspectors fixed salaries or it may reimburse them for their services by paying over part or all of any fees collected. It shall have power to fix reasonable fees for issuance of permits, inspections, and other services of the inspection department.

§ 160A-415. Conflicts of interest.

No member of an inspection department shall be financially interested in the furnishing of labor, material, or appliances for the construction, alteration, or maintenance of any building within the city's jurisdiction or any part or system thereof, or in the making of plans or specifications therefor, unless he is the owner of the building. No member of an inspection department shall engage in any work that is inconsistent with his duties or with the interest of the city.

§ 160A-416. Failure to perform duties.

If any member of an inspection department shall willfully fail to perform the duties required of him by law, or willfully shall improperly issue a permit, or shall give a certificate of compliance without first making the inspections required by law, or willfully shall improperly give a certificate of compliance, he shall be guilty of a misdemeanor.

§ 160A-417. Permits.

No person shall commence or proceed with
  (1) The construction, reconstruction, alteration, repair, movement to another site, removal, or demolition of any building or structure,
  (2) The installation, extension, or general repair of any plumbing system,
  (3) The installation, extension, alteration, or general repair of any heating or cooling equipment system, or
  (4) The installation, extension, alteration, or general repair of any electrical wiring, devices, appliances, or equipment,
without first securing from the inspection department with jurisdiction over the site of the work any and all permits required by the State Building Code and any other State or local laws applicable to the work. A permit shall be in writing and shall contain a provision that the work done shall comply with the State Building Code and all other applicable State and local laws. No permits shall be issued unless the plans and specifications are identified by the name and address of the author thereof, and if the General Statutes of North Carolina require that plans for certain types of work be prepared only by a registered architect or registered engineer, no permit shall be issued unless the plans and specifications bear the North Carolina seal of a registered architect or of a registered engineer. When any provision of the General Statutes of North Carolina or of any ordinance requires that work be done by a licensed specialty contractor of any kind, no permit for the work shall be issued unless the work is to be performed by such a duly licensed contractor. No permit issued under Articles 9 or 9C of Chapter 143 shall be required for any construction, installation, repair, replacement, or alteration costing five thousand dollars ($5,000) or less in any single family residence or farm building unless the work involves: the addition, repair or replacement of load bearing structures; the addition (excluding replacement of same size and capacity) or change in the design of plumbing; the addition, replacement or change in the design of heating, air conditioning, or electrical wiring, devices, appliances, or equipment; the use of materials not permitted by the North Carolina Uniform Residential Building Code; or the addition (excluding replacement of like grade of fire resistance) of roofing. Violation of this section shall constitute a misdemeanor.

§ 160A-418. Time limitations on validity of permits.

A permit issued pursuant to G.S. 160A-417 shall expire by limitation six months, or any lesser time fixed by ordinance of the city council, after the date of issuance if the work authorized by the permit has not been commenced. If after commencement the work is discontinued for a period of 12 months, the permit therefor shall immediately expire. No work authorized by any permit that has expired shall thereafter be performed until a new permit has been secured.

§ 160A-419. Changes in work.

After a permit has been issued, no changes or deviations from the terms of the application, plans and specifications, or the permit, except where changes or deviations are clearly permissible under the State Building Code, shall be made until specific written approval of proposed changes or deviations has been obtained from the inspection department.

§ 160A-420. Inspections of work in progress.

As the work pursuant to a permit progresses, local inspectors shall make as many inspections thereof as may be necessary to satisfy them that the work is being done according to the provisions of any applicable State and local laws and of the terms of the permit. In exercising this power, members of the inspection department shall have a right to enter on any premises within the jurisdiction of the department at all reasonable hours for the purposes of inspection or other enforcement action, upon presentation of proper credentials.

§ 160A-421. Stop orders.

Whenever any building or structure or part thereof is being demolished, constructed, reconstructed, altered, or repaired in a hazardous manner, or in substantial violation of any State or local building law, or in a manner that endangers life or property, the appropriate inspector may order the specific part of the work that is in violation or presents such a hazard to be immediately stopped. The stop order shall be in writing, directed to the person doing the work, and shall state the specific work to be stopped, the specific reasons therefor, and the conditions under which the work may be resumed. The owner or builder may appeal from a stop order involving alleged violation of the State Building Code or any approved local modification thereof to the North Carolina Commissioner of Insurance within a period of five days after the order is issued. Notice of appeal shall be given in writing to the Commissioner of Insurance, with a copy to the local inspector. The Commissioner of Insurance shall promptly conduct a hearing at which the appellant and the inspector shall be permitted to submit relevant evidence, and shall rule on the appeal as expeditiously as possible. Pending the ruling by the Commissioner of Insurance on an appeal no further work shall take place in violation of a stop order. Appeals from a stop order based on violation of any other local ordinance relating to buildings shall be taken to the local official designated by that ordinance and shall be taken, heard, and decided in the same manner as prescribed herein for appeals to the Commissioner. Violation of a stop order shall constitute a misdemeanor.

§ 160A-422. Revocation of permits.

The appropriate inspector may revoke and require the return of any permit by notifying the permit holder in writing stating the reason for the revocation. Permits shall be revoked for any substantial departure from the approved application, plans, or specifications; for refusal or failure to comply with the requirements of any applicable State or local laws; or for false statements or misrepresentations made in securing the permit. Any permit mistakenly issued in violation of an applicable State or local law may also be revoked.

§ 160A-423. Certificates of compliance.

At the conclusion of all work done under a permit, the appropriate inspector shall make a final inspection, and if he finds that the completed work complies with all applicable State and local laws and with the terms of the permit, he shall issue a certificate of compliance. No new building or part thereof may be occupied, and no addition or enlargement of an existing building may be occupied, and no existing building that has been altered or moved may be occupied, until the inspection department has issued a certificate of compliance. A temporary certificate of compliance may be issued permitting occupancy for a stated period of specified portions of the building that the inspector finds may safely be occupied prior to final completion of the entire building. Violation of this section shall constitute a misdemeanor.

§ 160A-424. Periodic inspections.

The inspection department shall make periodic inspections, subject to the council's directions, for unsafe, unsanitary, or otherwise hazardous and unlawful conditions in structures within its territorial jurisdiction. In addition, it shall make inspections when it has reason to believe that such conditions may exist in a particular structure. In exercising this power, members of the department shall have a right to enter on any premises within the jurisdiction of the department at all reasonable hours for the purposes of inspection or other enforcement action, upon presentation of proper credentials.

§ 160A-425. Defects in buildings to be corrected.

When a local inspector finds any defects in a building, or finds that the building has not been constructed in accordance with the applicable State and local laws, or that a building because of its condition is dangerous or contains fire hazardous conditions, it shall be his duty to notify the owner or occupant of the building of its defects, hazardous conditions, or failure to comply with law. The owner or occupant shall each immediately remedy the defects, hazardous conditions, or violations of law in the property he owns.

§ 160A-426. Unsafe buildings condemned.

Every building which shall appear to the inspector to be especially dangerous to life because of its liability to fire or because of bad condition of walls, overloaded floors, defective construction, decay, unsafe wiring or heating system, inadequate means of egress, or other causes, shall be held to be unsafe, and the inspector shall affix a notice of the dangerous character of the structure to a conspicuous place on the exterior wall of said building.

§ 160A-427. Removing notice from condemned building.

If any person shall remove any notice that has been affixed to any building or structure by a local inspector of any municipality and that states the dangerous character of the building or structure, he shall be guilty of a misdemeanor.

§ 160A-428. Action in event of failure to take corrective action.

If the owner of a building or structure that has been condemned as unsafe pursuant to G.S. 160A-426 shall fail to take prompt corrective action, the local inspector shall give him written notice, by certified or registered mail to his last known address or by personal service,

(1) That the building or structure is in a condition that appears to constitute a fire or safety hazard or to be dangerous to life, health, or other

(2) That a hearing will be held before the inspector at a designated place and time, not later than 10 days after the date of the notice, at which time the owner shall be entitled to be heard in person or by counsel and to present arguments and evidence pertaining to the matter; and

(3) That following the hearing, the inspector may issue such order to repair, close, vacate, or demolish the building or structure as appears appropriate.

If the name or whereabouts of the owner cannot after due diligence be discovered, the notice shall be considered properly and adequately served if a copy thereof is posted on the outside of the building or structure in question at least 10 days prior to the hearing and a notice of the hearing is published in a newspaper having general circulation in the city at least once not later than one week prior to the hearing.

§ 160A-429. Order to take corrective action.

If, upon a hearing held pursuant to the notice prescribed in G.S. 160A-428, the inspector shall find that the building or structure is in a condition that constitutes a fire or safety hazard or renders it dangerous to life, health, or other property, he shall make an order in writing, directed to the owner of such building or structure, requiring the owner to remedy the defective conditions by repairing, closing, vacating, or demolishing the building or structure or taking other necessary steps, within such period, not less than 60 days, as the inspector may prescribe; provided, that where the inspector finds that there is imminent danger to life or other property, he may order that corrective action be taken in such lesser period as may be feasible.

§ 160A-430. Appeal; finality of order if not appealed.

Any owner who has received an order under G.S. 160A-429 may appeal from the order to the city council by giving notice of appeal in writing to the inspector and to the city clerk within 10 days following issuance of the order. In the absence of an appeal, the order of the inspector shall be final. The city council shall hear an appeal within a reasonable time and may affirm, modify and affirm, or revoke the order.

§ 160A-431. Failure to comply with order.

If the owner of a building or structure fails to comply with an order issued pursuant to G.S. 160A-429 from which no appeal has been taken, or fails to comply with an order of the city council following an appeal, he shall be guilty of a misdemeanor and shall be punished in the discretion of the court.

§ 160A-432. Equitable enforcement.

Whenever any violation is denominated a misdemeanor under the provisions of this Part, the city, either in addition to or in lieu of other remedies, may initiate any appropriate action or proceedings to prevent, restrain, correct, or abate the violation or to prevent the occupancy of the building or structure involved.

§ 160A-433. Records and reports.

The inspection department shall keep complete and accurate records in convenient form of all applications received, permits issued, inspections and reinspections made, defects found, certificates of compliance granted, and all other work and activities of the department. These records shall be kept in the manner and for the periods prescribed by the North Carolina Department of

Cultural Resources. Periodic reports shall be submitted to the city council and to the Commissioner of Insurance as they shall by ordinance, rule, or regulation require.

§ 160A-434. Appeals in general.

Unless otherwise provided by law, appeals from any order, decision, or determination by a member of a local inspection department pertaining to the State Building Code or other State building laws shall be taken to the Commissioner of Insurance or other official specified in G.S. 143-139, by filing a written notice with him and with the inspection department within a period of 10 days after the order, decision, or determination. Further appeals may be taken to the State Building Code Council or to the courts as provided by law.

§ 160A-435. Establishment of fire limits.

The city council of every incorporated city shall pass one or more ordinances establishing and defining fire limits, which shall include the principal business portions of the city and which shall be known as primary fire limits. In addition, the council may, in its dicretion, establish and define one or more separate areas within the city as secondary fire limits.

§ 160A-436. Restrictions within primary fire limits.

Within the primary fire limits of any city, as established and defined by ordinance, no frame or wooden building or structure or addition thereto shall hereafter be erected, altered, repaired, or moved (either into the limits or from one place to another within the limits), except upon the permit of the local inspection department approved by the Commissioner of Insurance. The city council may make additional regulations for the prevention, extinguishment, or mitigation of fires within the primary fire limits.

§ 160A-437. Restriction within secondary fire limits.

Within any secondary fire limits of any city or town, as established and defined by ordinance, no frame or wooden building or structure or addition thereto shall be erected, altered, repaired, or moved except in accordance with any rules and regulations established by ordinance of the areas.

§ 160A-438. Failure to establish primary fire limits.

If the council of any city shall fail or refuse to establish and define the primary fire limits of the city as required by law, after having such failure or refusal called to their attention in writing by the State Commissioner of Insurance, the Commissioner shall have the power to establish the limits upon making a determination that they are necessary and in the public interest.

COUNTY INSPECTION DEPARTMENT ENABLING ACT

Chapter 153A.

Counties.

ARTICLE 18.

Planning and Regulation of Development.

Part 4. Building Inspection.

§ 153A-350. "Building" defined.

As used in this Part, the words "building" or "buildings" include other structures.

§ 153A-351. Inspection department; certification of electrical inspectors.

(a) A county may create an inspection department, consisting of one or more inspectors who may be given the titles of building inspector, electrical inspector, plumbing inspector, housing inspector, zoning inspector, heating and air-conditioning inspector, fire prevention inspector, deputy or assistant inspector, or any other title that is generally descriptive of the duties assigned. The department may be headed by a superintendent or director of inspections.

(a1) Every county shall perform the duties and responsibilities set forth in G.S. 153A-352 either by:

  (1) Creating its own inspection department;

  (2) Creating a joint inspection department in cooperation with one or more other units of local government, pursuant to G.S. 153A-353 or Part 1 of Article 20 of Chapter 160A; or,

  (3) Contracting with another unit of local government for the provision of inspection services pursuant to Part 1 of Article 20 of Chapter 160A.

Such action shall be taken no later than the applicable date in the schedule below, according to the county's population as published in the 1970 United States Census:

Counties over 75,000 population — July 1, 1979
Counties between 50,001 and 75,000 — July 1, 1981
Counties between 25,001 and 50,000 — July 1, 1983
Counties 25,000 and under — July 1, 1985.

In the event that any county shall fail to provide inspection services by the date specified above or shall cease to provide such services at any time thereafter, the Commissioner of Insurance shall arrange for the provision of such services, either through personnel employed by his Department or through an arrangement with other units of government. In either event, the Commissioner shall have and may exercise within the county's jurisdiction all powers made available to the board of county commissioners with respect to building inspection under Part 4 of Article 18 of this Chapter and Part 1 of Article 20 of Chapter 160A. Whenever the Commissioner has intervened in this manner, the county may assume provision of inspection services only after giving the Commissioner two years' written notice of its intention to do so; provided, however, that the Commissioner may waive this requirement or permit assumption at an earlier date if he finds that such earlier assumption will not unduly interfere with arrangements he has made for the provision of those services.

§ 153A-351.1. Qualifications of inspectors.

On and after the applicable date set forth in the schedule in G.S. 153A-351, no county shall employ an inspector to enforce the State Building Code as a member of a county or joint inspection department who does not have one of the following types of certificates issued by the North Carolina Code Officials Qualification Board attesting to his qualifications to hold such position: (i) a probationary certificate, valid for one year only; (ii) a standard certificate; or (iii) a limited certificate, which shall be valid only as an authorization for him to continue in the position held on the date specified in G.S. 143-151.10(c) and which shall become invalid if he does not successfully complete in-service training prescribed by the Qualification Board within the period specified in G.S. 143-151.10(c). An inspector holding one of the above certificates can be promoted to a position requiring a higher level certificate only upon issuance by the Board of a standard certificate or probationary certificate appropriate for such new position.

§ 153A-352. Duties and responsibilities.

The duties and responsibilities of an inspection department and of the inspectors in it are to enforce within the county's territorial jurisdiction State and local laws and local ordinances and regulations relating to:

(1) The construction of buildings;
(2) The installation of such facilities as plumbing systems, electrical systems, heating systems, refrigeration systems, and air-conditioning systems;
(3) The maintenance of buildings in a safe, sanitary, and healthful condition;
(4) Other matters that may be specified by the board of commissioners.

These duties and responsibilities include receiving applications for permits and issuing or denying permits, making necessary inspections, issuing or denying certificates of compliance, issuing orders to correct violations, bringing judicial actions against actual or threatened violations, keeping adequate records, and taking any other actions that may be required to adequately enforce the laws and ordinances and regulations. The board of commissioners may enact reasonable and appropriate provisions governing the enforcement of the laws and ordinances and regulations.

§ 153A-353. Joint inspection department; other arrangements.

A county may enter into and carry out contracts with one or more other counties or cities under which the parties agree to create and support a joint inspection department for enforcing those State and local laws and local ordinances and regulations specified in the agreement. The governing bodies of the contracting units may make any necessary appropriations for this purpose.

In lieu of a joint inspection department, a county may designate an inspector from another county or from a city to serve as a member of the county inspection department, with the approval of the governing body of the other county or city. The inspector, while exercising the duties of the position, is a county employee.

§ 153A-354. Financial support.

A county may appropriate any available funds for the support of its inspection department. It may provide for paying inspectors fixed salaries, or it may reimburse them for their services by paying over part or all of any fees collected. It may fix reasonable fees for issuing permits, for inspections, and for other services of the inspection department.

§ 153A-355. Conflicts of interest.

Unless he is the owner of the building, no member of an inspection department may be financially interested in furnishing labor, material, or appliances for the construction, alteration, or maintenance of any building within the county's territorial jurisdiction or any part or system thereof, or in making plans or specifications therefor. No member of any inspection department may engage in any work that is inconsistent with his duties or with the interest of the county.

§ 153A-356. Failure to perform duties.

If a member of an inspection department willfully fails to perform the duties required of him by law, or willfully improperly issues a permit, or gives a certificate of compliance without first making the inspections required by law, or willfully improperly gives a certificate of compliance, he is guilty of a misdemeanor.

§ 153A-357. Permits.

No person may commence or proceed with:
  (1) The construction, reconstruction, alteration, repair, movement to another site, removal, or demolition of any building;
  (2) The installation, extension, or general repair of any plumbing system;
  (3) The installation, extension, alteration, or general repair of any heating or cooling equipment system; or
  (4) The installation, extension, alteration, or general repair of any electrical wiring, devices, appliances, or equipment
without first securing from the inspection department with jurisdiction over the site of the work each permit required by the State Building Code and any other State or local law or local ordinance or regulation applicable to the work. A permit shall be in writing and shall contain a provision that the work done shall comply with the State Building Code and all other applicable State and local laws and local ordinances and regulations. No permit may be issued unless the plans and specifications are identified by the name and address of the author thereof; and if the General Statutes of North Carolina require that plans for certain types of work be prepared only by a registered architect or registered engineer, no permit may be issued unless the plans and specifications bear the North Carolina seal of a registered architect or of a registered engineer. If a provision of the General Statutes of North Carolina or of any ordinance requires that work be done by a licensed specialty contractor

of any kind, no permit for the work may be issued unless the work is to be performed by such a duly licensed contractor. No permit issued under Articles 9 or 9C of G.S. Chapter 143 shall be required for any construction, installation, repair, replacement, or alteration costing five thousand dollars ($5,000) or less in any single-family residence or farm building unless the work involves: the addition, repair or replacement of load bearing structures; the addition (excluding replacement of same size and capacity) or change in the design of plumbing; the addition, replacement or change in the design of heating, air conditioning, or electrical wiring, devices, appliances, or equipment; the use of materials not permitted by the North Carolina Uniform Residential Building Code; or the addition (excluding replacement of like grade of fire resistance) of roofing. Violation of this section constitutes a misdemeanor.

§ 153A-358. Time limitations on validity of permits.

A permit issued pursuant to G.S. 153A-357 expires six months, or any lesser time fixed by ordinance of the county, after the date of issuance if the work authorized by the permit has not commenced. If after commencement the work is discontinued for a period of 12 months, the permit therefor immediately expires. No work authorized by a permit that has expired may thereafter be performed until a new permit has been secured.

§ 153A-359. Changes in work.

After a permit has been issued, no change or deviation from the terms of the application, the plans and specifications, or the permit, except if the change or deviation is clearly permissible under the State Building Code, may be made until specific written approval of the proposed change or deviation has been obtained from the inspection department.

§ 153A-360. Inspections of work in progress.

As the work pursuant to a permit progresses, local inspectors shall make as many inspections of the work as may be necessary to satisfy them that it is being done according to the provisions of the applicable State and local laws and local ordinances and regulations and of the terms of the permit. In exercising this power, each member of the inspection department has a right, upon presentation of proper credentials, to enter on any premises within the territorial jurisdiction of the department at any reasonable hour for the purposes of inspection or other enforcement action.

§ 153A-361. Stop orders.

Whenever a building or part thereof is being demolished, constructed, reconstructed, altered, or repaired in a hazardous manner, or in substantial violation of a State or local building law or local building ordinance or regulation, or in a manner that endangers life or property, the appropriate inspector may order the specific part of the work that is in violation or that presents such a hazard to be immediately stopped. The stop order shall be in writing and directed to the person doing the work, and shall state the specific work to be stopped, the specific reasons for the stoppage, and the conditions under which the work may be resumed. The owner or builder may appeal from a stop order involving alleged violation of the State Building Code or any approved local modification thereof to the North Carolina Commissioner of Insurance within five days after the day the order is issued. The owner or builder shall give to the Commissioner of Insurance written notice of appeal, with a copy to the local inspector. The Commissioner shall promptly conduct a hearing at which the appellant and the inspector shall be permitted to submit relevant evidence, and the Commissioner shall rule on the appeal as expeditiously as possible. Pending the ruling by the Commissioner of Insurance on an appeal, no further work may take place in violation of a stop order. Appeals from a stop order based on violations of any other local ordinance relating to buildings shall be taken to the local official designated by that ordinance and shall be taken, heard, and decided in the same manner as prescribed herein for appeals to the Commissioner. Violation of a stop order constitutes a misdemeanor.

§ 153A-362. Revocation of permits.

The appropriate inspector may revoke and require the return of any permit by giving written notice to the permit holder, stating the reason for the revocation. Permits shall be revoked for any substantial departure from the approved application or plans and specifications, for refusal or failure to comply with the requirements of any applicable State or local laws or local ordinances or regulations, or for false statements or misrepresentations made in securing the permit. A permit mistakenly issued in violation of an applicable State or local law or local ordinance or regulation also may be revoked.

§ 153A-363. Certificates of compliance.

At the conclusion of all work done under a permit, the appropriate inspector shall make a final inspection. If he finds that the completed work complies with all applicable State and local laws and local ordinances and regulations and with the terms of the permit, he shall issue a certificate of compliance. No new building or part thereof may be occupied, no addition or enlargement of an existing building may be occupied, and no existing building that has been altered or removed may be occupied until the inspection department has issued a certificate of compliance. A temporary certificate of compliance may be issued permitting occupancy for a stated period of specified portions of the building that the inspector finds may safely be occupied before completion of the entire building. Violation of this section constitutes a misdemeanor.

§ 153A-364. Periodic inspections for hazardous or unlawful conditions.

The inspection department shall make periodic inspections, subject to the board of commissioners' directions, for unsafe, unsanitary, or otherwise hazardous and unlawful conditions in buildings within its territorial jurisdiction. In addition, it shall make any necessary inspections when it has reason to believe that such conditions may exist in a particular building. In exercising these powers, each member of the inspection department has a right, upon presentation of proper credentials, to enter on any premises within the territorial jurisdiction of the department at any reasonable hour for the purposes of inspection or other enforcement action.

§ 153A-365. Defects in buildings to be corrected.

If a local inspector finds any defect in a building, or finds that the building has not been constructed in accordance with the applicable State and local laws and local ordinances and regulations, or finds that a building because of its condition is dangerous or contains fire-hazardous conditions, he shall notify the owner or occupant of the building of its defects, hazardous conditions, or failure to comply with law. The owner and the occupant shall each immediately remedy the defects, hazardous conditions, or violations of law in the property each owns.

§ 153A-366. Unsafe buildings condemned.

The inspector shall condemn as unsafe each building that appears to him to be especially dangerous to life because of its liability to fire, bad conditions of walls, overloaded floors, defective construction, decay, unsafe wiring or heating system, inadequate means of egress, or other causes; and he shall affix a notice of the dangerous character of the building to a conspicuous place on its exterior wall.

§ 153A-367. Removing notice from condemned building.

If a person removes a notice that has been affixed to a building by a local inspector and that states the dangerous character of the building, he is guilty of a misdemeanor.

§ 153A-368. Action in event of failure to take corrective action.

If the owner of a building that has been condemned as unsafe pursuant to G.S. 153A-366 fails to take prompt corrective action, the local inspector shall by certified or registered mail to his last known address or by personal service give him written notice:

(1) That the building is in a condition that appears to constitute a fire or safety hazard or to be dangerous to life, health, or other property;

(2) That a hearing will be held before the inspector at a designated place and time, not later than 10 days after the date of the notice, at which time the owner is entitled to be heard in person or by counsel and to present arguments and evidence pertaining to the matter; and

(3) That following the hearing, the inspector may issue any order to repair, close, vacate, or demolish the building that appears appropriate.

If the name or whereabouts of the owner cannot after due diligence be discovered, the notice shall be considered properly and adequately served if a copy thereof is posted on the outside of the building in question at least 10 days before the day of the hearing and a notice of the hearing is published at least once not later than one week before the hearing.

§ 153A-369. Order to take corrective action.

If, upon a hearing held pursuant to G.S. 153A-368, the inspector finds that the building is in a condition that constitutes a fire or safety hazard or renders it dangerous to life, health, or other property, he shall issue a written order, directed to the owner of the building, requiring the owner to remedy the defective conditions by repairing, closing, vacating, or demolishing the building or taking other necessary steps, within such period, not less than 60 days, as the inspector may prescribe; provided, that where the inspector finds that there is imminent danger to life or other property, he may order that corrective action be taken in such lesser period as may be feasible.

§ 153A-370. Appeal; finality of order not appealed.

An owner who has received an order under G.S. 153A-369 may appeal from the order to the board of commissioners by giving written notice of appeal to the inspector and to the clerk within 10 days following the day the order is issued. In the absence of an appeal, the order of the inspector is final. The board of commissioners shall hear any appeal within a reasonable time and may affirm, modify and affirm, or revoke the order.

§ 153A-371. Failure to comply with order.

If the owner of a building fails to comply with an order issued pursuant to G.S. 153A-369 from which no appeal has been taken, or fails to comply with an order of the board of commissioners following an appeal, he is guilty of a misdemeanor.

§ 153A-372. Equitable enforcement.

Whenever a violation is denominated a misdemeanor under the provisions of this Part, the county, either in addition to or in lieu of other remedies, may initiate any appropriate action or proceeding to prevent, restrain, correct, or abate the violation or to prevent the occupancy of the building involved.

§ 153A-373. Records and reports.

The inspection department shall keep complete, and accurate records in convenient form of each application received, each permit issued, each inspection and reinspection made, and each defect found, each certificate of compliance granted, and all other work and activities of the department. These records shall be kept in the manner and for the periods prescribed by the North Carolina Department of Cultural Resources. The department shall submit periodic reports to the board of commissioners and to the Commissioner of Insurance as the board or the Commissioner may require.

§ 153A-374. Appeals.

Unless otherwise provided by law, any appeal from an order, decision, or determination of a member of a local inspection department pertaining to the State Building Code or any other State building law shall be taken to the Commissioner of Insurance or other official specified in G.S. 143-139, by filing a written notice with him and with the inspection department within 10 days after the day of the order, decision, or determination. Further appeals may be taken to the State Building Code Council or to the courts as provided by law.

§ 153A-375. Establishment of fire limits.

A county may by ordinance establish and define fire limits in any area within the county and not within a city. The limits may include only business and industrial areas. Within any fire limits, no frame or wooden building or addition thereto may be erected, altered, repaired, or moved (either into the fire limits or from one place to another within the limits) except upon the permit of the inspection department and approval of the Commissioner of Insurance. The board of commissioners may make additional regulations necessary for the prevention, extinguishment, or mitigation of fires within the fire limits.

MINIMUM HOUSING STANDARDS ENABLING ACT FOR MUNICIPALITIES AND COUNTIES

Chapter 160A.
Cities and Towns.
ARTICLE 19.
Planning and Regulation of Development.
Part 6. Minimum Housing Standards.

§ 160A-441. Exercise of police power authorized.

It is hereby found and declared that the existence and occupation of dwellings in this State that are unfit for human habitation are inimical to the welfare and dangerous and injurious to the health, safety and morals of the people of this State, and that a public necessity exists for the repair, closing or demolition of such dwellings. Whenever any city or county of this State finds that there exists in the city or county dwellings that are unfit for human habitation due to dilapidation, defects increasing the hazards of fire, accidents or other calamities, lack of ventilation, light or sanitary facilities, or due to other conditions rendering the dwellings unsafe or unsanitary, or dangerous or detrimental to the health, safety, morals, or otherwise inimical to the welfare of the residents of the city or county, power is hereby conferred upon the city or county to exercise its police powers to repair, close or demolish the dwellings in the manner herein provided. No ordinance enacted by the governing body of a county pursuant to this Part shall be applicable within the corporate limits of any city unless the city council of the city has by resolution expressly given its approval thereto.

In addition to the exercise of police power authorized herein, any city may by ordinance provide for the repair, closing or demolition of any abandoned structure which the city council finds to be a health or safety hazard as a result of the attraction of insects or rodents, conditions creating a fire hazard, dangerous conditions constituting a threat to children or frequent use by vagrants as living quarters in the absence of sanitary facilities. Such ordinance, if adopted, may provide for the repair, closing or demolition of such structure pursuant to the same provisions and procedures as are prescribed herein for the repair, closing or demolition of dwellings found to be unfit for human habitation.

§ 160A-442. Definitions.

The following terms shall have the meanings whenever used or referred to as indicated when used in this Part unless a different meaning clearly appears from the context:
   (1) "City" means any incorporated city or any county.
   (2) "Dwelling" means any building, or structure, or part thereof, used and occupied for human habitation or intended to be so used, and includes

any outhouses and appurtenances belonging thereto or usually enjoyed therewith.

(3) "Governing body" means the council, board of commissioners, or other legislative body, charged with governing a city or county.

(4) "Owner" means the holder of the title in fee simple and every mortgagee of record.

(5) "Parties in interest" means all individuals, associations and corporations who have interests of record in a dwelling and any who are in possession thereof.

(6) "Public authority" means any housing authority or any officer who is in charge of any department or branch of the government of the city, county, or State relating to health, fire, building regulations, or other activities concerning dwellings in the city.

(7) "Public officer" means the officer or officers who are authorized by ordinances adopted hereunder to exercise the powers prescribed by the ordinances and by this Part.

§ 160A-443. Ordinance authorized as to repair, closing and demolition; order of public officer.

Upon the adoption of an ordinance finding that dwelling conditions of the character described in G.S. 160A-441 exist within a city, the governing body of the city is hereby authorized to adopt and enforce ordinances relating to dwellings within the city's territorial jurisdiction that are unfit for human habitation. These ordinances shall include the following provisions:

(1) That a public officer be designated or appointed to exercise the powers prescribed by the ordinance.

(2) That whenever a petition is filed with the public officer by a public authority or by at least five residents of the city charging that any dwelling is unfit for human habitation or whenever it appears to the public officer (on his own motion) that any dwelling is unfit for human habitation, the public officer shall, if his preliminary investigation discloses a basis for such charges, issue and cause to be served upon the owner of and parties in interest in such dwellings a complaint stating the charges in that respect and containing a notice that a hearing will be held before the public officer (or his designated agent) at a place within the county in which the property is located fixed not less than 10 days nor more than 30 days after the serving of the complaint; that the owner and parties in interest shall be given the right to file an answer to the complaint and to appear in person, or otherwise, and give testimony at the place and time fixed in the complaint; and that the rules of evidence prevailing in courts of law or equity shall not be controlling in hearings before the public officer.

(3) That if, after notice and hearing, the public officer determines that the dwelling under consideration is unfit for human habitation, he shall state in writing his findings of fact in support of that determination and shall issue and cause to be served upon the owner thereof an order,

a. If the repair, alteration or improvement of the dwelling can be made at a reasonable cost in relation to the value of the dwelling (the ordinance of the city may fix a certain percentage of this value as being reasonable), requiring the owner, within the time specified, to repair, alter or improve the dwelling in order to render it fit for human habitation or to vacate and close the dwelling as a human habitation; or

b. If the repair, alteration or improvement of the dwelling cannot be made at a reasonable cost in relation to the value of the dwelling (the ordinance of the city may fix a certain percentage of this value as being reasonable), requiring the owner, within the time specified in the order, to remove or demolish such dwelling.

(4) That, if the owner fails to comply with an order to repair, alter or improve or to vacate and close the dwelling, the public officer may cause the dwelling to be repaired, altered or improved or to be vacated and closed; that the public officer may cause to be posted on the main entrance of any dwelling so closed, a placard with the following words: "This building is unfit for human habitation; the use or occupation of this building for human habitation is prohibited and unlawful." Occupation of a building so posted shall constitute a misdemeanor.

(5) That, if the owner fails to comply with an order to remove or demolish the dwelling, the public officer may cause such dwelling to be removed or demolished. The duties of the public officer set forth in subdivisions (4) and (5) shall not be exercised until the governing body shall have by ordinance ordered the public officer to proceed to effectuate the purpose of this Article with respect to the particular property or properties which the public officer shall have found to be unfit for human habitation and which property or properties shall be described in the ordinance. No such ordinance shall be adopted to require demolition of a dwelling until the owner has first been given a reasonable opportunity to bring it into conformity with the housing code. This ordinance shall be recorded in the office of the register of deeds in the county wherein the property or properties are located and shall be indexed in the name of the property owner in the grantor index.

(6) That the amount of the cost of repairs, alterations or improvements, or vacating and closing, or removal or demolition by the public officer shall be a lien against the real property upon which the cost was incurred, which lien shall be filed, have the same priority, and be collected as the lien for special assessment provided in Article 10 of this Chapter. If the dwelling is removed or demolished by the public officer, he shall sell the materials of the dwelling and shall credit the proceeds of the sale against the cost of the removal or demolition and any balance remaining shall be deposited in the superior court by the public officer, shall be secured in a manner directed by the court, and shall be disbursed by the court to the persons found to be entitled thereto by final order or decree of the court. Nothing in this section shall be construed to impair or limit in any way the power of the city to define and declare nuisances and to cause their removal or abatement by summary proceedings, or otherwise.

§ 160A-444. Standards.

An ordinance adopted by a city under this Part shall provide that the public officer may determine that a dwelling is unfit for human habitation if he finds that conditions exist in the dwelling that render it dangerous or injurious to the health, safety or morals of the occupants of the dwelling, the occupants of neighboring dwellings, or other residents of the city. Defective conditions may include the following (without limiting the generality of the foregoing): defects therein increasing the hazards of fire, accident, or other calamities; lack of adequate ventilation, light, or sanitary facilities; dilapidation; disrepair; structural defects; uncleanliness. The ordinances may provide additional standards to guide the public officers, or his agents, in determining the fitness of a dwelling for human habitation.

§ 160A-445. Service of complaints and orders.

Complaints or orders issued by a public officer pursuant to an ordinance adopted under this Part shall be served upon persons either personally or by registered or certified mail. If the identities of any owners or the whereabouts of persons are unknown and cannot be ascertained by the public officer in the exercise of reasonable diligence, and the public officer makes an affidavit to that effect, then the serving of the complaint or order upon the unknown owners or other persons may be made by publication in a newspaper having general circulation in the city at least once no later than the time at which personal service would be required under the provisions of this Part. When service is made by publication, a notice of the pending proceedings shall be posted in a conspicuous place on the premises thereby affected.

§ 160A-446. Remedies.

(a) The governing body may provide for the creation and organization of a housing appeals board to which appeals may be taken from any decision or order of the public officer, or may provide for such appeals to be heard and determined by its zoning board of adjustment.

(b) The housing appeals board, if created, shall consist of five members to serve for three-year staggered terms. It shall have the power to elect its own officers, to fix the times and places for its meetings, to adopt necessary rules of procedure, and to adopt other rules and regulations for the proper discharge of its duties. It shall keep an accurate record of all its proceedings.

(c) An appeal from any decision or order of the public officer may be taken by any person aggrieved thereby or by any officer, board or commission of the city. Any appeal from the public officer shall be taken within 10 days from the rendering of the decision or service of the order by filing with the public officer and with the board a notice of appeal which shall specify the grounds upon which the appeal is based. Upon the filing of any notice of appeal, the public officer shall forthwith transmit to the board all the papers constituting the record upon which the decision appealed from was made. When an appeal is from a decision of the public officer refusing to allow the person aggrieved thereby to do any act, his decision shall remain in force until modified or reversed. When any appeal is from a decision of the public officer requiring the person aggrieved to do any act, the appeal shall have the effect of suspending the requirement until the hearing by the board, unless the public officer certifies to the board, after the notice of appeal is filed with him, that because of facts stated in the certificate (a copy of which shall be furnished the appellant), a suspension of his requirement would cause imminent peril to life or property. In that case the requirement shall not be suspended except by a restraining order, which may be granted for due cause shown upon not less than one day's written notice to the public officer, by the board, or by a court of record upon petition made pursuant to subsection (f) of this section.

(d) The appeals board shall fix a reasonable time for hearing appeals, shall give due notice to the parties, and shall render its decision within a reasonable time. Any party may appear in person or by agent or attorney. The board may reverse or affirm, wholly or partly, or may modify the decision or order appealed from, and may make any decision and order that in its opinion ought to be made in the matter, and to that end it shall have all the powers of the public officer, but the concurring vote of four members of the board shall be necessary to reverse or modify any decision or order of the public officer. The board shall have power also in passing upon appeals, when practical difficulties or unnecessary hardships would result from carrying out the strict letter of the ordinance, to adapt the application of the ordinance to the necessities of the case to the end that the spirit of the ordinance shall be observed, public safety and welfare secured, and substantial justice done.

(e) Every decision of the board shall be subject to review by proceedings in the nature of certiorari instituted within 15 days of the decision of the board, but not otherwise.

(f) Any person aggrieved by an order issued by the public officer or a decision rendered by the board may petition the superior court for an injunction restraining the public officer from carrying out the order or decision and the court may, upon such petition, issue a temporary injunction restraining the public officer pending a final disposition of the cause. The petition shall be filed within 30 days after issuance of the order or rendering of the decision. Hearings shall be had by the court on a petition within 20 days, and shall be given preference over other matters on the court's calendar. The court shall hear and determine the issues raised and shall enter such final order or decree as law and justice may require. It shall not be necessary to file bond in any amount before obtaining a temporary injunction under this subsection.

(g) If any dwelling is erected, constructed, altered, repaired, converted, maintained, or used in violation of this Part or of any ordinance or code adopted under authority of this Part or any valid order or decision of the public officer or board made pursuant to any ordinance or code adopted under authority of this Part, the public officer or board may institute any appropriate action or proceedings to prevent the unlawful erection, construction, reconstruction, alteration or use, to restrain, correct or abate the violation, to prevent the occupancy of the dwelling, or to prevent any illegal act, conduct or use in or about the premises of the dwelling.

§ 160A-447. Compensation to owners of condemned property.

Nothing in this Part shall be construed as preventing the owner or owners of any property from receiving just compensation for the taking of property by the power of eminent domain under the laws of this State, nor as permitting any property to be condemned or destroyed except in accordance with the police power of the State.

§ 160A-448. Additional powers of public officer.

An ordinance adopted by the governing body of the city may authorize the public officer to exercise any powers necessary or convenient to carry out and effectuate the purpose and provisions of this Part, including the following powers in addition to others herein granted:
  (1) To investigate the dwelling conditions in the city in order to determine which dwellings therein are unfit for human habitations;
  (2) To administer oaths, affirmations, examine witnesses and receive evidence;
  (3) To enter upon premises for the purpose of making examinations in a manner that will do the least possible inconvenience to the persons in possession;
  (4) To appoint and fix the duties of officers, agents and employees necessary to carry out the purposes of the ordinances; and
  (5) To delegate any of his functions and powers under the ordinance to other officers and other agents.

§ 160A-449. Administration of ordinance.

The governing body of any city adopting an ordinance under this Part shall, as soon as possible thereafter, prepare an estimate of the annual expenses or costs to provide the equipment, personnel and supplies necessary for periodic examinations and investigations of the dwellings in the city for the purpose of determining the fitness of dwellings for human habitation, and for the enforcement and administration of its ordinances adopted under this Part. The city is authorized to make appropriations from its revenues necessary for this purpose and may accept and apply grants or donations to assist it in carrying out the provisions of the ordinances.

§ 160A-450. Supplemental nature of Part.

Nothing in this Part shall be construed to abrogate or impair the powers of the courts or of any department of any city to enforce any provisions of its charter or its ordinances or regulations, nor to prevent or punish violations thereof; and the powers conferred by this Part shall be in addition and supplemental to the powers conferred by any other law.